Ahura Mazda and the Divine Order
The Ancient Wisdom of Zoroastrianism
By Nina Vale

VELLAZ

Summary

Prologue

In the sands of ancient Persia, where the skies embrace the earth and the heat of the sacred fire dances with the desert winds, a secret lies, waiting to be rediscovered. You, who now hold these pages, are invited to cross the threshold of a time where the visible and the invisible intertwine in an eternal dance. Here, the voices of the past murmur stories of a prophet, Zarathustra, whose gaze pierced beyond the illusions of the world, reaching the heart of a truth that transcends time.

It is a world where Ahura Mazda, the Supreme Wisdom, battles against the shadows of Angra Mainyu, the spirit of destruction and lies. But this battle does not take place only among the stars or in the depths of myths; it unfolds in every thought, word, and gesture. The universe Zarathustra revealed is not distant. It pulses in every choice you make, in every path you decide to follow.

Here, the sacred fire is not just a flame, but the very essence of the light that guides humanity's steps amid darkness. And the darkness, born from the depths of Angra Mainyu, whispers doubts, temptations, and desires that can lead even the purest soul astray. Its struggle is silent but relentless, echoing in the uncertainties that dwell in the heart of mankind.

As you enter this universe, you will understand that the fate of the cosmos depends on the will of those who inhabit the earth. Every gesture, every word uttered, contributes to a delicate balance, sustaining the eternal struggle between Asha, the divine order, and Druj, the disorder that seeks to subvert creation. It is through your actions that the light of Ahura Mazda can triumph, just as every deviation contributes to the darkness that attempts to engulf the world.

But do not be mistaken: this is not a narrative of certainties or easy endings. It is a journey that questions, challenges, and transforms. The passage through the mysteries of Zoroastrianism is an invitation to look beyond the visible, to confront what lies deepest in the human soul and in the fabric of the universe. Are you prepared to open your eyes and face the forces that shape your destiny and the fate of everything around you? Then move forward, knowing that each line written here speaks directly to your being, like an echo of the ancient voice that whispered to the prophet in his visions.

Luiz Santos

Chapter 1
Zoroastrianism

In the distant past, amidst the shifting sands and fertile valleys of ancient Persia—modern-day Iran—a profound spiritual awakening began to unfold. It was a time when the world was woven together by tales of gods and spirits, each embodying the raw forces of nature. This was a land where fire, water, and earth held deep significance, where temples dedicated to various deities dotted the landscape, and sacred rituals bound communities together. Within this vibrant tapestry of beliefs, Zoroastrianism emerged, carrying with it a vision of the universe that would reshape the course of history.

Central to this transformation was Zarathustra, a figure whose life straddled the realm of myth and reality. Known in the West as Zoroaster, his presence looms over the birth of a new spiritual tradition. Born into a society that revered a pantheon of gods—each with their own domain and power—Zarathustra found himself at odds with the prevailing religious norms. The ancient Persians worshiped deities like Mithra, the protector of truth, and Anahita, the goddess of water and fertility. These beliefs had been passed down through generations, providing structure and meaning to their world. Yet, Zarathustra's heart yearned for a deeper understanding, a singular truth that could transcend the multiplicity of gods.

Zarathustra's journey began in this world of ancient beliefs. He grew up among the pastoral tribes of the region, where cattle-herding and seasonal migrations defined life's rhythms. From a young age, he displayed an insatiable curiosity about the nature of existence. But it was around his thirtieth year that his life took a pivotal turn. According to Zoroastrian tradition, he withdrew into solitude, seeking clarity away from the distractions of everyday life. It was during this period of isolation that he experienced a series of divine visions, the most significant of which was a direct encounter with Ahura Mazda, the Wise Lord.

In this encounter, Ahura Mazda revealed a cosmic truth that shattered the old ways of thinking. He was not one among many deities, but the supreme, omniscient creator, embodying light, wisdom, and goodness. Zarathustra learned of the cosmic struggle between Ahura Mazda and Angra Mainyu, the spirit of darkness and chaos. This was no ordinary rivalry between gods; it was a universal battle between Asha—truth and order—and Druj—falsehood and chaos. The world, Zarathustra realized, was a battleground where each human being had a role in the eternal struggle, their choices contributing to the victory of either light or darkness.

Zarathustra's teachings emphasized a radical shift in perspective: the focus moved from appeasing multiple deities to embracing a singular path of righteousness. He spoke of a divine order that governed all creation, urging his followers to live by the principles of Asha—good thoughts, good words, and good deeds. This moral triad would become a cornerstone of Zoroastrian practice, guiding believers toward a life in harmony with the divine. It was a call to ethical living, where each action bore consequences that echoed through both the material and spiritual realms.

The prophet's early years of preaching, however, were marked by struggle and rejection. The priests and chieftains of the time saw in his message a threat to their traditions and authority. Zarathustra faced ridicule and persecution, yet he remained steadfast, driven by the conviction that his revelations held the key to a higher truth. He traveled from village to village, sharing his vision of a universe where the forces of light and darkness contended for supremacy, and where each soul played a part in the grand design.

Despite these hardships, a small group of followers began to gather around him—people who were drawn to the clarity of his message and the promise of a world governed by justice and divine wisdom. Among these early converts were those who had grown weary of the violence and uncertainties that characterized their age. They found hope in Zarathustra's words, which spoke of a cosmic purpose that transcended the transient struggles of earthly life.

Zarathustra's message also carried a promise of renewal—not just for individuals but for society as a whole. He envisioned a world where humans, through their choices, could align themselves with Ahura Mazda's divine plan, contributing to the eventual triumph of light over darkness. This vision offered a sense of agency to the faithful, emphasizing that their daily actions could tilt the balance of cosmic forces.

As time passed, his followers became the nucleus of what would grow into a far-reaching religious tradition. Their gatherings and discussions of the teachings of Ahura Mazda laid the groundwork for a faith that would influence the spiritual landscape of Persia for centuries. The prophet's words, initially whispered in the secluded valleys and among humble herdsmen, began to spread, carried by those who believed in the promise of a new order.

Yet, the journey was just beginning. Zarathustra's struggles to find acceptance in a world resistant to change highlighted the challenges inherent in the birth of any new faith. The old gods did not give way easily, and the priesthood, bound to the traditions of sacrifice and ritual, saw in Zarathustra's monotheism a challenge to their authority. But through persistence, the prophet's voice would eventually find a more receptive ear, setting the stage for the transformation of ancient Persian beliefs and the establishment of Zoroastrianism as a major spiritual force.

As the dawn of Zoroastrianism broke over the horizon of ancient Persia, its teachings held a promise of unity and purpose—one that would inspire generations to come and leave a lasting imprint on the spiritual history of the region. The story of this awakening, rooted in the timeless questions of existence and the nature of good and evil, had only begun to unfold.

Zarathustra's life, from the moment of his mystical vision, became a quest to illuminate the path laid out by Ahura Mazda. His revelations were not merely philosophical musings—they were direct insights into the nature of existence, the workings of the cosmos, and the moral responsibilities of humanity. This new vision offered a radical departure from the religious norms of his time. It proposed a singular, universal order governed by a supreme deity, Ahura Mazda, and challenged the polytheistic traditions that had long shaped Persian society.

Zarathustra's journey as a prophet was not easy. After his initial encounter with Ahura Mazda, he returned to his people with a fervor that was unsettling to many. He began preaching about the existence of two primal spirits: Spenta Mainyu, the spirit of good, creation, and truth, and Angra Mainyu, the destructive spirit of falsehood and chaos. This dualism was not an equal struggle between opposing forces, but rather a cosmic order where good held the promise of eventual triumph through human agency. Zarathustra's voice carried the conviction that every individual had a role in this grand cosmic battle, where the choices between Asha (truth) and Druj (deceit) determined not only their personal fate but the fate of the world itself.

Despite the clarity and depth of his message, Zarathustra faced immense resistance. The priests of the old order, those who presided over the sacrifices to the ancient gods, saw in him a threat to their power and influence. To them, his call to reject rituals that did not align with the worship of Ahura Mazda was sacrilege. They derided him as a heretic, and the tribal chieftains, who relied on the blessings of their gods to maintain control over their lands and people, turned him away. The struggle to convert a society so deeply rooted in its ancient ways tested Zarathustra's resolve. His teachings, which emphasized the inner purity of thought, word, and action, contrasted sharply with the external, material focus of traditional sacrifices.

Amidst this struggle, a turning point came when Zarathustra found a patron in King Vishtaspa, a regional ruler who saw the transformative potential in his message. The stories of their meeting are interwoven with myth and reverence. It is said that Zarathustra, through his teachings and perhaps through miraculous acts, convinced Vishtaspa of the truth of Ahura Mazda's message. This royal endorsement provided Zarathustra with the support he needed to spread his doctrine more widely, and his faith began to take root beyond the humble beginnings of a few faithful followers.

With Vishtaspa's conversion, Zoroastrianism began to spread through the court and the lands under the king's influence. The prophet's teachings offered a new vision of governance, one where rulers had a divine duty to uphold justice and Asha, fostering a society aligned with the principles of truth. This alliance between prophet and king was instrumental in shifting the perception of Zoroastrianism from a subversive doctrine to a guiding philosophy for leadership and governance. It transformed the way justice was administered and set a precedent for a moral code that placed the well-being of the community above the whims of individual power.

Zarathustra's ideas of social justice extended beyond the court. His teachings called for the protection of the weak and the respect of all living beings as part of the divine creation. In a society that often prioritized strength and conquest, this emphasis on compassion and moral integrity was revolutionary. It spoke to those who had been marginalized by the existing social order, offering them a sense of dignity and purpose within the cosmic framework. His message reached farmers, artisans, and herdsmen—people whose labor was undervalued but who found, in Zarathustra's vision, a place of honor in the struggle for Asha.

Central to Zarathustra's teachings was the idea that humans, through their thoughts, words, and deeds, could influence the cosmic struggle between good and evil. This principle of free will was at the heart of Zoroastrian ethics. Zarathustra preached that each individual had the power to choose their path and that their choices would resonate throughout the cosmos, aiding Ahura Mazda's creation or succumbing to the destructive forces of Angra Mainyu. This belief imbued life with a profound sense of responsibility, where every decision could either uphold or disrupt the divine order.

Vishtaspa's court became a center for the study and dissemination of Zoroastrian ideas. It was here that Zarathustra's teachings were formalized, taking on a structure that would eventually become the foundation of the Avesta, the sacred scriptures of Zoroastrianism. Though these teachings were initially passed down orally, the royal support helped ensure their preservation, giving them a foothold that would withstand the ebb and flow of history. Scholars, priests, and followers gathered to learn the new doctrines, committing to memory the hymns and prayers that extolled Ahura Mazda's creation and the moral paths that humans must follow.

Yet, the prophet's journey did not end with Vishtaspa's conversion. He continued to travel and teach, his followers growing in number and influence. His message spread across the lands, finding resonance among tribes and communities who were drawn to the promise of a just world governed by the principles of Asha. Through dialogue, debate, and unwavering faith, Zarathustra carved a new path through the ancient cultural landscape of Persia.

Zarathustra's death, much like his life, is wrapped in mystery. Some accounts suggest he was murdered while praying, a martyr for his unwavering faith. Others hint at a peaceful passing, surrounded by those who would carry his teachings into the future. Regardless of the manner of his end, his legacy endured. The seeds he planted took root in the hearts of his followers, growing into a faith that would endure for millennia, surviving invasions, conquests, and cultural shifts.

Zoroastrianism, born from Zarathustra's solitary visions and spread through the support of a converted king, became a religion that spoke to the depths of the human condition. It addressed the eternal questions of good and evil, the nature of divine justice, and the role of humanity in a world fraught with moral challenges. And it began with one man's revelation—a vision of a world where truth could shine through the darkness, guiding humanity toward a better, more harmonious existence. The story of Zoroastrianism's early days is thus a tale of struggle and triumph, of a prophet who, against all odds, illuminated a path toward spiritual enlightenment that would resonate through the ages.

Chapter 2
The Sacred Texts - The Avesta

In the heart of Zoroastrian tradition lies the Avesta, the sacred collection of hymns, prayers, and rituals that embodies the core teachings of Zarathustra. This ancient scripture serves as the spiritual guidebook for followers of Ahura Mazda, a repository of divine wisdom, cosmic truths, and the moral principles that shape Zoroastrian life. The Avesta is more than a text; it is a vessel through which the words of Zarathustra have been preserved and passed down through centuries of change, turmoil, and resilience. It is in the Avesta that the mysteries of creation, the nature of good and evil, and the path toward righteousness are written in verses that echo with the voice of a distant past.

The Avesta is divided into several sections, each serving a distinct purpose within the religious framework. Among its most important parts is the Yasna, a liturgical text used in religious ceremonies, which includes the Gathas—the hymns believed to have been composed by Zarathustra himself. The Gathas are the oldest portion of the Avesta, their verses steeped in the poetic language of ancient Persia. Through these hymns, Zarathustra communicates his direct experiences with the divine, his visions of Ahura Mazda, and his reflections on the struggle between Asha and Druj. The Gathas are not merely prayers; they are dialogues with the divine, where the prophet grapples with the mysteries of existence and the nature of the universe.

Another key component of the Avesta is the Yashts, a collection of hymns dedicated to various divine beings and aspects of the natural world. These texts are rich in mythological detail, invoking the spirits and deities that inhabit the Zoroastrian cosmology. Through the Yashts, followers seek the blessings of powerful entities like Mithra, the god of covenant and truth, and Anahita, the goddess of waters and fertility. The Yashts celebrate the interconnectedness of nature and the divine, emphasizing the Zoroastrian reverence for creation. These hymns, filled with vivid imagery of rivers, mountains, and celestial bodies, reflect a worldview in which every element of nature is imbued with sacred significance.

The Vendidad, another critical part of the Avesta, serves a different purpose. Unlike the poetic and devotional tone of the Gathas and Yashts, the Vendidad is a legal and ritualistic text, outlining the rules for maintaining purity and warding off evil influences. It provides detailed instructions on the rites of purification, the treatment of sacred elements like fire and water, and the proper conduct for dealing with death and the afterlife. The Vendidad is a practical guide for the Zoroastrian faithful, offering a path to maintaining spiritual and physical cleanliness in a world where the forces of Angra Mainyu are ever-present. It highlights the importance of ritual in daily life, where actions must align with the divine order to ensure the prosperity of the community.

The structure of the Avesta reflects the complex nature of Zoroastrian worship, balancing the mystical with the practical, the poetic with the prescriptive. Its verses are recited during ceremonies conducted by priests, known as Mobeds, who are trained in the art of chanting these ancient words. The recitation of the Avesta is not merely a reading but a ritual act that bridges the earthly and the divine, creating a space where the faithful can connect with Ahura Mazda and the spiritual realms. The rhythm and intonation of the chants are considered to hold power, a means of invoking the divine presence and reinforcing the cosmic order of Asha.

Throughout history, the preservation of the Avesta has been a story of survival against the forces of time and conquest. Much of the original Avesta was lost during periods of invasion and destruction, especially after the fall of the Sassanian Empire and the subsequent Islamic conquest of Persia. What remains of the Avesta today is a fraction of its once-vast corpus, but it carries the weight of millennia. The surviving texts were painstakingly preserved by Zoroastrian priests who safeguarded these scriptures through oral tradition and later transcription. The resilience of these texts speaks to the dedication of the Zoroastrian community, who viewed the preservation of the Avesta as essential to maintaining their connection with the ancient truths revealed by Zarathustra.

The Avesta's importance extends beyond its role in rituals; it is also a spiritual compass for the individual. It offers guidance on how to live a life aligned with the principles of truth, purity, and reverence for creation. Its verses encourage the faithful to contemplate the nature of the soul, the responsibilities of free will, and the eternal consequences of one's actions. Through the teachings of the Avesta, Zoroastrians are reminded that their choices contribute to the cosmic struggle between good and evil, and that the pursuit of Asha is a daily endeavor that shapes both their destiny and the fate of the world.

In its totality, the Avesta is more than a book; it is a living testament to the enduring spirit of Zoroastrianism. Its words are recited in fire temples where the sacred flame burns as a symbol of Ahura Mazda's light and wisdom. The Avesta remains a source of strength for a community that has endured displacement and diaspora, a reminder of a heritage that stretches back to the dawn of civilization. For the Zoroastrian faithful, it is a link to their ancestors, to Zarathustra's vision, and to the eternal struggle for a world governed by justice and truth. Through the Avesta, the ancient voices of Persia continue to speak, guiding those who seek to understand the mysteries of existence and the path to spiritual enlightenment.

In the verses of the Avesta, the story of creation, the nature of the divine, and the responsibilities of human life come together in a harmonious symphony, a narrative that has shaped the spiritual journey of countless souls. This sacred text, with its blend of cosmic vision and practical guidance, remains a cornerstone of Zoroastrian identity—a beacon of light that continues to shine through the mists of time, offering wisdom to those who listen.

The Avesta, as a collection of sacred texts, is not merely a record of prayers and hymns; it is a repository of Zoroastrian philosophy and a profound exploration of the cosmic truths revealed by Zarathustra. The teachings within these ancient verses delve into the fundamental nature of existence, the eternal struggle between good and evil, and the responsibilities of humankind in upholding the divine order. As one explores the Avesta in depth, the texts reveal a world where every action, word, and thought bears weight in the cosmic balance between Asha and Druj—truth and deceit.

The Gathas, attributed directly to Zarathustra, are central to this philosophical foundation. Written in an archaic Avestan language, the hymns of the Gathas convey the essence of Zarathustra's spiritual revelations. Here, he speaks of Ahura Mazda as the embodiment of wisdom and light, guiding the faithful toward a life aligned with Asha. Zarathustra's words call upon individuals to use their free will to choose the path of righteousness, thus playing a part in the cosmic battle against Angra Mainyu, the spirit of destruction. These hymns explore themes such as the creation of the world, the nature of divine justice, and the fate of the soul, making them the heart of Zoroastrian theology.

In the verses of the Gathas, Zarathustra asks profound questions about the nature of the universe and humanity's place within it. He contemplates the nature of the soul, the origin of creation, and the dual forces that shape reality. For instance, he describes the moment when the two primal spirits—Spenta Mainyu, the bounteous spirit of Ahura Mazda, and Angra Mainyu, the spirit of chaos—chose their respective paths, setting into motion the cosmic struggle that defines existence. Through these teachings, the faithful are reminded that their own choices mirror this ancient decision, as they continuously decide between the paths of light and darkness.

Beyond the Gathas, the Yashts provide a deeper understanding of the divine beings that assist Ahura Mazda in maintaining the order of the cosmos. Each hymn is dedicated to a particular Yazata, or divine entity, celebrating their role in upholding Asha. Among these, Mithra stands out as the protector of truth and contracts, embodying the light that pierces through darkness. Anahita, the goddess of waters, represents purity and the nourishing power of rivers and rains. These figures are not distant deities but are intimately connected to the elements of the natural world, reflecting Zoroastrianism's deep respect for nature and the interconnectedness of all life.

The narratives within the Yashts are rich with allegorical battles and cosmic events. For instance, the Tishtrya Yasht tells the story of Tishtrya, the star that brings rain, fighting against the demonic drought spirit Apaosha. This mythological struggle symbolizes the eternal battle between life-giving forces and those that seek to bring barrenness and death. Such stories are not merely mythic tales but serve as spiritual lessons, illustrating the Zoroastrian belief that every act of goodness contributes to the maintenance of cosmic balance.

The Vendidad, with its more practical focus, provides a guide to the moral and ritual purity essential for resisting the influence of Angra Mainyu. It outlines the rites for maintaining bodily cleanliness and for purifying spaces tainted by death or demonic forces. This emphasis on purity reflects a deeper Zoroastrian understanding of the physical world as a sacred creation that must be protected. The Vendidad's laws touch upon every aspect of daily life—how to care for the earth, how to treat animals, and how to ensure that fire, the symbol of Ahura Mazda's presence, remains pure and unpolluted. In this way, the Vendidad serves as both a spiritual and ecological guide, emphasizing the importance of respecting the environment as part of one's religious duty.

Among the most intriguing aspects of the Avesta are the passages that address the creation of the world and the role of humanity within it. In the creation myth, Ahura Mazda crafts the universe as an ordered structure, introducing the elements one by one: sky, water, earth, plants, animals, and, finally, humankind. Each part of creation is imbued with the principle of Asha, reflecting the divine order that sustains life. Yet, with creation came the challenge of Angra Mainyu, who seeks to corrupt and destroy this order. The Avesta teaches that humans, as the last creation, have a unique role: they are the stewards of this world, tasked with defending it against chaos through their actions.

This sense of cosmic responsibility is reinforced in the Avesta's descriptions of the afterlife, particularly the journey of the soul after death. Upon dying, each soul faces judgment at the Chinvat Bridge, where its deeds are weighed to determine whether it will cross into the House of Song—a realm of light and joy—or fall into the darkness of the House of Lies. This vision of the afterlife serves as a powerful incentive for Zoroastrians to live a life of virtue, knowing that their actions directly affect their spiritual destiny. The teachings in the Avesta about the soul's journey underscore the importance of living according to the principles of truth, justice, and reverence for the divine.

The Avesta's rich symbolism and teachings are not only directed toward the community but also toward the individual's inner journey. The text encourages reflection on the nature of one's own thoughts and intentions, reminding the faithful that the battle between Asha and Druj takes place within every heart and mind. It is in the individual's choices that the grand cosmic drama finds its most intimate expression, where every moment holds the potential for spiritual growth or decline.

The Avesta, in its entirety, thus represents a bridge between the divine and the earthly, the ancient and the eternal. Its verses continue to resonate with those who seek wisdom from Zarathustra's teachings, offering guidance through the complexities of life and the mysteries of existence. For the Zoroastrian community, these sacred texts are not relics of a distant past but living words that inspire a way of life. Through the Avesta, the light of Ahura Mazda continues to shine, illuminating a path of righteousness that stretches beyond time, connecting the present to a lineage of ancient seekers of truth.

Chapter 3
Cosmology

In the vast tapestry of Zoroastrianism, the cosmos emerges as a dynamic arena where the eternal struggle between good and evil unfolds. This worldview, shaped by the teachings of Zarathustra and preserved within the verses of the Avesta, presents the universe as a battleground defined by cosmic dualism. At its heart lies Ahura Mazda, the supreme deity who embodies wisdom, light, and order. Opposing him is Angra Mainyu, the destructive spirit who seeks to spread chaos and darkness. This duality is not merely symbolic—it permeates every aspect of creation, from the celestial realms to the inner struggles of human souls.

Ahura Mazda, the Wise Lord, stands as the creator of all that is good. He is not bound by time or space, existing beyond the material world yet deeply connected to it. His divine light, known as Hvar or the Sun, is seen as a manifestation of his eternal presence, illuminating the universe and guiding humanity toward truth. In Zoroastrian cosmology, Ahura Mazda is surrounded by the Amesha Spentas, or "Holy Immortals," each representing an aspect of the divine order he established. These seven divine entities include Vohu Manah (Good Mind), Asha Vahishta (Best Truth), and Spenta Armaiti (Holy Devotion), among others, and they serve as guardians of various elements of creation, embodying the principles that uphold the cosmic balance.

Opposed to this celestial order is Angra Mainyu, also known as Ahriman, the spirit of destruction and deceit. Unlike Ahura Mazda, Angra Mainyu is not a creator but a corrupter. His very essence embodies Druj, the force of lies and disorder that seeks to undermine the harmony of the universe. Zoroastrianism portrays Angra Mainyu as a malevolent force that strives to introduce suffering and chaos into the world, attacking both physical creation and the spiritual purity of beings. This struggle is not portrayed as a battle between equals; rather, it is a conflict where Ahura Mazda's ultimate victory is assured, but the timeline of this victory depends on the choices made by humans.

The Zoroastrian view of the universe is deeply structured, with each element of creation playing a specific role in this cosmic struggle. Ahura Mazda's creation unfolds in a series of stages, beginning with the spiritual world and followed by the material. The spiritual realm, known as Mēnōg, represents the ideal state of creation, uncorrupted by the influences of Angra Mainyu. It is the realm where the Amesha Spentas reside, maintaining the blueprint of divine order. The material world, or Getig, is where the physical manifestations of this order take shape—where the sky, earth, water, and all living creatures were created by Ahura Mazda.

However, with the creation of the material world, Angra Mainyu's corruption begins. He infiltrates the physical realm, bringing sickness, decay, and death—forces that were absent in the pure spiritual domain. This invasion marks the beginning of the struggle that defines human existence: a world caught between the purity of Ahura Mazda's original vision and the defilement wrought by Angra Mainyu. The duality between Mēnōg and Getig illustrates the Zoroastrian belief that the material world, though corrupted, is not beyond redemption. Through righteous actions and adherence to Asha, humans can work to restore the balance and purity of creation.

Within this cosmic framework, the concepts of Asha and Druj hold central importance. Asha, often translated as "truth" or "order," is the principle that governs the universe, representing the divine law and the rightful way of living. It is the path set by Ahura Mazda, guiding everything from the movement of stars to the moral choices of human beings. Asha is not simply a philosophical ideal; it is the force that sustains life, health, and prosperity. It governs the cycles of nature and the harmony of the seasons, ensuring that the cosmic order remains intact. In every act of honesty, charity, or justice, Zoroastrians believe they are reinforcing Asha's power.

Conversely, Druj represents falsehood, chaos, and decay. It is the force that opposes Asha at every turn, manifesting in both physical ailments and moral corruption. Disease, famine, and conflict are seen as manifestations of Druj's influence over the material world. The challenge for humanity, according to Zoroastrian teachings, lies in recognizing the presence of Druj and choosing to combat it through their thoughts, words, and deeds. By doing so, they align themselves with the cosmic struggle and play a role in ensuring that the balance of the universe leans toward the side of light and order.

This dualistic cosmology extends to the structure of time itself. Zoroastrianism envisions time as divided into three great epochs: the creation, the present period of conflict, and the final renovation of the world. The present time is characterized by the struggle between Asha and Druj, where each human action has the potential to tip the scales toward either light or darkness. It is a period of trials, where the faithful must remain vigilant against the deceptions of Angra Mainyu. Yet, the ultimate outcome of this cosmic battle is not in doubt. Ahura Mazda's divine wisdom assures that the forces of good will eventually triumph, leading to the Frashokereti, or the renewal of the world.

In this future era, according to Zoroastrian belief, the world will be purified of all corruption. Angra Mainyu and his demonic forces will be vanquished, and Asha will be fully restored. All souls will be reunited with their perfected forms, and the material and spiritual realms will become one. The universe will return to its original state of purity, free from the influence of chaos and evil. This vision of the future provides Zoroastrians with a sense of hope and purpose, as their everyday actions contribute to the fulfillment of this cosmic destiny.

The Zoroastrian cosmology is thus a profound narrative of light and darkness, of divine wisdom guiding the cosmos and human beings who hold the power to choose their role in this great drama. It is a worldview that emphasizes the interconnectedness of all life and the importance of maintaining the natural order. Through their respect for the elements—fire, water, earth—and their commitment to truth and justice, Zoroastrians see themselves as participants in a cosmic mission to preserve the balance of creation. This understanding of the universe shapes every aspect of their religious practice, from the prayers recited before a sacred flame to the ethical decisions made in daily life.

In this grand vision of the cosmos, Ahura Mazda's light continues to shine as a beacon of hope, guiding souls through the darkness and reminding them of the promise of a world redeemed. Through the principles of Asha, each act of kindness and integrity contributes to the slow but certain victory over chaos, echoing through the timeless struggle between order and entropy. It is within this cosmic narrative that the faithful find their purpose—a purpose that transcends time and binds them to the eternal struggle for a world where light prevails over shadow, and truth dispels the falsehood that seeks to consume it.

The cosmology of Zoroastrianism does not only exist on a grand, universal scale but extends deeply into the daily lives and practices of its followers. It is a worldview that shapes the way Zoroastrians perceive their surroundings, their relationships, and their role within the intricate tapestry of creation. Each element of their faith is tied to the cosmic battle between Asha (order) and Druj (chaos), influencing how Zoroastrians conduct themselves in the face of moral and existential challenges. This cosmic vision is not confined to temples or scripture but resonates in every aspect of Zoroastrian life, offering a framework through which the faithful navigate their existence.

One of the most significant aspects of Zoroastrian cosmology is the concept of Asha, a principle that embodies truth, order, and the divine law set by Ahura Mazda. Asha is not merely an abstract idea; it is a guiding force that shapes the universe's structure and the ethical conduct expected of every Zoroastrian.

The faithful are called to align themselves with Asha in all their actions, striving to live in harmony with the natural world and its divine order. This extends to everyday practices, such as maintaining cleanliness, offering prayers before the sacred flame, and treating all life with respect. To live according to Asha is to contribute to the cosmic struggle in favor of light and righteousness, pushing back against the encroaching forces of Druj.

The concept of Druj, on the other hand, represents disorder, falsehood, and the destructive chaos introduced by Angra Mainyu. Druj manifests not only in the metaphysical realm as a corrupting influence but also in the material world, through acts of deceit, violence, and disrespect for the natural order. For Zoroastrians, resisting Druj is a daily battle that takes place in the mind, in speech, and in action. It requires mindfulness and a constant awareness of the moral implications of one's choices. Acts that harm others, deceive, or disrespect the sanctity of life are considered to be alignments with Druj, weakening the presence of Asha in the world.

Zoroastrian rituals and religious practices are designed to reinforce the cosmic principles of Asha, creating a sacred space that mirrors the divine order of the universe. One of the most central elements of Zoroastrian worship is fire, which symbolizes the light of Ahura Mazda and serves as a constant reminder of the divine presence in the material world. In fire temples, Zoroastrians gather to pray before a sacred flame, maintaining its purity as a gesture of devotion to Asha. The fire is kept burning continuously, reflecting the eternal nature of Ahura Mazda's light, and is treated with the utmost reverence, never allowed to be polluted by unclean substances.

In daily life, Zoroastrians perform simple rituals that reinforce their connection to the cosmic order. Prayers are recited multiple times a day, often facing a source of light, whether it be the rising sun or a lit candle, symbolizing a turning toward truth and away from the darkness of Druj. These prayers are considered acts of alignment with the divine, moments where the faithful reaffirm their commitment to living according to Asha. Even in mundane activities like eating or working, Zoroastrians are taught to maintain a mindset of gratitude and respect for the blessings of Ahura Mazda, ensuring that their actions remain in harmony with the cosmic order.

The importance of free will in Zoroastrian cosmology is a recurring theme, as each individual is seen as an active participant in the ongoing cosmic battle. This belief in human agency is central to the Zoroastrian understanding of good and evil. Unlike many ancient belief systems where fate is predetermined by the gods, Zoroastrianism places the power of choice squarely in the hands of each person. Followers are encouraged to reflect deeply on their actions and their consequences, knowing that every choice either strengthens Asha or allows Druj to gain ground. This emphasis on free will provides a moral framework that is both empowering and demanding, as it places the responsibility for the world's fate in the hands of its inhabitants.

This philosophy extends to the way Zoroastrians view nature and the environment. The earth, water, plants, and animals are all considered sacred creations of Ahura Mazda, deserving of care and respect. This reverence for nature is not simply ecological but is tied to the cosmic battle against chaos. Pollution, waste, and disrespect for natural resources are seen as forms of Druj, acts that disrupt the divine harmony of the world. For Zoroastrians, the act of tending to a garden, conserving water, or caring for animals is more than just good stewardship—it is a spiritual duty that aligns them with Asha and contributes to the restoration of cosmic balance.

The influence of Zoroastrian cosmology is also evident in the community's approach to life's challenges and adversities. The struggles of daily life, whether they be illness, loss, or moral dilemmas, are understood as reflections of the broader cosmic struggle. In facing such challenges, Zoroastrians draw strength from their belief in Ahura Mazda's ultimate wisdom and the promise that, despite temporary setbacks, the forces of good will ultimately prevail. This faith in the triumph of light over darkness offers solace and resilience, encouraging believers to persevere in their efforts to live righteously, even when confronted with difficult circumstances.

The teachings of the Avesta, including its vivid descriptions of the cosmic struggle, play a central role in shaping this perspective. For instance, passages from the Vendidad emphasize the importance of purity and vigilance against spiritual and physical corruption, reinforcing the idea that every act of care for oneself and others is a contribution to Asha's strength. These teachings serve as a reminder that the sacred is woven into the fabric of everyday life, that the choices made in even the smallest moments have cosmic significance.

Ultimately, the Zoroastrian view of the cosmos offers a vision of interconnectedness—where every being, every element, and every moment plays a part in a grand narrative that stretches beyond time. This sense of cosmic duty gives a profound sense of purpose to the lives of the faithful, reminding them that their actions resonate far beyond the immediate world. It fosters a community bound not only by shared rituals and beliefs but by a shared mission to preserve the divine order against the encroaching shadows of chaos.

In this intricate dance between light and darkness, Zoroastrians find a path that is both demanding and deeply meaningful. The world, with all its beauty and challenges, becomes a stage where the drama of Asha and Druj plays out, and where each individual, through their thoughts, words, and deeds, contributes to the unfolding story of the universe. It is a worldview that invites reflection, reverence, and a commitment to a life of integrity, offering a spiritual compass that guides the faithful through the complexities of existence, always with an eye toward the greater cosmic struggle that shapes the destiny of all creation.

Chapter 4
Ahura Mazda - The Supreme Deity

Ahura Mazda, the supreme deity of Zoroastrianism, stands as the embodiment of wisdom, light, and truth. He is the creator of all that is good in the universe, a being whose essence is intertwined with the concept of Asha, the divine order that sustains life and maintains balance in the cosmos. Unlike the capricious deities of other ancient pantheons, Ahura Mazda's nature is singularly focused on the promotion of harmony, justice, and moral clarity. He is not only a distant cosmic force but a personal guide for those who seek to understand the mysteries of existence and align themselves with the principles that govern the universe.

The name Ahura Mazda itself is rich with meaning. Derived from Avestan, "Ahura" means "Lord" or "Spirit," and "Mazda" translates to "Wisdom" or "Knowledge." Together, the name conveys a sense of a divine intelligence that governs the universe with purpose and foresight. In the teachings of Zarathustra, Ahura Mazda is not just a creator but the very source of all wisdom, the architect of the stars and the order of the natural world. He is portrayed as a deity who possesses Haurvatat (Wholeness) and Ameretat (Immortality), qualities that signify his eternal and unchanging nature. This makes him distinct from the deities of pre-Zoroastrian Persia, whose power was often tied to specific realms of nature or social roles.

Zoroastrian cosmology places Ahura Mazda at the center of creation, depicting him as the originator of both the spiritual and material worlds. Before the material universe took shape, Ahura Mazda created the spiritual realm, a perfect and eternal domain where the principles of Asha reigned supreme. This act of creation was not a distant event but an ongoing process, where Ahura Mazda's wisdom continues to guide the unfolding of the cosmos. In Zoroastrian thought, every star that shines in the night sky and every natural law that governs life is a manifestation of his divine order. The beauty of the world, from the flowing rivers to the cycles of the seasons, is seen as a reflection of Ahura Mazda's creative will.

One of the most profound aspects of Ahura Mazda's nature is his relationship with humanity. Zarathustra taught that Ahura Mazda endowed humans with Vohu Manah, or Good Mind, which enables them to distinguish between right and wrong. This gift is what allows humans to participate in the cosmic struggle between Asha and Druj, using their free will to choose the path of righteousness. Unlike other ancient gods who demanded blind obedience, Ahura Mazda seeks a conscious relationship with his followers, urging them to understand the moral dimensions of their choices and their responsibility in the preservation of the world. Through this relationship, Zoroastrians are invited to become co-workers with Ahura Mazda in the fight against chaos, contributing to the ultimate victory of light over darkness.

Ahura Mazda's role as a moral guide is further reflected in his interactions with the Amesha Spentas, the "Beneficent Immortals" who serve as aspects of his divine will. These beings are not separate gods but rather facets of Ahura Mazda's creative power, each embodying a particular virtue or element of the world. For example, Asha Vahishta represents the highest truth and the cosmic order, while Spenta Armaiti embodies devotion and reverence. These entities serve as intermediaries between Ahura Mazda and the material world, guiding humans toward a life that aligns with the principles of Asha. Together, they form a divine council that upholds the integrity of creation, ensuring that Ahura Mazda's vision of a just and harmonious universe is realized.

This divine hierarchy, with Ahura Mazda at its head, reflects the structured nature of the Zoroastrian worldview. The presence of the Amesha Spentas emphasizes that Ahura Mazda's influence extends into every aspect of existence, from the natural cycles of life to the ethical frameworks that guide human behavior. When Zoroastrians offer prayers to Ahura Mazda, they are also invoking these divine qualities, seeking to bring their own lives into harmony with the cosmic virtues that the Amesha Spentas represent. The prayers and rituals directed toward Ahura Mazda thus serve as acts of alignment, where the faithful seek to reflect the divine order in their own thoughts, words, and deeds.

Ahura Mazda's central role in Zoroastrianism is not just as a deity of worship but as a symbol of the eternal struggle for truth and righteousness. His existence as the ultimate source of light and wisdom provides a foundation for understanding the moral universe in which Zoroastrians live. Through their devotion to Ahura Mazda, believers are reminded of their duty to uphold Asha in the face of Druj's encroachment, to be vigilant against falsehood, and to strive for a life that embodies integrity and compassion. This relationship with the divine is deeply personal, offering each individual the opportunity to partake in the cosmic order through their own actions.

The concept of Ahura Mazda also brings a unique perspective to the nature of divinity itself. Unlike many other traditions that depict gods as fallible or driven by human-like desires, Ahura Mazda represents an ideal of perfection. He is without flaw or weakness, embodying the highest ideals of wisdom and justice. This vision of a deity who is pure in thought, word, and action sets a standard for the faithful, encouraging them to aspire toward similar virtues in their own lives. Through this aspiration, Zoroastrians see themselves as capable of contributing to the cosmic order, embodying the divine qualities that Ahura Mazda represents.

In Zoroastrian temples, Ahura Mazda is not depicted in human form but is symbolized through the sacred fire, a reminder of his eternal presence and the light of wisdom that he bestows. The fire, burning continuously on altars, serves as a tangible connection to the divine, a symbol of Ahura Mazda's guiding light that dispels the darkness of ignorance. This symbolism reinforces the idea that the divine is not distant but ever-present, a source of inspiration that illuminates the path of Asha for those who seek it.

Ahura Mazda's essence as the creator and sustainer of life, as the ultimate arbiter of truth, and as the force that drives the cosmos forward, is the core of Zoroastrian spirituality. His teachings through Zarathustra offer a vision of a world where order, justice, and compassion reign, a world where each individual has the power to contribute to the greater good. Through this relationship with Ahura Mazda, Zoroastrians find a sense of purpose, a moral compass that guides them through the complexities of existence, always pointing toward the promise of a universe where light prevails over shadow and wisdom triumphs over ignorance.

The worship of Ahura Mazda within Zoroastrianism is not only a practice of reverence but a profound expression of devotion that intertwines daily life with the cosmic order. Zoroastrians see their relationship with Ahura Mazda as a partnership in the ongoing struggle for the preservation of Asha, the divine truth and order. This connection is nurtured through rituals, prayers, and ethical conduct, shaping a spiritual path where the presence of Ahura Mazda guides both communal and individual life.

Central to Zoroastrian worship is the practice of daily prayers, known as Gāhs, which are recited five times a day, each aligned with specific phases of the day. These prayers serve to keep the faithful in constant communion with Ahura Mazda, reminding them of their role in upholding Asha in every thought, word, and deed. Reciting these prayers is more than a formal ritual—it is an act of aligning oneself with the divine light, reinforcing the ideals of wisdom and righteousness that Ahura Mazda embodies. The Gāhs are typically directed toward natural elements like fire, water, and earth, recognizing them as creations of Ahura Mazda and reaffirming the importance of living in harmony with the natural world.

Rituals involving fire play a particularly significant role in this worship. Fire is considered the purest symbol of Ahura Mazda's essence, representing the eternal flame of wisdom and light that he brings into the world. In Zoroastrian fire temples, or Atash Behrams, the sacred flame is tended to by Mobeds (priests), who ensure it is kept burning continuously. The fire itself becomes a medium through which worshippers connect with Ahura Mazda, offering prayers before the flame and reflecting on its symbolism as a beacon of truth. The act of tending to the fire—whether in the grand temples or in small household shrines—embodies the effort to keep the spirit of Asha alive, a reminder that the divine presence must be cultivated with care and devotion.

Devotional practices to Ahura Mazda extend beyond the confines of ritual spaces and permeate the daily lives of the faithful. One of the core expressions of this devotion is the adherence to the triad of Humata, Hukhta, and Hvarshta—Good Thoughts, Good Words, and Good Deeds. This triad forms the ethical foundation of Zoroastrian life, guiding how believers interact with one another and the world. These principles are not abstract ideals but practical commitments that shape everyday actions, from honesty in business dealings to kindness in family relationships. By embodying these virtues, Zoroastrians see themselves as participants in the cosmic mission to spread Ahura Mazda's light and uphold the moral fabric of the world.

The Yasna, a central part of the Avesta and key to Zoroastrian worship, is a ritual that directly engages with Ahura Mazda's presence. Performed by priests, it includes offerings of haoma, a sacred plant, and recitations of hymns that praise Ahura Mazda and his creation. The Yasna ceremony is seen as a reenactment of the divine order, a way of bringing the community into alignment with the rhythms of the cosmos. During the ceremony, the recitation of the Gathas—hymns attributed to Zarathustra himself—invokes Ahura Mazda's wisdom and reiterates the eternal principles that should guide human life. This ritual serves as a collective affirmation of faith, reinforcing the unity between the divine, nature, and the community.

The relationship with Ahura Mazda also shapes Zoroastrian festivals, which mark important moments in the natural and spiritual cycles of life. Celebrations like Nowruz (the Persian New Year) and Mehragan are not just cultural events but spiritual occasions to express gratitude for Ahura Mazda's creation. During these times, communities gather to perform prayers, share feasts, and reflect on the values of generosity, renewal, and balance. These festivals are moments when the Zoroastrian calendar and the rhythms of the natural world come together, emphasizing the unity of the material and spiritual realms as part of Ahura Mazda's design.

Beyond rituals and prayers, the influence of Ahura Mazda is felt in the ethical and legal systems that govern Zoroastrian communities. Zarathustra's teachings, which highlight the divine attributes of truth and justice, provide a framework for resolving disputes and guiding community conduct. Zoroastrian law, as outlined in texts like the Vendidad, reflects the belief that legal matters must be approached with fairness and respect for the dignity of each individual. The principles of justice are seen as an extension of Asha, embodying Ahura Mazda's vision for a world where harmony prevails over discord. Through this, the faithful are reminded that upholding the law is a form of devotion, a means of enacting Ahura Mazda's will in their everyday interactions.

This deep-seated respect for Ahura Mazda's guidance is also evident in the Zoroastrian approach to life's transitions, such as birth, marriage, and death. During these life events, special prayers and ceremonies are performed to seek Ahura Mazda's blessing and to ensure that each phase of life is aligned with Asha. The Naujote ceremony, a rite of initiation for children, symbolizes the acceptance of Ahura Mazda's path, as the initiate dons the sudreh (sacred shirt) and kusti (sacred cord), which serve as reminders of their commitment to the principles of the faith. In this way, the connection to Ahura Mazda is woven into the very fabric of a Zoroastrian's life, from the first steps of childhood to the final moments of the earthly journey.

The devotional relationship with Ahura Mazda also shapes the Zoroastrian understanding of community and charity. Acts of charity are seen as direct expressions of the divine will, reinforcing the belief that helping others contributes to the maintenance of Asha. Community welfare projects, support for the less fortunate, and the care of communal fire temples are considered sacred duties, carried out with the intention of honoring Ahura Mazda's teachings. In this way, the worship of Ahura Mazda transcends individual piety and becomes a shared effort to create a society that reflects divine order and compassion.

Even as Zoroastrians have faced challenges through history, including persecution and diaspora, the worship of Ahura Mazda has remained a central pillar of their identity. The practices and values that revolve around this worship have been adapted to new contexts, allowing the faithful to maintain their connection to the divine even as their circumstances change. Today, whether in a small fire temple in rural Iran or a community center in a bustling city of the diaspora, Zoroastrians continue to find in Ahura Mazda a source of strength, wisdom, and hope.

This enduring relationship with Ahura Mazda reflects a vision of the divine that is not confined to the heavens but is intimately present in the lives of those who seek to understand and live by the principles of Asha. Through prayer, ritual, and the ethical pursuit of a just life, Zoroastrians remain connected to the guiding light of Ahura Mazda, finding in him the wisdom to navigate the complexities of the world and the inspiration to contribute to the cosmic struggle for a reality governed by truth and righteousness. As long as this flame of devotion burns, the presence of Ahura Mazda continues to illuminate the path of those who strive to uphold the ancient values of a tradition that has endured for millennia.

Chapter 5
Angra Mainyu and the Forces of Evil

In the dualistic framework of Zoroastrianism, Angra Mainyu—often known as Ahriman—stands as the dark counterpart to Ahura Mazda, representing the embodiment of chaos, falsehood, and destruction. While Ahura Mazda symbolizes wisdom, order, and the guiding light of creation, Angra Mainyu is the force that seeks to undermine and corrupt this divine vision. His very nature is opposed to Asha, the cosmic order, and he embodies Druj, the deceit that threatens the harmony of the universe. This opposition between Ahura Mazda and Angra Mainyu forms the foundation of the Zoroastrian worldview, presenting the cosmos as a battleground where the forces of good and evil contend for supremacy.

Angra Mainyu's origin story is not one of creation but of rebellion against the natural order established by Ahura Mazda. He is not a deity with a domain over a particular aspect of life; rather, he represents the negation of life itself. His existence is defined by an eternal drive to spread chaos, decay, and suffering, working tirelessly to oppose every act of creation and harmony brought forth by Ahura Mazda. This opposition is not merely philosophical but is understood as a literal and ongoing struggle that manifests in both the spiritual and material worlds.

The nature of Angra Mainyu is rooted in the concept of Druj, which translates to falsehood, disorder, and corruption. Druj is the antithesis of Asha, and Angra Mainyu's power lies in his ability to sow confusion and moral deviation. Where Asha brings clarity and truth, Druj brings deception, leading humans away from the path of righteousness. This spiritual conflict is not limited to abstract realms; it influences the everyday experiences of individuals, making every decision a potential site of cosmic conflict. In Zoroastrian belief, the presence of sickness, death, and natural disasters are seen as signs of Angra Mainyu's attempts to warp and disrupt Ahura Mazda's perfect creation.

The symbolism of darkness is central to understanding Angra Mainyu's role within Zoroastrian thought. Darkness represents ignorance, despair, and the absence of divine guidance. It is the state of existence where the light of Ahura Mazda's wisdom is blocked, allowing Druj to spread unchecked. In ancient Zoroastrian imagery, Angra Mainyu is often associated with shadows, hidden dangers, and the threats that lurk beyond the edges of human understanding. He is the embodiment of fear and chaos, exploiting the uncertainties of life to lead souls away from the truth.

Angra Mainyu's influence is not limited to external dangers but extends deeply into the moral and spiritual realm of individuals. He is believed to attack the mind and spirit, using temptation, greed, and hatred to cloud judgment and lead people astray. This inner struggle is seen as a reflection of the larger cosmic battle, where each person's choices contribute to either the strength of Asha or the spread of Druj. In Zoroastrian tradition, succumbing to anger, envy, or dishonesty is viewed as yielding to Angra Mainyu's influence, allowing the seeds of corruption to take root in the soul. Therefore, resisting these impulses is seen as an act of spiritual warfare, aligning oneself with Ahura Mazda's will.

Despite his destructive nature, Angra Mainyu is not considered equal to Ahura Mazda in power or wisdom. Zoroastrian teachings emphasize that while Angra Mainyu can cause immense suffering and disruption, his power is fundamentally flawed because it is rooted in negativity and destruction rather than creation. Unlike Ahura Mazda, who has a clear and positive vision for the universe, Angra Mainyu can only react to what has already been created, seeking to mar and distort it. This imbalance is a source of hope for Zoroastrians, as it suggests that the eventual triumph of good over evil is not just possible but assured. The belief that Ahura Mazda's wisdom will ultimately prevail is central to Zoroastrian eschatology, offering a vision of a future where the darkness of Angra Mainyu is dispelled completely.

Angra Mainyu's role in the cosmic struggle is also reflected in the Zoroastrian understanding of the afterlife and the fate of souls. Upon death, every soul faces judgment at the Chinvat Bridge, where their deeds are weighed to determine their alignment with either Asha or Druj. Those who have lived a life of virtue and truth are welcomed into the House of Song, a realm of light and peace under Ahura Mazda's dominion. Conversely, those who have succumbed to the influences of Angra Mainyu find themselves in the House of Lies, a realm of suffering where Druj holds sway. This concept of a spiritual reckoning emphasizes the enduring impact of Angra Mainyu's deception, showing that the choices made in life have eternal consequences.

The teachings of Zarathustra offer guidance on how to confront and resist the influence of Angra Mainyu. The recitation of prayers, the performance of rituals, and the adherence to the principles of Humata, Hukhta, Hvarshta—Good Thoughts, Good Words, and Good Deeds—are seen as protective acts that shield the soul from corruption. By focusing on the positive aspects of life and striving to live in alignment with Asha, Zoroastrians believe they can weaken the hold of Angra Mainyu and contribute to the eventual restoration of the world's purity. Ritual purity, therefore, is not just a personal or communal practice but a direct method of counteracting the dark influence of Angra Mainyu, maintaining a connection with the divine.

While Angra Mainyu's presence is a source of suffering, Zoroastrian teachings emphasize the importance of facing this adversity with courage and resilience. The struggle against Angra Mainyu is not seen as a burden but as a divine opportunity for spiritual growth. It is through resisting the temptations of Druj and choosing to act with integrity that humans fulfill their role in the cosmic drama. Each act of kindness, each choice to speak the truth, is a victory for Asha and a defiance of Angra Mainyu's influence. This belief gives Zoroastrians a sense of purpose, turning even the smallest decisions into meaningful contributions to the larger struggle for the soul of the universe.

In the narrative of Zoroastrian cosmology, Angra Mainyu serves as a reminder of the challenges inherent in the pursuit of a righteous life. He is the shadow that contrasts with Ahura Mazda's light, the opposition that defines the stakes of human existence. His role in the cosmic balance illustrates the dynamic nature of Zoroastrianism's vision of the universe, where struggle and choice shape the destiny of both individuals and the world itself. The figure of Angra Mainyu, while fearsome, ultimately reinforces the Zoroastrian message that through vigilance, wisdom, and devotion, the forces of truth and light will prevail.

Angra Mainyu's role in Zoroastrianism is not only as the embodiment of cosmic evil but as a strategist whose primary goal is to corrupt and destabilize Ahura Mazda's creation. His methods are insidious, targeting both the physical and spiritual realms to bring suffering, decay, and moral confusion. Understanding these strategies is crucial for Zoroastrians, as it allows them to recognize the subtle ways in which Angra Mainyu attempts to undermine Asha and to strengthen their own spiritual defenses against his influence.

One of the central strategies employed by Angra Mainyu is the sowing of doubt and despair within the human mind. Unlike Ahura Mazda, whose wisdom guides with clarity and truth, Angra Mainyu thrives in ambiguity and uncertainty. He exploits moments of weakness, aiming to make individuals question their own worth, their connection to Ahura Mazda, and the path of righteousness. This psychological warfare is seen in the temptations that lead people to embrace greed, hatred, or envy—emotions that cloud judgment and weaken the will to pursue Asha. In Zoroastrian thought, maintaining a clear mind through prayer, meditation, and ethical reflection is considered essential for resisting these negative influences.

Angra Mainyu's influence is also visible in the physical world through the introduction of disease, natural disasters, and other forms of suffering. These disruptions are not viewed as random occurrences but as manifestations of Druj, the force that opposes the natural order. Illness and decay are seen as assaults on the harmony that Ahura Mazda intended for the material world. To combat these threats, Zoroastrian rituals often include purification practices aimed at restoring balance and repelling the corrupting touch of Angra Mainyu. These rituals serve as both spiritual and physical shields, reinforcing the community's connection to Asha and their resilience against the forces of disorder.

The struggle against Angra Mainyu extends to the social and communal level, where his influence can manifest through discord and injustice. Zoroastrian teachings warn that societal strife—such as unjust leadership, corruption, and the breakdown of communal values—are signs of Angra Mainyu's presence. In a community torn by deceit and inequality, Druj finds fertile ground to grow. Thus, Zoroastrian leaders and followers alike are tasked with fostering justice and honesty, ensuring that their societies reflect the principles of Asha. This focus on ethical governance and fairness serves as a counterbalance to the chaos that Angra Mainyu seeks to spread, reinforcing the idea that social harmony is integral to the cosmic struggle.

Angra Mainyu's strategies also involve direct attacks on the sacred practices that sustain Zoroastrian life. He seeks to desecrate the elements that hold spiritual significance, such as fire, water, and earth, by encouraging acts that pollute or disrespect these sacred creations. In Zoroastrianism, these elements are considered to be pure manifestations of Ahura Mazda's will, and any harm done to them is seen as an act of alignment with Druj. This is why Zoroastrians place such importance on environmental purity and why rituals are designed to protect the sanctity of these natural elements. By preserving the purity of fire, maintaining clean water, and respecting the land,

Zoroastrians actively resist Angra Mainyu's attempts to distort the world.

Beyond these physical and societal strategies, Angra Mainyu's most dangerous tactic may be his attempt to distort moral perception. He works to blur the lines between right and wrong, tempting individuals to rationalize their harmful actions and thus stray from the path of Asha. This moral confusion is a hallmark of Druj's influence, leading people to act in ways that harm themselves and others while believing they are justified. Zoroastrian teachings emphasize the importance of maintaining a disciplined mind and a firm grasp of ethical principles to counter this threat. Through the guidance of the Avesta and the wisdom of the Amesha Spentas, the faithful learn to discern the true nature of their actions and to reject the subtle deceptions of Angra Mainyu.

Zoroastrianism offers specific methods for overcoming these influences, focusing on the cultivation of spiritual strength. One of the most significant practices is the Kusti ritual, in which believers recite prayers while untying and retying a sacred cord around their waist. This ritual is a daily reaffirmation of the individual's commitment to Asha, a physical gesture that symbolizes the binding of oneself to the principles of truth and order. The repeated recitation of Ashem Vohu, a prayer that praises the value of truth, serves as a mantra to keep the mind focused on the path of righteousness, pushing back against the temptations that Angra Mainyu might introduce.

Moreover, the community plays a crucial role in supporting individuals in their battle against Angra Mainyu's deceptions. Through communal worship, the recitation of the Gathas, and shared rituals in fire temples, Zoroastrians find collective strength. The fire temple itself, with its ever-burning flame, becomes a place where the light of Ahura Mazda is made manifest, providing a refuge against the darkness that Angra Mainyu represents. These communal practices remind Zoroastrians that they are not alone in their struggles, that each act of worship is a contribution to the cosmic battle for the soul of the world.

Zoroastrianism also teaches that the struggle against Angra Mainyu requires a long-term perspective, an understanding that the ultimate triumph of good will not be immediate. The concept of Frashokereti, the eventual renewal and purification of the world, provides a vision of hope and assurance that despite the suffering and challenges posed by Angra Mainyu, Ahura Mazda's order will ultimately prevail. This eschatological belief shapes the Zoroastrian response to hardship, encouraging perseverance in the face of adversity. It serves as a reminder that every effort to maintain Asha, however small, contributes to the larger divine plan and the eventual defeat of darkness.

In the grand cosmic narrative of Zoroastrianism, Angra Mainyu is a formidable adversary, yet one whose power is inherently flawed because it is rooted in destruction rather than creation. His strategies may disrupt the harmony of the world, but they cannot extinguish the light of Ahura Mazda. The Zoroastrian focus on ethical living, purity, and devotion to truth serves as a constant resistance to Angra Mainyu's influence, embodying the belief that even in the midst of struggle, the light of wisdom and goodness will endure.

Angra Mainyu's presence, while a source of trials, ultimately highlights the importance of human choice in Zoroastrian thought. It underscores the belief that the world's fate is intertwined with the actions of its inhabitants. Every time a Zoroastrian resists temptation, upholds justice, or performs a prayer before the sacred fire, they push back against the shadows that Angra Mainyu casts. This daily struggle is a testament to the resilience of the human spirit and its capacity to choose light over darkness, reflecting the deeper truth that even in the face of the greatest adversities, the pursuit of Asha remains a path that cannot be dimmed.

Chapter 6
The Creation of the World

Zoroastrianism's vision of creation is a story woven with divine intention, cosmic struggle, and the emergence of a world that holds both beauty and challenge. This creation narrative is a cornerstone of Zoroastrian theology, revealing how Ahura Mazda's wisdom shaped the universe and set in motion the great conflict between Asha, the cosmic order, and Druj, the forces of chaos. According to the Avesta, the sacred texts of Zoroastrianism, the act of creation was not just a moment of bringing forth life, but a deliberate strategy to counteract the threat posed by Angra Mainyu, the spirit of destruction and falsehood.

The process of creation, as detailed in Zoroastrian teachings, unfolds in seven stages, each representing a vital aspect of the material and spiritual world. These stages are closely tied to the Amesha Spentas, the seven divine emanations of Ahura Mazda, who serve as guardians over different aspects of creation. The first stage begins with the creation of the sky, which forms the protective dome over the world. This sky is envisioned as a solid and pure crystal, a symbol of the divine light that shields the earth from the influence of chaos. Under this celestial canopy, Ahura Mazda then brought forth the waters, filling the world with rivers, lakes, and seas, which were meant to nurture life and sustain the earth's balance.

The third stage of creation was the formation of the earth itself—a vast and immovable land, representing stability and order. This land was not yet populated with life, but it provided the foundation upon which the rest of creation would flourish.

Ahura Mazda then created the plant kingdom, which filled the earth with greenery, providing nourishment and life-giving oxygen. Plants, in Zoroastrian thought, are seen as sacred, embodying a connection to the divine order of Asha. They symbolize the inherent purity of nature and its role in sustaining the physical and spiritual well-being of the world.

Following the plants, Ahura Mazda introduced the animal kingdom, creating the first bull—Gavaevodata, a mythological being that represents the essence of all living creatures. This primordial bull symbolizes fertility, strength, and the potential for life to thrive across the earth. Its creation marked the beginning of a world where living beings could exist in harmony with the divine plan. However, this harmony was not to go unchallenged, as Angra Mainyu sought to corrupt and harm the bull, leading to the spread of diseases and suffering among animals. Despite these attempts, the divine essence of the bull contributed to the continuation of life, showing that even in the face of destruction, the creative spirit of Ahura Mazda could not be fully undone.

The fifth stage of creation brought forth humanity, with Ahura Mazda shaping Gayomart, the first human, who embodied the purity and potential of mankind. Gayomart was created to be the guardian of Asha on earth, a being whose purpose was to maintain the balance of the world through right action and thought. In Zoroastrianism, humans are seen as integral to the cosmic order, possessing the unique ability to choose between good and evil, Asha and Druj. This capacity for free will makes humanity a crucial ally in Ahura Mazda's struggle against Angra Mainyu. The fate of the world, and the eventual victory of light over darkness, is thus intertwined with the choices made by humans, who are called upon to protect creation and live according to the divine truth.

The sixth stage involved the creation of fire, a sacred element that symbolizes Ahura Mazda's divine light and wisdom. Fire, in Zoroastrianism, is not only a physical phenomenon but a spiritual presence, embodying the purity and creative energy of the divine. It serves as a bridge between the material world and the spiritual realms, a tangible manifestation of Ahura Mazda's guiding presence. Fire is central to Zoroastrian rituals, where it is treated with great reverence, kept pure, and used as a means to connect the faithful with the eternal flame of divine wisdom. In the story of creation, fire plays a protective role, offering warmth and light that counters the cold and darkness associated with Angra Mainyu.

The final stage of creation was the introduction of the Amesha Spentas to the material world. Each of these divine beings took on the guardianship of one aspect of creation, ensuring that Asha remained strong even as Angra Mainyu sought to spread his influence. Haurvatat (Wholeness) and Ameretat (Immortality) watched over water and plants, preserving their purity. Vohu Manah (Good Mind) guided humanity, helping them make choices that aligned with divine wisdom. This divine council ensured that the forces of light would not be overwhelmed, providing spiritual support to every part of Ahura Mazda's creation.

Yet, with the completion of the material world, Angra Mainyu awoke from his darkness and launched his assault on this new reality. He brought forth his own demonic forces to attack each stage of creation, introducing diseases into the waters, corruption into the earth, and fear into the hearts of humans. This marked the beginning of the Gumezishn, the cosmic mingling of good and evil. It is a time of conflict, where the pure creation of Ahura Mazda is continuously tested by the disruptions of Angra Mainyu. The struggle between these opposing forces defines the human experience, as every aspect of life becomes a site of contest between Asha and Druj.

Despite the turmoil caused by Angra Mainyu's attack, the creation narrative offers a vision of hope and resilience. The plants, animals, and humans—though vulnerable to corruption— are also capable of healing and regeneration through their alignment with Asha. Zoroastrians believe that through rituals, prayers, and ethical living, they can restore the purity that Angra Mainyu attempts to taint. The Amesha Spentas, acting as divine protectors, continue to guide humanity, reinforcing the idea that each person's actions have cosmic significance.

The creation story thus serves as a powerful reminder of the interconnectedness of all life and the importance of maintaining the balance of the natural world. It teaches that the material world is not a place to be escaped or dismissed but a realm where the divine can be encountered and served. By understanding their role in this creation, Zoroastrians see themselves as stewards of a divine heritage, tasked with protecting the earth, fostering growth, and preserving the spiritual light that Ahura Mazda has bestowed upon them.

This narrative, with its layers of myth and symbolism, is more than a story of beginnings—it is a call to action. It challenges each believer to recognize the sacredness of the world around them and to take part in the ongoing effort to protect it from the forces that seek to undo its harmony. In the rituals performed before the sacred fire, in the care taken to preserve water and land, and in the commitment to honesty and integrity, Zoroastrians continue to honor the creation that Ahura Mazda brought into being, affirming their place within the ancient struggle between light and shadow.

The Zoroastrian story of creation goes beyond the mere formation of the universe; it delves into the responsibilities that arise for humanity and the profound implications of being the guardians of Ahura Mazda's divine order. In this intricate vision, creation is a dynamic process where humans are not passive observers but active participants, tasked with maintaining the balance of Asha, the cosmic order. This duty is not just a spiritual obligation but a direct response to the constant attempts of Angra Mainyu to undermine the world through chaos and corruption.

At the center of this cosmic mission is the role of Gayomart, the first human, whose essence embodies the potential of humanity. Gayomart's existence represents the purity and innocence of Ahura Mazda's creation, a state untouched by the deceit of Druj. When Angra Mainyu launched his assault on creation, he targeted Gayomart, seeking to extinguish this pure being. Although Gayomart succumbed to Angra Mainyu's influence and died, the death of this primordial human was not a defeat but a transformation. From the remains of Gayomart, life flourished—his seed became the source of human life, and his purity continued to shape the moral and spiritual potential of humankind.

This concept of life emerging from the struggle is pivotal to Zoroastrianism. It suggests that even in moments of darkness and loss, the divine spark within humanity remains resilient. The descendants of Gayomart inherit the dual legacy of purity and struggle, carrying within them the potential for both good and evil. Zoroastrian teachings emphasize that this inheritance is not a passive trait but a responsibility—each individual is charged with the task of choosing Asha over Druj, ensuring that the world moves closer to the divine vision that Ahura Mazda intended.

The relationship between the physical and spiritual realms is further highlighted in the way Zoroastrians perceive the natural world. The earth, plants, animals, and humans are interconnected, forming a web of life that must be protected from the pollution and decay spread by Angra Mainyu. This reverence for nature is seen in the care Zoroastrians take in their everyday interactions with the environment, where acts of conservation and respect are viewed as extensions of their spiritual duty. For instance, rituals involving the preservation of sacred fires or the careful use of water sources are not merely cultural practices but affirmations of the divine essence within the natural world.

Human responsibility as guardians of the earth is also tied to the Zoroastrian understanding of Frashokereti, the eventual renewal of the world. This eschatological concept envisions a time when Asha will fully triumph over Druj, restoring creation to its original purity. However, this restoration is not seen as an inevitable event that unfolds without human involvement. Instead, it requires the continuous effort of the faithful, whose actions help to cleanse the world from the impurities introduced by Angra Mainyu. Each good deed, each act of compassion or environmental stewardship, is considered a contribution to this cosmic renewal, reinforcing the belief that humanity's role is essential in the grand design.

Zoroastrian scriptures also emphasize the concept of Amesha Spentas, the divine emanations of Ahura Mazda, and their relationship to the elements of creation. These beings, such as Spenta Armaiti, who embodies the spirit of the earth, and Haurvatat and Ameretat, who preside over water and plants, work alongside humanity in the maintenance of Asha. By respecting and honoring these aspects of creation, Zoroastrians believe they can strengthen the presence of Asha in the world, making it more resistant to the corrupting forces of Angra Mainyu. This understanding of the Amesha Spentas as both spiritual guides and protectors of nature illustrates the depth of the Zoroastrian commitment to a harmonious existence.

Zoroastrian rituals reflect this cosmic duty through acts of purification and reverence. One such practice is the Zoroastrian ritual of the consecration of fire, which involves the careful tending and honoring of sacred flames. In these rituals, the fire is treated as a living embodiment of Ahura Mazda's presence on earth, its purity symbolizing the untainted essence of creation. The ritual involves the recitation of specific hymns, which are believed to cleanse the space of any influence of Druj, reasserting the dominance of Asha within the physical realm. By maintaining the purity of fire, Zoroastrians create a space where the divine order is preserved, offering a place of refuge against the ever-present threat of chaos.

The significance of these rituals extends to the treatment of the deceased, where the concepts of purity and cosmic responsibility take on a somber tone. Zoroastrians practice sky burial, where the bodies of the dead are exposed to the elements in structures known as Dakhmas or "Towers of Silence." This practice arises from the belief that death, as a manifestation of Angra Mainyu's influence, could contaminate the earth if not managed properly. By allowing the natural elements and scavenging birds to purify the remains, Zoroastrians ensure that the earth remains untainted, aligning their practices with their reverence for nature and the cosmic order. This approach demonstrates a profound awareness of the interconnectedness of all life and the need to respect the sanctity of Ahura Mazda's creation even in death.

The moral dimensions of this creation story are not limited to ritual but extend into the everyday actions of believers. Zoroastrian teachings hold that to live in accordance with Asha is to actively contribute to the prosperity of the earth and the well-being of others. Acts such as cultivating the land, caring for animals, and engaging in honest work are seen as reflections of divine intent. This perspective gives a spiritual significance to mundane tasks, transforming the ordinary into a means of participating in the cosmic mission. It is through these actions that the Zoroastrian faithful maintain their role as stewards of creation, ensuring that the light of Ahura Mazda continues to shine in the material world.

The struggle between Asha and Druj is thus embodied in the choices each person makes, extending the narrative of creation into the lived reality of Zoroastrian communities. Every ethical decision is a small battle in the larger war between order and chaos, and every individual action has the potential to either affirm or disrupt the divine balance. This belief in the significance of human choice offers both a challenge and a promise: a challenge to remain vigilant in the face of the temptations posed by Angra Mainyu, and a promise that through their efforts, humanity can help guide the world toward a future where the purity of Asha prevails.

In this grand vision of creation, Zoroastrianism offers a worldview that sees the material and spiritual realms as intertwined, where the physical world is a sacred space that reflects the divine order. The story of the world's creation, with its emphasis on human responsibility and cosmic struggle, calls believers to be active participants in the unfolding of the divine plan. It invites them to see their lives not as isolated events but as integral parts of a story that began with Ahura Mazda's vision and continues through the efforts of every individual who chooses to uphold the principles of truth, order, and reverence for life.

The narrative of creation, with its emphasis on stewardship and cosmic duty, serves as a guide for the faithful in navigating the complexities of existence. It reminds them that even in a world marked by the shadow of Angra Mainyu, the presence of Asha remains within reach, waiting to be strengthened by those who dare to act with integrity and compassion. Through this understanding, the Zoroastrian faithful find purpose, knowing that their actions contribute not only to their own spiritual growth but to the ongoing effort to restore the world to its intended state of harmony and light.

Chapter 7
Asha and Druj - Order and Chaos

In Zoroastrianism, the concepts of Asha and Druj represent the fundamental dualities that shape the cosmos and the moral landscape of human existence. Asha embodies truth, order, and the divine law, guiding the universe towards harmony and righteousness. Druj, its antithesis, symbolizes falsehood, chaos, and corruption, striving to distort the purity of creation. These forces are not abstract ideas but active principles that manifest in every aspect of life, from the natural world to the innermost thoughts of individuals. Understanding Asha and Druj is essential for grasping the Zoroastrian vision of a world where every action, word, and thought contributes to the balance between light and darkness.

Asha, often translated as "truth" or "righteousness," is the principle that governs the orderly functioning of the universe. It is the guiding force behind the cycles of nature, the structure of the cosmos, and the moral law that Ahura Mazda established through creation. Asha is more than a set of rules; it represents the inherent harmony that exists when the world functions as it was intended. This principle is reflected in the beauty of the natural world—the predictable movement of the stars, the rhythm of the seasons, and the flourishing of life. It is also present in the ethical behavior of humans, who are called to align themselves with this cosmic order through their choices.

The idea of Asha is central to Zoroastrian ethics and spirituality. It provides a framework for understanding the right way to live, emphasizing values such as honesty, justice, and reverence for all forms of life. When Zoroastrians speak of living according to Asha, they mean living in a way that respects the natural world, supports the community, and honors the divine presence in every being. Asha is the path of the virtuous, the foundation upon which a life of integrity and spiritual clarity is built. It is through the pursuit of Asha that individuals find purpose, becoming co-creators with Ahura Mazda in maintaining the balance of the world.

In contrast, Druj represents the force of disorder and falsehood. It is the source of all lies, deceit, and moral corruption that undermine the fabric of creation. While Asha seeks to build and sustain, Druj aims to destroy and distort. Angra Mainyu, the spirit of evil, embodies Druj and works to spread its influence across the material and spiritual realms. Druj is present wherever chaos, violence, or injustice reigns—where truth is obscured, and where the natural order is disrupted. Zoroastrian teachings warn that Druj can creep into the heart of individuals through selfishness, anger, and deceit, turning them away from the light of Asha.

The struggle between Asha and Druj is not confined to the cosmic level; it plays out within each person's mind and soul. Zoroastrianism teaches that humans, endowed with free will by Ahura Mazda, have the power to choose between these two paths. This choice is at the core of their spiritual journey, determining their role in the greater cosmic struggle. Asha calls them to act with integrity and compassion, to be stewards of the earth, and to uphold justice. Druj tempts them with shortcuts, false promises, and actions that harm others. Every decision becomes a battle, with the fate of the individual's soul and the balance of the world hanging in the balance.

In practical terms, the influence of Asha and Druj extends to how Zoroastrians interact with their environment and community. Acts of kindness, such as feeding the hungry, protecting animals, and offering hospitality, are seen as affirmations of Asha. These actions reflect a commitment to the wellbeing of others and the maintenance of the divine order. Conversely, acts that cause harm, whether through lies, theft, or neglect of the natural world, are considered manifestations of Druj. Such behaviors disrupt the harmony that Asha seeks to maintain, creating disorder in both the physical and spiritual realms.

This dualistic worldview is closely tied to Zoroastrian rituals and daily practices. Prayers, such as the recitation of the Ashem Vohu, directly invoke the power of Asha, emphasizing the importance of truth and the believer's dedication to living in accordance with it. These prayers serve as a reminder of the ongoing battle between order and chaos, encouraging individuals to keep their thoughts aligned with the principles of Asha. Rituals of purification, including the use of consecrated water and fire, are ways of physically and spiritually cleansing oneself from the influence of Druj, reinforcing the purity that Asha demands.

Zoroastrian scriptures, particularly the Gathas of Zarathustra, explore the tension between Asha and Druj in poetic and philosophical terms. Zarathustra's hymns frequently address the moral dilemmas faced by his followers, urging them to choose Asha in their actions and to recognize the dangers of falling under Druj's sway. He speaks of a world where humans are called to be ashavans—those who walk the path of Asha—standing against the dregvants, those who embody the lies of Druj. This distinction is not only about morality but about one's alignment with cosmic purpose, contributing to either the sustenance or the undermining of creation.

The concepts of Asha and Druj also shape the Zoroastrian understanding of the afterlife. The Chinvat Bridge, the bridge of judgment that souls must cross after death, reflects this duality. Those who have lived in accordance with Asha find the bridge broad and easy to cross, leading them to the House of Song, a realm of light and joy under Ahura Mazda's care. Those who have succumbed to Druj face a narrow, treacherous crossing, falling into the House of Lies, where their souls experience the suffering caused by their own actions. This vision of judgment reinforces the importance of living a life that aligns with Asha, as the consequences extend far beyond this earthly existence.

The interplay between Asha and Druj also offers a framework for understanding the challenges of the world. Suffering, natural disasters, and societal conflicts are seen as manifestations of Druj's influence, reminders of the ongoing battle that shapes the cosmos. Zoroastrians are taught to respond to these challenges not with despair, but with resilience and a renewed commitment to the principles of Asha. By remaining steadfast in the face of hardship, they believe they can help turn the tide against Druj, contributing to the eventual triumph of good over evil.

In this intricate balance between Asha and Druj, Zoroastrianism presents a vision of life where every moment holds significance, where the simplest actions can tip the scales toward light or darkness. It is a worldview that emphasizes personal responsibility, community, and the sacredness of creation. For the faithful, the path of Asha is not an easy one—it requires discipline, clarity, and a constant vigilance against the temptations of Druj. Yet, it is also a path filled with purpose, offering the promise that by living in harmony with the divine order, they are not only shaping their own fate but participating in the greater cosmic story, one that leads toward the ultimate restoration of the world.

The principles of Asha and Druj are not merely abstract concepts within Zoroastrianism; they are deeply integrated into the daily lives and practices of its followers. Zoroastrians view their actions, thoughts, and choices as direct contributions to the cosmic struggle between these forces. Living in alignment with Asha involves more than understanding its meaning; it requires actively applying its values in every aspect of life, from personal behavior to community responsibilities. This commitment shapes how Zoroastrians conduct themselves, fostering a culture where each decision is a deliberate act of supporting Asha and resisting the pervasive influence of Druj.

Asha guides Zoroastrians to act with integrity, to speak truthfully, and to maintain a sense of duty towards others and the environment. The triad of Humata, Hukhta, Hvarshta—Good

Thoughts, Good Words, and Good Deeds—is central to this practice. This triad serves as a simple yet profound ethical framework that shapes how individuals engage with the world. Good thoughts are seen as the seed of all virtuous action, fostering a mind that remains clear of envy, hatred, and deceit. Good words reflect the commitment to honesty and kindness in speech, ensuring that communication serves as a means of building trust and understanding. Good deeds encompass actions that are beneficial to others and that contribute to the maintenance of order in the world, from helping the needy to protecting nature.

These principles are reinforced through daily rituals and prayers that emphasize mindfulness of Asha's presence. The recitation of the Ashem Vohu prayer, which extols the value of truth and righteousness, serves as a reminder to align oneself with Asha's path. By regularly engaging in such prayers, Zoroastrians keep their focus on the ideals of truth and order, striving to manifest these qualities in their interactions with others. Ritual purity is seen as an extension of this alignment, where practices such as washing before prayer or maintaining the cleanliness of one's home are considered acts that honor Asha's desire for a harmonious world.

In contrast, the influence of Druj is countered through vigilance against the thoughts and behaviors that can lead to corruption and chaos. Zoroastrians recognize that Druj often manifests subtly, through temptations to lie, act selfishly, or harm others. The battle against Druj is fought on a personal level, where individuals strive to maintain control over their impulses and resist the allure of shortcuts or actions that would compromise their integrity. Zoroastrian teachings emphasize that every act of dishonesty or cruelty strengthens Druj's presence in the world, making the struggle against these impulses a deeply spiritual endeavor.

This personal struggle extends into the social sphere, where Asha serves as a foundation for justice and communal harmony. Zoroastrian communities are guided by principles of fairness, hospitality, and support for those in need. Social gatherings, including those held in fire temples, are not just opportunities for worship but for reinforcing communal bonds through shared values. In these spaces, the principles of Asha guide interactions, promoting a culture where mutual respect and collective responsibility are paramount. By maintaining justice within their communities, Zoroastrians believe they create a microcosm of the ideal order that Asha represents, pushing back against the disorder that Druj seeks to introduce.

Rituals, such as the Yasna ceremony, play a crucial role in reinforcing the cosmic balance between Asha and Druj. The Yasna, a central rite involving the recitation of sacred texts and offerings, is performed to invoke the presence of Ahura Mazda and the Amesha Spentas. During the ritual, participants seek to purify themselves and their surroundings, creating a space where Asha's influence can manifest. This purification is not only a physical act but a spiritual one, aiming to dispel the shadows of Druj that may linger in the minds and hearts of those present. The ritual's structure symbolizes the re-establishment of divine order, reminding participants of their role in the ongoing struggle for a world governed by truth and light.

Beyond formal rituals, the application of Asha in daily life is seen in practices such as truth-telling and conflict resolution. Zoroastrian teachings emphasize that lying, even in small matters, introduces a measure of Druj into the world, disturbing the harmony that Asha seeks to maintain. This commitment to truthfulness fosters a culture where transparency and honesty are deeply valued. In resolving conflicts, Zoroastrians are encouraged to seek peaceful solutions that uphold justice, reflecting the belief that maintaining harmony among people is as vital as maintaining harmony in nature.

Environmental stewardship is another important expression of Asha, with the care for the natural world being seen as a spiritual duty. Zoroastrians believe that the earth, water, fire, and air are sacred creations of Ahura Mazda, deserving of respect and protection. This reverence extends to all living beings, where compassion towards animals and the preservation of natural resources are seen as ways of upholding Asha's principles. Acts such as planting trees, conserving water, and minimizing waste are viewed as direct contributions to the fight against Druj, reflecting the belief that maintaining the purity of nature is part of maintaining the purity of one's soul.

The Zoroastrian calendar, marked by festivals such as Nowruz and Mehregan, further integrates the principles of Asha into the rhythm of life. These festivals celebrate the cycles of nature and the victories of light over darkness, serving as times for renewal and reflection. During these celebrations, the community gathers to offer thanks for the blessings of creation and to renew their commitment to living in accordance with Asha. Such moments strengthen the bonds between individuals and their environment, reminding them of the broader cosmic story in which they play a part.

The emphasis on Asha as a way of life also shapes Zoroastrian attitudes towards death and the afterlife. Death is viewed as a transition where the choices made during life determine the soul's experience in the spiritual realms. Those who have lived according to Asha are believed to cross the Chinvat Bridge with ease, entering a realm of light where they join the presence of Ahura Mazda. This belief reinforces the importance of maintaining a life that aligns with Asha, as the consequences of one's actions extend beyond the earthly life into the spiritual destiny of the soul.

Zoroastrianism's approach to moral discipline is not one of fear but of hope and purpose. The teachings of Zarathustra inspire followers to see their everyday choices as opportunities to affirm their place in the cosmic struggle. Whether through small acts of kindness, the pursuit of justice, or the dedication to purity in thought and action, each moment is a chance to contribute to the triumph of Asha. This perspective encourages a sense of agency, where the faithful understand that their efforts, however humble, are part of a larger divine mission.

In this way, Zoroastrian life becomes a continuous dialogue with the forces of order and chaos, where Asha is a guiding light that offers clarity amidst the complexities of existence. The Zoroastrian community, bound together by shared rituals and ethical commitments, finds strength in the knowledge that their collective actions can shape the balance of the world. It is through this unity, grounded in the pursuit of Asha, that they face the challenges posed by Druj, transforming even the most ordinary moments into expressions of a cosmic vision that reaches beyond time and space, towards a future where light and truth prevail.

Chapter 8
Fire

In the heart of Zoroastrianism, fire burns as a symbol of divine presence, embodying the light, warmth, and purity that Ahura Mazda bestows upon the world. Fire is not merely a physical element; it is a spiritual force that represents the eternal flame of truth and the essence of Asha, the cosmic order. Revered as a direct manifestation of Ahura Mazda, fire holds a central place in Zoroastrian rituals, serving as a bridge between the material and spiritual realms. Its role extends beyond the sacred spaces of temples, weaving into the everyday lives of believers as a source of inspiration and a symbol of the divine connection that sustains the universe.

The concept of fire in Zoroastrianism is deeply intertwined with the principle of Asha. Just as Asha represents the truth and order of the cosmos, fire symbolizes the pure light of knowledge that dispels the shadows of ignorance and falsehood. In this way, fire serves as a constant reminder of the divine truth that guides the universe. It is believed that through the sacred flames, Ahura Mazda's presence can be perceived on Earth, providing a spiritual anchor for those who seek wisdom and enlightenment. This makes the fire not only a focal point for worship but a symbol of the inner light that each individual must cultivate to live in harmony with Asha.

The most revered fires are found in the Atash Behrams, or fire temples, which serve as the spiritual centers of Zoroastrian communities. These temples house the sacred fire that is meticulously tended by priests, known as Mobeds. The fire within an Atash Behram is considered the highest grade of sacred flame, known as Atash Adaran, and its care involves strict rituals to maintain its purity. Priests ensure that the fire is never extinguished, feeding it with sandalwood and frankincense to sustain its brightness. The unbroken continuity of the flame symbolizes the eternal nature of Ahura Mazda's wisdom, standing as a beacon of divine presence amidst the challenges of the material world.

The fire itself is treated with the utmost respect, as it is considered a living symbol of the divine. Rituals are performed to ensure that the flame remains unpolluted, with strict guidelines about who may approach it and how offerings are made. The Yasna, a key Zoroastrian ritual that includes the recitation of hymns and the preparation of haoma, a sacred plant-based drink, is often performed in front of the sacred flame. This ceremony seeks to honor Ahura Mazda and the Amesha Spentas, invoking their presence and reinforcing the connection between the earthly and spiritual realms. The recitation of the Avesta before the fire serves as an act of alignment, where the words of the sacred texts resonate with the purity of the flame, reinforcing the principles of Asha.

The role of fire extends beyond the temples into the daily lives of Zoroastrians, where household fires are treated with a similar reverence. Families often keep a small flame or lamp burning in their homes, using it as a focal point for their daily prayers. This practice reflects the belief that even the smallest flame holds a spark of the divine, and by honoring it, the faithful can maintain a connection with Ahura Mazda's wisdom. In the home, the fire becomes a symbol of continuity, representing the passing of tradition from one generation to the next, and serving as a reminder of the ever-present light that guides the family's spiritual and moral journey.

Zoroastrianism's emphasis on the purity of fire is closely tied to its teachings about maintaining both physical and spiritual cleanliness. Fire is considered inherently pure, and its role as a purifier is central to many Zoroastrian rituals. It is believed that fire can cleanse both physical spaces and spiritual impurities, making it a vital part of rituals such as those for birth, marriage, and death. When a new child is welcomed into the community or a couple is married, the fire is invoked as a witness, its purity symbolizing the hope for a life filled with Asha. Similarly, at the end of life, fire plays a role in the ceremonies that honor the deceased, ensuring that the transition from the material world respects the sacredness of creation.

The symbolism of fire as a purifier also extends to the natural world. In Zoroastrian environmental practices, fire's role as a cleanser reflects the broader belief in the sanctity of the elements. Zoroastrians are taught to avoid actions that would pollute fire, such as throwing waste or unclean substances into it. Instead, offerings made to the sacred flame must be pure and worthy, reflecting the respect for the divine element. This practice embodies the idea that respecting fire is a way of respecting Ahura Mazda's creation, reinforcing the connection between the material and spiritual realms.

Beyond its ritualistic role, fire serves as a metaphor for the spiritual journey of each individual. Just as the sacred flames are tended with care to maintain their brightness, Zoroastrians are encouraged to cultivate their inner flame, the light of wisdom and truth within themselves. The teachings of Zarathustra emphasize that the human soul is like a flame, capable of burning brightly if it is nourished by good thoughts, good words, and good deeds. This inner light is what allows each person to resist the influences of Druj and to walk the path of Asha, transforming their life into a testament to the divine order.

The presence of fire as a symbol of life and energy extends to Zoroastrian festivals, such as Sadeh and Nowruz, where fire plays a central role in celebrations. During Sadeh, which marks the discovery of fire and the triumph of warmth over winter's cold, large bonfires are lit to symbolize the light of knowledge overcoming darkness. This festival is a communal expression of the belief that fire's warmth and light are gifts from Ahura Mazda, capable of sustaining life through the hardships of the world. Similarly, during Nowruz, the Persian New Year, the lighting of fires symbolizes the renewal of life and the cleansing of the past, preparing the community for a new cycle of growth and hope.

Fire's role in Zoroastrianism is thus multifaceted—at once a physical element, a symbol of divine truth, and a spiritual guide. Its importance is woven through the daily acts of worship, the grand rituals of the temples, and the intimate moments of family life. For Zoroastrians, the sight of a flame is a reminder that Ahura Mazda's wisdom is ever-present, guiding them through the darkness of uncertainty and the challenges posed by Angra Mainyu. It embodies the enduring belief that as long as the flame of truth burns, there remains hope for a world where Asha prevails over Druj, where order, compassion, and light are preserved amidst the complexities of existence.

In revering fire, Zoroastrians maintain a connection to their ancient heritage, a tradition that has survived the passage of millennia. The sacred flame, whether blazing in a grand temple or flickering in a modest home, is a symbol of resilience, embodying the enduring spirit of a faith that finds the divine in the most elemental forces of nature. Through their devotion to fire, the followers of Zarathustra honor not only the god who created the world but the very essence of life that animates the universe, a flame that continues to light the path towards understanding, wisdom, and a world guided by the principles of Asha.

The veneration of fire in Zoroastrianism is not solely about its symbolism, but also about the practical and sacred rituals that center around this element. These rituals are deeply woven into the fabric of Zoroastrian life, reflecting a profound understanding of fire as a link between the material and spiritual realms. Beyond being a symbol of Ahura Mazda's presence, fire is actively engaged in daily prayers, ceremonial practices, and life cycle events, reinforcing its role as a conduit of divine energy and a guardian of spiritual purity.

In Zoroastrian worship, the different types of sacred fires are categorized according to their spiritual significance, each serving a unique role in religious practice. The highest grade is the Atash Behram, known as the "Victorious Fire." This fire is found in the most revered fire temples and is regarded as the pinnacle of Zoroastrian sanctity. The process of consecrating an Atash Behram is intricate and time-consuming, involving the purification of fire taken from sixteen different sources, including a craftsman's forge, a funeral pyre, and the household hearth. This process symbolizes the gathering of diverse elements of the world and uniting them under the purifying force of the divine flame, representing a microcosm of the order that Asha brings to the universe.

The ritual care of an Atash Behram is carried out by specially trained priests who are responsible for maintaining the fire's purity. These priests, known as Mobeds, perform daily ceremonies that include the recitation of the Avesta and the offering of sandalwood and incense, which serve to feed the flame. The continuous burning of the fire is a powerful symbol of the eternal nature of Ahura Mazda's light, a reminder that even in a world shadowed by Angra Mainyu's influence, the divine presence endures. The role of the Mobeds in this context is not just practical but deeply spiritual—they serve as intermediaries who ensure that the connection between the divine and earthly realms remains strong and unbroken.

Beyond the Atash Behram, other grades of sacred fire, such as the Atash Adaran and Atash Dadgah, are found in smaller temples and home shrines. While they are less complex in their consecration, these fires are treated with the same reverence. The Atash Adaran, often referred to as the "Fire of Fires," serves communities that may not have access to an Atash Behram. The Atash Dadgah, or "Installed Fire," can be kept in family homes, offering a more intimate space for daily devotion. In these settings, the fire serves as a focal point for personal prayers and a symbol of the family's commitment to Asha. These home fires are tended with care, and families often perform a simple ritual of adding wood or incense while reciting blessings, keeping the connection to the sacred alive in everyday life.

The importance of fire in Zoroastrian rituals extends to life cycle events, where it plays a central role in marking transitions and invoking divine blessings. In marriage ceremonies, the couple stands before a sacred flame as they exchange vows, symbolizing the purity of their union and the light they bring into each other's lives. The fire acts as a witness, its presence a reminder that their commitment is not only to one another but also to the principles of truth and order that fire represents. Similarly, during the Navjote ceremony—an initiation rite where children are formally welcomed into the Zoroastrian faith—the sacred fire is a central element, symbolizing the child's entry into a life guided by the light of Asha.

At the end of life, fire also plays a role in the funerary practices of Zoroastrians, though with a different focus. Due to the belief in the purity of fire, it must not be polluted by the dead, who are seen as under the temporary influence of Angra Mainyu. Thus, rather than cremation, Zoroastrians traditionally practice sky burials on Dakhmas, or "Towers of Silence." Yet, fire remains part of the death rituals through prayers performed near a consecrated flame, which are meant to aid the soul's passage across the Chinvat Bridge and into the afterlife. The fire's role in these prayers reinforces its function as a guide and protector, helping to purify the path that the soul must traverse.

During communal gatherings and festivals, the lighting of fires serves as a collective reaffirmation of faith and unity. One of the most significant festivals, Sadeh, celebrates the discovery of fire, with large bonfires symbolizing humanity's triumph over darkness and cold. The festival brings communities together, where participants gather around the flames, reciting prayers, singing hymns, and sharing food. The fire is a focal point of joy and reverence, a communal offering to Ahura Mazda that strengthens the bonds between participants. This act of gathering around the fire symbolizes a shared commitment to uphold Asha in the face of the challenges brought by Druj, turning the simple act of lighting a flame into a powerful statement of hope and resilience.

Another key celebration, Nowruz, the Zoroastrian New Year, involves rituals that cleanse the home and mind in preparation for renewal. The lighting of Chaharshanbe Suri fires—small bonfires that people leap over—is a common practice during this time, symbolizing the burning away of past misfortunes and impurities, making way for the blessings of a new year. The ritual, though joyous and festive, is rooted in the ancient belief that fire can purify and transform, turning what is old and worn into a fertile ground for new beginnings. This emphasis on renewal through fire reflects the broader Zoroastrian view that the light of Asha can transform the world, one action at a time.

Fire's significance in Zoroastrianism is also expressed through its relationship with other elements, such as water and earth, in rituals that emphasize the balance of nature. The use of fire and water together in ceremonies, such as the Abyan, reflects the belief that these elements, when kept pure, maintain the cosmic balance established by Ahura Mazda. Water, like fire, is considered a carrier of divine blessings, and rituals often involve sprinkling consecrated water around a sacred flame, symbolizing the interplay of light and life. This connection between fire and water highlights the Zoroastrian commitment to environmental stewardship, where preserving the purity of nature is seen as essential to maintaining spiritual harmony.

Through these rituals, fire becomes more than a mere symbol—it is a dynamic participant in the spiritual life of the community. Its presence in the heart of rituals and in the everyday spaces of life serves as a constant reminder of the divine light that guides the faithful. It reinforces the idea that maintaining Asha is a continuous process, one that requires both individual devotion and collective effort. Each time a flame is lit, it represents a renewal of the commitment to the principles of truth, order, and compassion that Zoroastrianism holds dear.

The reverence for fire and its role in rituals encapsulates the core of Zoroastrian belief: that the world, though challenged by forces of darkness, is sustained through the light of wisdom and the actions of those who choose to live in alignment with Asha. By tending to the sacred flames, Zoroastrians not only honor their ancient traditions but also affirm their role as keepers of the light. In this way, the rituals surrounding fire serve as a testament to the enduring strength of a faith that finds the divine in the elements, and in the everyday acts of devotion that keep the flame of hope burning brightly, even amidst the trials of existence.

Chapter 9
Ethics

Zoroastrianism places a profound emphasis on ethics, positioning moral conduct at the core of its spiritual practice. Unlike religions that focus heavily on ritual or dogma, Zoroastrianism teaches that the essence of faith lies in how one lives—through thoughts, words, and actions that align with the divine order of Asha. The pursuit of a virtuous life is not merely a personal quest for righteousness but a cosmic responsibility, as each individual's choices contribute to the balance between good and evil, between Asha and Druj. Central to this ethical framework is the triad known as Humata, Hukhta, Hvarshta— Good Thoughts, Good Words, and Good Deeds—guiding Zoroastrians in every aspect of their lives.

Good Thoughts, or Humata, form the foundation of the Zoroastrian ethical code. Zoroastrians believe that the mind is the starting point of all actions, and cultivating pure thoughts is essential for living in accordance with Asha. This principle emphasizes the importance of mental discipline, encouraging individuals to guard against thoughts of hatred, envy, and deceit. It is taught that a mind aligned with truth naturally leads to positive speech and behavior, shaping a life that contributes to the wellbeing of others. By fostering clarity and integrity in their thoughts, Zoroastrians see themselves as directly participating in the cosmic struggle against Druj, maintaining the inner purity that is necessary for the outward expression of virtue.

The second element, Hukhta, or Good Words, extends the principle of Asha into the realm of speech. Zoroastrianism places great importance on the power of words, recognizing them as tools that can either uplift or harm. Speaking truthfully is seen as a reflection of the divine light within, an affirmation of one's commitment to Asha. Zoroastrians are encouraged to use their words to build harmony, offer encouragement, and resolve conflicts peacefully. Slander, false accusations, and deceitful speech are considered acts that strengthen Druj, introducing chaos into human relationships and the broader community. Thus, maintaining honesty and kindness in speech is not just a matter of personal integrity but a way of contributing to the order that Ahura Mazda envisioned for the world.

Hvarshta, or Good Deeds, completes the triad, emphasizing that thoughts and words must be matched by actions that reflect ethical values. In Zoroastrian teachings, deeds are the tangible expressions of one's inner beliefs, turning abstract principles into concrete realities. Good deeds encompass a wide range of actions, from caring for the needy to protecting the environment and engaging in honest work. Acts of charity, known as Dastur, are particularly encouraged, reflecting the belief that helping others reinforces the divine order of Asha. Zoroastrians view their efforts to alleviate suffering as direct contributions to the cosmic struggle against the forces of evil, creating ripples of positivity that extend beyond individual lives.

This triad serves as a practical guide for Zoroastrians, offering a straightforward but profound framework for daily decision-making. By constantly aligning their thoughts, words, and actions with these ideals, they seek to embody the values that Zarathustra preached and to live in harmony with Ahura Mazda's vision. The ethical life is thus seen as an ongoing process, one that requires vigilance and self-reflection. Zoroastrian teachings emphasize the importance of Fravashi, or the inner guardian spirit, which guides the individual in discerning right from wrong. This inner voice is considered a gift from Ahura Mazda, a spark of divine wisdom that helps believers navigate the complexities of life and make choices that uphold Asha.

Beyond personal conduct, Zoroastrian ethics extend to social relationships and responsibilities. The family unit is considered a sacred space where the principles of Humata, Hukhta, and Hvarshta are first learned and practiced. Respect for elders, care for children, and mutual support between spouses are seen as foundational to a life of integrity. Families are encouraged to create environments where truthfulness and kindness are the norms, setting an example that extends into the broader community. The Zoroastrian community, or Anjuman, becomes a larger family bound together by shared values, where the wellbeing of one is seen as interconnected with the wellbeing of all.

Justice is another cornerstone of Zoroastrian ethics, closely tied to the principle of Asha. Zoroastrianism teaches that upholding justice is a sacred duty, one that mirrors the divine justice of Ahura Mazda. This involves not only seeking fairness in one's own dealings but also standing against oppression and injustice wherever they are encountered. Zoroastrian law, as outlined in ancient texts like the Vendidad, provides guidance on ethical behavior in areas such as commerce, marriage, and communal disputes. While these laws have evolved over time, the underlying principle remains that justice should serve the purpose of restoring harmony and balance, rather than merely punishing wrongdoing. This focus on restorative justice aligns with the belief that even those who have strayed can be guided back to the path of Asha through wisdom and compassion.

Zoroastrian ethics also emphasize the importance of work and the dignity of labor. Zarathustra's teachings promote the idea that honest work is a form of worship, a way of contributing to the wellbeing of the world. Whether through farming, crafting, or providing services, Zoroastrians are taught to see their work as a means of sustaining the divine order. This perspective transforms daily labor into a spiritual practice, where the effort to do one's best is seen as an offering to Ahura Mazda. In contrast, laziness and dishonesty in work are viewed as expressions of Druj, undermining the harmony that honest labor brings to society.

Environmental ethics are also integral to the Zoroastrian way of life. The natural world, as part of Ahura Mazda's creation, is to be treated with respect and care. Zoroastrians believe that polluting the earth, water, or air is not only an offense against the environment but a disruption of Asha itself. Practices such as conserving water, protecting animals, and maintaining cleanliness in living spaces are seen as reflections of spiritual purity. These actions are not just ecological but deeply religious, reaffirming the Zoroastrian commitment to preserving the balance of creation. The reverence for nature is a reminder that humanity's role is not to dominate the earth but to act as its stewards, maintaining the sacred order established by Ahura Mazda.

Zoroastrian ethical teachings extend to the treatment of others, emphasizing the value of compassion and the responsibility to care for those who are less fortunate. Acts of charity, such as providing for the poor or supporting community projects, are considered ways to manifest the light of Asha in the world. This focus on social responsibility creates a sense of solidarity within Zoroastrian communities, where each person's wellbeing is seen as interconnected with the collective. Through these acts of kindness, Zoroastrians believe they are not only fulfilling their moral duty but also strengthening the presence of good in the world, contributing to the larger cosmic struggle between Asha and Druj.

Zoroastrianism's emphasis on ethics and moral conduct provides a vision of life where every action, no matter how small, has cosmic significance. The principles of Humata, Hukhta, and Hvarshta offer a path that is both simple and profound, guiding believers to live in a way that honors the divine order and contributes to the greater good. This focus on living a life of integrity transforms faith from a set of beliefs into a lived reality, where each thought, word, and deed is a testament to one's commitment to Ahura Mazda and the enduring struggle for a world where truth and light prevail over falsehood and darkness.

Zoroastrian ethics, grounded in the principles of Humata, Hukhta, Hvarshta—Good Thoughts, Good Words, and Good Deeds—extend beyond ancient precepts to adapt to the challenges of modern life. As the world evolves, Zoroastrians continue to draw from their deep-rooted values to navigate contemporary issues, ensuring that their actions align with Asha, the cosmic order. This adaptability allows Zoroastrian communities to uphold their ancient ethical foundations while responding to new social, environmental, and moral dilemmas in a dynamic world.

One of the key ways in which Zoroastrian ethics manifest in the modern era is through social responsibility and the adaptation of community values to changing circumstances. In today's globalized society, where Zoroastrians often live as minorities, the principles of mutual support and charity take on new significance. The tradition of Dastur—acts of kindness and charity—remains a vital practice, but now it also includes efforts such as supporting Zoroastrian educational initiatives, providing aid to the elderly, and contributing to humanitarian efforts beyond their immediate community. This extension of compassion reflects the idea that Asha's light should reach all corners of society, offering help to those in need regardless of their background.

Zoroastrian communities have adapted their charitable efforts to address modern challenges like economic inequality, access to education, and healthcare. Many Zoroastrian organizations have established scholarship programs, healthcare facilities, and social services that benefit both Zoroastrians and the broader communities in which they live. These efforts are seen as modern expressions of ancient teachings, where the practice of generosity and the upliftment of others align with the timeless commitment to righteousness. In this way, Zoroastrians view their social contributions not just as acts of goodwill, but as crucial elements in the broader struggle to maintain Asha in a world that often leans towards chaos and division.

The principles of truthfulness and integrity, as embodied in Hukhta, also play a significant role in the Zoroastrian approach to modern professional life. In an era where ethical challenges in business and governance are common, Zoroastrians strive to maintain high standards of honesty and transparency in their work. This commitment to ethical conduct extends to fair business practices, ethical investment, and an emphasis on integrity in professional relationships. Zoroastrians are taught to view their professions as extensions of their spiritual path, where every decision reflects their commitment to Asha. By prioritizing fairness and ethical behavior, they seek to create workplaces and business environments that align with the values of order and justice, standing against the deceptions that might otherwise compromise their integrity.

In the face of rapid technological advancement, Zoroastrian ethical teachings offer guidance on issues such as digital communication and the responsible use of technology. The principle of Hukhta—Good Words—extends to the realm of online interactions, encouraging Zoroastrians to engage in respectful and truthful communication even in digital spaces. This reflects a broader commitment to maintaining Asha in all aspects of life, including those that have emerged with modernity. By emphasizing the importance of truth and respect in digital dialogues, Zoroastrians seek to create a positive influence in a space where misinformation and negativity can easily spread, using their principles to guide their engagement with the virtual world.

Environmental stewardship, rooted in the Zoroastrian reverence for the natural world, has become increasingly relevant as ecological challenges grow more urgent. Zoroastrian teachings have long emphasized the sacredness of water, earth, and fire, considering pollution of these elements a violation of divine order. In the modern context, this respect translates into active involvement in environmental conservation and sustainability efforts. Many Zoroastrians participate in initiatives aimed at reducing pollution, conserving water, and promoting renewable energy. They view these actions as extensions of their duty to protect Ahura Mazda's creation, reinforcing the ancient belief that humans are stewards of the earth, responsible for maintaining the balance that Asha demands.

Zoroastrian communities have also adapted their practices to address global issues such as climate change, recognizing that preserving the environment is a way to uphold their spiritual principles. For example, initiatives to reduce waste and promote sustainable living are increasingly integrated into Zoroastrian communal life, including events and celebrations where efforts are made to minimize the environmental impact. By focusing on sustainability, Zoroastrians see themselves as part of a broader movement to restore the harmony of the natural world, aligning their ancient values with the ecological needs of the present.

The teachings of Humata—Good Thoughts—also influence the way Zoroastrians approach mental and emotional wellbeing in the modern era. As awareness of mental health grows, Zoroastrians emphasize the importance of maintaining a clear and peaceful mind, in alignment with the tradition of cultivating positive thoughts. This approach encourages mindfulness, meditation, and the recitation of prayers as ways to nurture mental clarity and resilience. Zoroastrian spiritual practices, such as the daily recitation of the Ashem Vohu and reflection before the sacred fire, are seen as methods to center the mind and strengthen the spirit, offering tools for coping with the stresses of contemporary life.

Furthermore, Zoroastrian ethics provide a framework for navigating the complexities of social diversity and multiculturalism. Living in diaspora communities, Zoroastrians often engage with people of various faiths and cultural backgrounds. Their teachings encourage respect for others' beliefs and an openness to dialogue, reflecting Zarathustra's emphasis on the value of wisdom and understanding. Zoroastrians are guided to maintain their identity while building bridges with others, seeing these interactions as opportunities to embody the principles of Asha in diverse settings. This balance of tradition and openness allows Zoroastrians to preserve their heritage while contributing positively to the societies in which they live.

As Zoroastrianism faces the challenges of preserving its identity in a rapidly changing world, the principles of Humata, Hukhta, Hvarshta remain as relevant as ever. Efforts to transmit these values to younger generations are central to the community's survival. Education about Zoroastrian history, theology, and ethics is often emphasized in youth programs, ensuring that new generations understand the importance of aligning their lives with Asha. These educational efforts often include discussions on how ancient principles apply to modern dilemmas, providing young Zoroastrians with a sense of continuity and purpose. By engaging with their traditions in a meaningful way, younger Zoroastrians learn to see their heritage not as a relic of the past, but as a living guide to a righteous life.

The community's focus on intergenerational dialogue ensures that ethical teachings are adapted to meet contemporary realities while remaining true to their spiritual roots. Elders share their wisdom and experience, while younger members bring new perspectives, creating a dynamic process of learning and adaptation. This dialogue reinforces the belief that the essence of Zoroastrian ethics—compassion, truthfulness, respect for nature, and dedication to the wellbeing of others—transcends time, offering a timeless blueprint for a good life, no matter the era or location.

Through this ongoing engagement with their ethical teachings, Zoroastrians continue to affirm their role as protectors of Asha in a world where Druj, the force of chaos and falsehood, still poses challenges. The principles of Humata, Hukhta, Hvarshta offer a way to navigate modernity while remaining grounded in ancient wisdom, guiding every thought, word, and action. This continuity allows Zoroastrians to remain steadfast in their commitment to a life that honors the divine order, contributing to a world where light prevails over darkness, and where the values of truth, integrity, and compassion endure amidst the complexities of the present day.

Chapter 10
Women

The role of women in Zoroastrianism is both complex and significant, shaped by ancient teachings that have evolved through centuries of cultural and social changes. The position of women in Zoroastrian tradition has roots in the teachings of Zarathustra, who, according to the Gathas, emphasized the spiritual equality of men and women. Zarathustra's vision offered a view where women, like men, were seen as moral agents capable of choosing between Asha (truth and order) and Druj (falsehood and chaos). This foundational belief set the stage for a tradition where women's contributions to religious life, family, and society were acknowledged and valued.

In pre-Islamic Persia, Zoroastrianism played a significant role in shaping societal norms and laws, including those that defined the status and rights of women. Historical records from ancient Persia, such as the Achaemenid and Sassanian eras, indicate that Zoroastrian women held positions of influence within their families and communities. They had rights to property and could engage in business, an uncommon status compared to other ancient societies. Women were often involved in the economic life of the household, managing estates and participating in trade. This economic autonomy is reflected in the Zoroastrian emphasis on the family unit as a foundation of society, where both men and women contributed to its prosperity and moral fabric.

Zarathustra's teachings also placed a significant emphasis on marriage as a sacred institution, where the roles of both partners were seen as essential to maintaining Asha within the household. Marriage was viewed not only as a social contract but as a spiritual partnership aimed at fostering harmony and upholding the divine order. In this context, women played a vital role in the religious upbringing of children and in maintaining the rituals and purity practices that connected the family to the Zoroastrian faith. The home itself was considered a space where the sacred flame of Ahura Mazda could be honored through daily prayers and rituals, and women often served as the custodians of these practices, ensuring that the light of Asha was preserved in their domestic sphere.

Despite this emphasis on spiritual equality, the realities of women's roles in Zoroastrian society were shaped by the broader social structures of the time. The Sassanian legal codes, which were heavily influenced by Zoroastrian doctrine, did include provisions that reflected a patriarchal structure, such as laws related to inheritance and family hierarchy. For example, while women could inherit property, the distribution often favored male heirs. These legal frameworks, while offering women certain rights, also delineated their roles in ways that reinforced male leadership within both the household and the community. However, these structures did not negate the spiritual agency of women, who continued to be seen as vital participants in the religious life of their families and communities.

The role of women in religious practice also extended to their participation in rituals and festivals. While the priesthood remained predominantly male, women had important roles in family rituals and community celebrations. During festivals like Nowruz and Mehregan, which celebrate the renewal of life and the triumph of light, women actively participated in the preparation of sacred spaces, the creation of offerings, and the recitation of prayers. These activities underscored the belief that women's spiritual contributions were integral to the maintenance of Asha, not only within their families but within the larger Zoroastrian community.

In addition to their role in maintaining religious practices, Zoroastrian women were also recognized for their wisdom and moral guidance. Historical texts and oral traditions preserve stories of women who advised kings, led households with compassion, and served as examples of moral strength. These narratives celebrate the virtues of integrity, courage, and resilience, emphasizing that women's spiritual strength was just as crucial as their roles in family life. Figures such as Pourandokht and Azarmidokht, Sassanian queens who ruled during times of political turmoil, are remembered as leaders who embodied the principles of justice and order central to Zoroastrian teachings.

The teachings of Humata, Hukhta, Hvarshta—Good Thoughts, Good Words, and Good Deeds—provided a moral framework that applied equally to men and women, encouraging all followers to strive for a life aligned with Asha. This equality in spiritual responsibility reinforced the idea that women were not secondary in the eyes of Ahura Mazda but were capable of achieving spiritual greatness. Zarathustra's emphasis on individual choice and moral agency extended to all, suggesting that every person, regardless of gender, had a role in the cosmic battle between light and darkness.

In Zoroastrian mythology, women also play significant symbolic roles, representing both the nurturing aspects of nature and the resilience of the human spirit. The Amesha Spenta Spenta Armaiti, often associated with earth and devotion, is seen as a feminine divine force, embodying the qualities of love, patience, and loyalty to Ahura Mazda's creation. This divine aspect emphasizes the idea that the virtues associated with women are integral to the Zoroastrian vision of a balanced and harmonious universe. Spenta Armaiti's role in the divine order serves as a reminder of the importance of nurturing and sustaining the world, qualities that Zoroastrian women are encouraged to emulate in their care for family, community, and nature.

Moreover, the Zoroastrian emphasis on the purity of thought and action found expression in practices that guided women's roles in maintaining both physical and spiritual cleanliness. Rituals such as purification after childbirth, and the adherence to specific practices during menstruation, were seen as ways to align with the principles of purity central to Zoroastrian thought. While these practices reinforced a sense of ritual separation, they also highlighted the unique responsibilities of women in preserving the sanctity of life and the home. These rituals, though sometimes viewed as restrictive, were often interpreted within the community as opportunities for spiritual reflection and renewal, connecting individual practices with the broader cosmic order.

Throughout history, Zoroastrian women have navigated their roles within the framework of tradition while adapting to new social and cultural contexts. As Zoroastrianism faced challenges from external influences, including the arrival of Islam in Persia, women played a crucial role in preserving the cultural and religious practices of their community. In times of adversity, they became keepers of oral traditions, storytellers who passed down the Gathas and the stories of Zarathustra to their children, ensuring that the essence of the faith remained alive even when public practice became difficult. This role as guardians of memory and tradition underscores the enduring resilience of Zoroastrian women, who have continuously adapted their roles to support their faith's survival.

Zoroastrianism's approach to women, with its blend of spiritual equality and social tradition, offers a nuanced perspective that has allowed the faith to endure through many centuries. The teachings of Zarathustra provided a foundation that recognized the spiritual potential of women, even as societal structures shaped their roles in specific ways. This balance between ancient teachings and evolving social realities has defined the journey of Zoroastrian women, who have remained active participants in their communities, contributing to the preservation of Asha and the values that their faith holds dear.

In understanding the role of women within Zoroastrianism, it becomes clear that their contributions are woven into the very fabric of the tradition. Their presence, both as keepers of household rituals and as symbols of divine virtues, continues to shape the spiritual life of the community. As Zoroastrianism faces the challenges of maintaining its identity in the modern world, the legacy of women's spiritual strength and resilience remains a guiding light, reflecting the enduring belief that the path of Asha is one that all are called to walk, in unity and with a shared commitment to the truth that binds the cosmos together.

The contributions of Zoroastrian women have played a pivotal role in shaping the faith's resilience and continuity through history, offering both spiritual and cultural strength to their communities. As Zoroastrianism spread beyond the borders of ancient Persia, particularly during periods of migration and diaspora, women often found themselves at the forefront of preserving the religion's customs and values. Their efforts ensured that the teachings of Zarathustra remained alive, adapting to new challenges while keeping the essence of the tradition intact. This chapter explores the evolving role of Zoroastrian women, highlighting their leadership, the challenges they faced, and their ongoing struggle for recognition and equality within the broader framework of their faith.

In the centuries following the Islamic conquest of Persia, Zoroastrian communities experienced significant upheaval. Many were displaced or migrated, with a large number settling in India, where they became known as the Parsis. This migration was a turning point for Zoroastrian women, who had to adapt to a new cultural environment while maintaining their religious identity. Within this diaspora, women emerged as key figures in the home, ensuring that the rituals, prayers, and oral traditions of their ancestors were passed on to the next generation. They became storytellers, preserving the tales of Zarathustra and the ancient Persian kings, thereby keeping alive the cultural memory of a community in exile.

This role as preservers of tradition extended to the transmission of the Avesta and the daily practice of prayers before the sacred fire. Despite not being part of the priesthood, Zoroastrian women in the diaspora played a critical role in nurturing the religious devotion of their families. They taught their children the fundamental tenets of the faith, including the principles of Humata, Hukhta, Hvarshta—Good Thoughts, Good Words, and Good Deeds. Through their commitment to these values, women ensured that Zoroastrian ethical teachings remained a central part of family life, even as their communities adapted to the challenges of living in a new and often unfamiliar cultural context.

As the Parsis established themselves in India, women's roles evolved in response to the changing social landscape. In the colonial period, Parsi women began to gain access to education and professional opportunities, contributing to their communities not only as keepers of tradition but as leaders in social and economic spheres. Education empowered a new generation of Zoroastrian women, who became active in fields such as healthcare, education, and social reform. Their efforts in founding schools, hospitals, and charitable organizations were instrumental in strengthening both their own communities and the society around them. These initiatives reflected the Zoroastrian emphasis on charity and community service, values deeply embedded in their religious teachings.

Prominent figures, such as Bhikaiji Cama, who became a leading figure in India's independence movement, exemplify the spirit of Zoroastrian women who blended their commitment to their faith with a broader vision of social justice and progress. Cama's activism, along with that of other Zoroastrian women, highlighted a tradition of engagement with the wider world, where the values of Asha—truth, order, and justice—were applied to social and political causes. This blending of religious devotion and social action demonstrated that the principles taught by Zarathustra were not confined to ritual but could inspire transformative change in society.

In addition to their public roles, Zoroastrian women continued to navigate the expectations of their traditional communities, where cultural norms often placed them in defined roles within the household. These expectations sometimes created tensions as women sought to balance the respect for tradition with their desire for greater autonomy. Issues such as marriage within the faith, inheritance rights, and participation in community leadership often highlighted the challenges of maintaining traditional values while adapting to modern ideals of gender equality. For example, in traditional Zoroastrian communities, rules regarding marriage to non-Zoroastrians have been a point of contention, affecting both the status of women within the community and their children's recognition as Zoroastrians.

The struggle for gender equality within the community has seen progress over the years, with debates around these issues reflecting broader societal shifts. Many Zoroastrian women have advocated for reforms that recognize their right to full participation in religious and communal life. These efforts have included calls for greater involvement in the management of fire temples and the inclusion of women in roles traditionally reserved for men, such as the recitation of specific prayers or involvement in community councils. While these changes have met with varying degrees of acceptance, they reflect an ongoing dialogue within the community about how to honor tradition while embracing the evolving roles of women.

In recent decades, the role of Zoroastrian women has continued to expand as globalization and the dispersion of communities across the world have reshaped the Zoroastrian diaspora. Today, Zoroastrian women are found leading community organizations, participating in international conferences, and contributing to academic research that explores the history and philosophy of their faith. They bring perspectives that emphasize the need for inclusivity and adaptation, addressing the challenges of maintaining a small and scattered population. Through platforms like the World Zoroastrian Organization and regional associations, women have played a crucial role in shaping the discourse around the future of their faith, ensuring that Zoroastrianism remains relevant for the next generation.

This engagement is particularly important as the global Zoroastrian community faces the challenge of declining numbers.

Many Zoroastrian women are at the forefront of efforts to attract and educate young people about their heritage, blending traditional teachings with modern contexts. This involves creating educational programs, organizing cultural events, and using digital platforms to connect Zoroastrians across the world. By leveraging these tools, Zoroastrian women continue to play their role as educators and keepers of tradition, ensuring that the stories, values, and practices that have sustained their community are accessible to those who seek to learn.

Yet, the path is not without challenges. The question of gender equality continues to provoke discussion, especially regarding the interpretation of religious texts and the role of women in rituals traditionally led by male priests. These debates are part of a broader conversation about how Zoroastrianism can remain true to its ancient roots while evolving to reflect contemporary values. For many Zoroastrian women, this journey is not about abandoning tradition but about reimagining it in ways that allow for greater participation and recognition of their contributions. They seek a space where their voices are heard as equals, both in the sacred and communal aspects of their faith.

The journey of Zoroastrian women, from ancient Persia to modern diaspora communities, reflects the enduring strength and adaptability of their spirit. Through times of upheaval and transformation, they have remained steadfast in their dedication to preserving the light of Asha. Their resilience and leadership have ensured that the teachings of Zarathustra continue to inspire a vision of life where truth, justice, and compassion guide every action. As Zoroastrian communities look to the future, the role of women remains as vital as ever, offering a reminder that the principles of equality and moral strength that Zarathustra preached are timeless, capable of guiding a faith that is both ancient and ever-renewing.

By embracing their heritage while advocating for change, Zoroastrian women embody the spirit of Asha in a way that speaks to both the past and the future. Their journey serves as a testament to the power of faith to adapt, survive, and thrive, even in the face of challenges. They continue to illuminate the path forward, keeping alive the ancient flame that has burned for millennia—a flame that symbolizes not only the divine presence of Ahura Mazda but the enduring light of wisdom, strength, and hope that Zoroastrian women bring to their families, their communities, and the world.

Chapter 11
Purification Rituals

In Zoroastrianism, the concept of purity is central to maintaining a connection with Ahura Mazda and the cosmic order of Asha. Purification rituals are seen as essential to preserving both physical and spiritual cleanliness, protecting the faithful from the corrupting influences of Angra Mainyu, the spirit of chaos and evil. These practices embody a worldview where maintaining purity is not just a matter of physical hygiene, but a spiritual duty that upholds the divine balance of the universe. Through these rituals, Zoroastrians reinforce their commitment to living in harmony with Asha, ensuring that their actions, thoughts, and environments remain aligned with the divine order.

One of the fundamental practices in Zoroastrian purification is the padyab, or ablution, a ritual that involves the washing of hands and face before prayers or sacred activities. The act of performing a padyab is a reminder of the importance of maintaining external and internal cleanliness, symbolizing the removal of impurities before approaching the divine. This ritual is often performed before reciting prayers from the Avesta, preparing the individual to engage with the sacred texts with a pure mind and body. By consciously engaging in this simple act of purification, Zoroastrians seek to clear away both physical dirt and the distractions of daily life, creating a space for spiritual focus and reflection.

Beyond the personal practice of ablution, Zoroastrianism includes more elaborate purification rituals that are performed on specific occasions or in response to particular needs. One such ritual is the Nahn, a more comprehensive purification involving the washing of the entire body with consecrated water. The Nahns are often performed during significant life events, such as before marriage ceremonies or during periods of illness, where spiritual and physical renewal is sought. The use of consecrated water, blessed by a Mobed (priest), reinforces the belief that water is a sacred element, a medium through which the divine can cleanse and restore the individual. By immersing themselves in this ritual, Zoroastrians seek to realign their bodies and souls with the purity of Ahura Mazda's creation.

The role of fire in purification also features prominently in Zoroastrian rites. Fire, as the earthly representative of Ahura Mazda's light, serves as a purifier that can cleanse spaces, objects, and people of spiritual impurities. The sacred fire present in temples is believed to emit a spiritual energy that dispels the influence of Druj (deception and evil). During rituals, priests may wave a flame or incense burner over objects or individuals to purify them, a practice that symbolizes the power of divine light to restore balance and order. This use of fire extends to daily rituals in the home, where small lamps or candles are lit during prayers to invite the protective presence of Ahura Mazda into the household.

Another important purification ritual is the Barsom ceremony, where bundles of consecrated twigs, typically from the pomegranate or tamarisk tree, are used to bless the faithful and sacred spaces. The Barsom represents the plant life that is part of Ahura Mazda's creation, and its use in rituals symbolizes the interconnectedness of the natural and spiritual worlds. During the Barsom ceremony, the Mobed holds the bundle while reciting prayers, invoking blessings upon the participants and seeking to drive away any spiritual impurities. The ritual serves as a reminder of the Zoroastrian respect for nature, emphasizing that all elements of creation play a role in maintaining the cosmic balance of Asha.

Purification rituals in Zoroastrianism also extend to the care of sacred spaces, including temples and places where rituals are performed. It is believed that these spaces must be kept free of pollution, both physical and spiritual, to ensure that the divine presence can dwell within. Zoroastrians take great care to ensure that fire temples are maintained with strict cleanliness, and special rites are performed to purify the sacred fire itself. The attention to maintaining these spaces reflects the belief that purity is not just an individual responsibility, but a communal effort that supports the spiritual health of the entire community. By keeping their places of worship pure, Zoroastrians create environments where the divine light of Ahura Mazda can shine without obstruction, providing a refuge from the chaos of the world.

Purification is also central to Zoroastrian rites surrounding the transition between life and death. When a person passes away, Zoroastrian tradition holds that their physical body becomes impure as it is affected by decay, a process associated with Angra Mainyu. To prevent this impurity from spreading, a series of rituals is performed to purify the environment and guide the soul to the afterlife. The body is washed with bull's urine, known as nirang, and then laid to rest in a Dakhma (Tower of Silence), where it is exposed to the sun and birds of prey. This process ensures that the elements of earth, water, and fire remain untainted by decay, reflecting the belief that nature must remain pure, even in death.

The use of bull's urine in purification, although unfamiliar to modern sensibilities, is deeply rooted in Zoroastrian cosmology. It is considered a powerful agent of purification, representing the life-giving and purifying aspects of nature. It is used not only in death rituals but also in the preparation of spaces and objects for religious ceremonies. Through such practices, Zoroastrians engage with elements of their ancient heritage, maintaining traditions that have been passed down for millennia, even as they adapt them to contemporary life.

Purity in Zoroastrianism is not limited to physical acts of washing and ritual but extends to thoughts and intentions, reinforcing the spiritual dimension of these practices. The emphasis on purity of mind aligns with the ethical principles of Humata (Good Thoughts), which teaches that true purity begins within. Zoroastrians believe that negative thoughts, such as anger or jealousy, can disrupt the harmony of Asha, just as physical impurities can affect the body. Therefore, the practice of mindfulness and the cultivation of positive thoughts are seen as essential components of maintaining spiritual purity. This holistic approach to purity ensures that Zoroastrian rituals are not merely external practices, but expressions of a deeper commitment to a life lived in alignment with divine principles.

The significance of these purification rituals lies in their ability to connect the believer with the sacred, turning everyday actions into opportunities for spiritual renewal. Whether through the simple act of washing before prayer or the elaborate rites of a Nahns, Zoroastrians are constantly reminded of their role in preserving the purity of the world. This practice of ongoing purification reflects the dynamic nature of Asha, which must be actively maintained against the encroaching influence of Druj. It is through these rituals that Zoroastrians reaffirm their commitment to the cosmic order, recognizing that their actions contribute to the broader struggle between light and darkness.

Through the lens of purification, Zoroastrianism offers a vision of a world where spiritual and material realms are intertwined, where the physical act of cleansing is a reflection of a deeper, spiritual aspiration. The rituals, while ancient, carry a timeless relevance, reminding the faithful that purity is a path to divine connection. As Zoroastrians navigate the complexities of modern life, these practices provide a touchstone, a way to maintain their identity and their bond with Ahura Mazda in a world that is ever-changing.

The depth and intricacy of Zoroastrian purification rituals reveal a profound understanding of the spiritual significance behind every action. These practices, rooted in the belief that maintaining both physical and spiritual cleanliness is essential for upholding Asha, serve as a bridge between the everyday and the divine. As these rituals have evolved, they have taken on layers of meaning that connect the Zoroastrian faithful with their ancient heritage while providing a framework for engaging with the challenges of the modern world. In this chapter, we delve deeper into some of the most significant purification rites, exploring their symbolic meanings and the ways in which they reinforce the spiritual integrity of individuals and communities.

Among the most significant purification rites in Zoroastrianism is the Bareshnum, an elaborate ritual that represents the pinnacle of spiritual cleansing. The Bareshnum is reserved for serious situations, such as when a person has come into contact with a corpse or another source of significant spiritual impurity. The ritual involves a nine-day process in which the individual undergoes repeated ablutions with consecrated water and sand, guided by a Mobed (priest) who ensures that each step is conducted according to the sacred texts. The process also includes the recitation of prayers from the Avesta, invoking Ahura Mazda's aid in restoring purity. During the Bareshnum, the person remains in isolation, reflecting on their spiritual state and seeking to realign themselves with the cosmic order. This period of introspection emphasizes that purification is not merely about physical acts, but about achieving a deeper spiritual renewal.

The ritual of Bareshnum is highly symbolic, illustrating the Zoroastrian view of purification as a process of reestablishing the divine balance disrupted by exposure to death or decay. The use of consecrated elements like water and sand in the ritual signifies the unbroken connection between the spiritual and natural worlds. Water, considered a sacred gift from Ahura Mazda, cleanses the body while symbolizing the washing away of spiritual impurities. The use of sand represents the connection to the earth, reminding the participant of their role as a steward of nature, tasked with maintaining its purity. Through these elements, the Bareshnum ritual becomes a microcosm of the cosmic struggle between Asha and Druj, where each act of purification contributes to the broader goal of sustaining divine order.

A related practice is the Kusti ritual, which is performed daily by all Zoroastrians as a reminder of their commitment to purity. The Kusti is a sacred cord made of wool, worn around the waist, that symbolizes the division between good and evil, light and darkness. It is traditionally worn over the Sudreh, a white cotton shirt that represents the purity of the soul. The ritual involves untying and retying the Kusti while reciting prayers, usually performed several times a day, including at dawn, midday, and sunset. During the ritual, the individual faces a source of light, such as the sun or a lamp, symbolizing their alignment with the divine light of Ahura Mazda.

The act of untying the Kusti is seen as a symbolic release of impure thoughts or actions, while the retying represents a renewed commitment to Asha. This daily practice serves as a form of ongoing spiritual maintenance, ensuring that the individual remains focused on their ethical responsibilities. The Kusti ritual is an accessible way for Zoroastrians to integrate the principles of their faith into everyday life, emphasizing that the pursuit of purity is a continuous process that requires vigilance and intention. The simplicity of the Kusti ritual, coupled with its profound spiritual meaning, illustrates the Zoroastrian belief that even small actions can have a significant impact in the struggle to maintain order and truth in the world.

In addition to personal purification practices, Zoroastrianism emphasizes the purification of sacred objects and spaces, ensuring that they remain suitable for divine presence. One of the key rituals for purifying spaces is the Parahom ceremony, which is performed in temples or during community gatherings. This ceremony involves the preparation of a sacred mixture of milk, pomegranate leaves, and consecrated water, which is sprinkled around the space while prayers are recited. The Parahom ritual is used to cleanse areas that have been exposed to impurities or to prepare a space for a special ceremony. The use of pomegranate leaves is particularly significant, as the pomegranate is a symbol of life and fertility in Zoroastrian culture, representing the renewal of purity within the space.

The ritual of Hamazor also plays a role in communal purification, though its focus is more on the unity and strength of the community itself. Hamazor is a greeting ritual performed during gatherings, where individuals clasp hands and exchange blessings for health and prosperity. This act of physical connection symbolizes the spiritual unity of the community and the shared commitment to upholding Asha. While not a purification ritual in the physical sense, Hamazor reflects the Zoroastrian belief that maintaining harmony among individuals is essential for sustaining the purity of the community. The ritual reinforces the idea that spiritual purity extends beyond the individual to encompass relationships and the collective wellbeing of the faithful.

Another essential aspect of Zoroastrian purification is the maintenance of Dakhmas, or Towers of Silence, where the bodies of the deceased are placed for sky burial. While this practice has declined in many regions, it remains a symbol of the Zoroastrian emphasis on keeping the elements—earth, water, fire, and air—free from the pollution of death. The Dakhmas are constructed in a way that allows sunlight and scavenger birds to naturally decompose the body, thus preserving the purity of the earth and preventing contamination. This practice reflects the belief that the natural world must be respected and that death, while a passage for the soul, should not disrupt the divine order of nature. For communities that no longer practice sky burials, modified rites are performed to ensure that the spirit of this ancient tradition is maintained.

In contemporary times, Zoroastrians have adapted many of these ancient rituals to fit new contexts, particularly as the community has spread across diverse geographic and cultural landscapes. While the full Bareshnum ritual is rarely performed today due to its complexity, elements of its practice, such as specific prayers and acts of ablution, have been integrated into simpler forms that can be performed in daily life. Similarly, the principles behind the purification of sacred spaces continue to guide the design and maintenance of Zoroastrian temples and community centers, where rituals like the Parahom ensure that these places remain sanctuaries of divine light.

The adaptation of purification rituals reflects the resilience of Zoroastrian traditions, where the core spiritual values are preserved even as the practices themselves evolve. Zoroastrians living in modern urban environments, for example, have found ways to maintain their daily Kusti prayers and purity practices despite the constraints of contemporary life. For many, these adapted rituals serve as a reminder of their connection to a spiritual heritage that spans millennia, providing a sense of continuity and grounding amidst the rapid changes of the modern world.

Through these purification rituals, Zoroastrians continually renew their bond with Ahura Mazda and reaffirm their role as guardians of Asha. The practices, whether simple daily ablutions or intricate communal ceremonies, serve as a testament to the enduring belief that purity is the foundation of spiritual strength. By maintaining this purity, Zoroastrians contribute to the cosmic struggle against Angra Mainyu, upholding a vision of life where light and truth are preserved against the forces of darkness and deceit.

The enduring relevance of these rituals lies not in their form alone, but in the values they embody. They teach that purity is both a state of being and a path of continuous effort, a journey that each individual and community undertakes to sustain the light of Asha in their lives. Through the act of purification, Zoroastrians remember that they are part of a greater cosmic order, connected to a tradition that calls upon them to be mindful stewards of the world, always seeking to maintain the balance between the sacred and the everyday.

Chapter 12
Festivals and Celebrations

Zoroastrian festivals represent a harmonious blend of spirituality, nature, and the cycles of life, acting as powerful reminders of the cosmic order established by Ahura Mazda. These celebrations, deeply rooted in the principles of Asha, are designed to align the faithful with the rhythms of the natural world, honoring the divine and reinforcing the community's connection to the universe. Through these festivals, Zoroastrians express gratitude, seek renewal, and celebrate the triumph of light over darkness. Each festival holds a unique place within the Zoroastrian calendar, offering moments for reflection, joy, and collective worship.

Among the most significant Zoroastrian festivals is Nowruz, the Persian New Year, which marks the arrival of spring and the renewal of life. Celebrated on the vernal equinox, Nowruz is a time when day and night are balanced, symbolizing the equilibrium between the forces of good and evil. The festival's origins predate Zoroastrianism, but it was embraced and enriched by the faith, which infused it with themes of rebirth and spiritual awakening. During Nowruz, Zoroastrians prepare their homes with meticulous care, performing deep cleanings known as khaneh takani, a symbolic act of purifying both the physical space and the soul in preparation for the new year. This practice reflects the Zoroastrian emphasis on purity, making Nowruz not only a celebration of nature's rebirth but also a personal and spiritual renewal for the faithful.

Central to the Nowruz celebration is the preparation of the Haft-Seen, a table adorned with seven symbolic items, each beginning with the Persian letter "S." These items, including sabzeh (sprouted wheat or lentils), senjed (dried oleaster fruit), seeb (apple), seer (garlic), somāq (sumac), serkeh (vinegar), and samanu (sweet pudding), represent different aspects of life and the hopes for the coming year—growth, health, prosperity, and wisdom. In some traditions, the Haft-Seen may also include a holy book, such as the Avesta, to signify the spiritual aspect of the celebration. Lighting candles around the Haft-Seen serves as a reminder of the ever-present light of Ahura Mazda, guiding the faithful through life's challenges and bringing hope for the future. This focus on light and new beginnings is a reflection of Zoroastrian cosmology, where every act that upholds Asha contributes to the renewal of creation.

Another key element of Nowruz is the Chaharshanbe Suri, or the Festival of Fire, which takes place on the last Wednesday before the new year. During this festival, Zoroastrians jump over small bonfires, chanting phrases that express the wish for their ailments to be taken away by the fire, while receiving its warmth and vitality. The bonfire jumping is symbolic of the transformative power of fire, which, in Zoroastrian belief, represents the purifying light of Ahura Mazda. This ritual serves as a way to leave behind the burdens of the past year and step into the new year with renewed energy. It also highlights the enduring Zoroastrian respect for fire as a symbol of spiritual purity, a theme that runs through many aspects of the faith.

Mehregan is another important Zoroastrian festival, celebrated in honor of Mithra, the divine being associated with covenants, friendship, and the light of the sun. Falling in autumn, Mehregan is a time for giving thanks for the harvest and the abundance of the earth. It reflects the Zoroastrian belief in the interconnectedness of all life and the responsibility of humans to protect and nurture nature. Traditionally, Zoroastrians gather with their families and communities during Mehregan to offer prayers, share meals, and recite passages from the Avesta that praise Mithra and the natural world. The celebration is marked by the sharing of fruits, flowers, and incense, symbolizing the gifts of nature and the renewal of spiritual bonds within the community.

Mehregan is also a time for acts of charity, reflecting the Zoroastrian value of generosity. During this festival, Zoroastrians are encouraged to support those in need, ensuring that the blessings of the harvest are shared among all. This practice emphasizes the ethical dimension of Zoroastrian festivals, where celebration is always intertwined with the responsibility to uphold Asha in both personal and social life. By practicing generosity and kindness during Mehregan, Zoroastrians strengthen the bonds of community and reaffirm their commitment to the values that define their faith.

Yalda, the longest night of the year, is another celebration that holds deep spiritual meaning in the Zoroastrian tradition. Occurring on the winter solstice, Yalda represents the struggle between light and darkness, a theme central to Zoroastrian cosmology. On this night, Zoroastrians gather with their loved ones, staying awake through the long hours to witness the triumph of the sun over the darkness as dawn approaches. It is a time for storytelling, reciting poetry, and reflecting on the cycles of life and nature. The symbolism of Yalda as a time when light begins its slow return mirrors the eternal Zoroastrian belief in the eventual triumph of good over evil. It reminds the faithful that even in the darkest times, the promise of light remains.

During Yalda, special foods are prepared, such as pomegranates, nuts, and watermelon, which are believed to bring warmth and protection against the harshness of winter. The red seeds of the pomegranate symbolize the life-giving blood, while the bright colors of the fruit are a reminder of the sun's eventual return. The communal nature of Yalda gatherings emphasizes the importance of solidarity and mutual support within the Zoroastrian community, reinforcing the idea that facing challenges together strengthens the bonds that sustain spiritual resilience.

Zoroastrian festivals also include Gahambars, which are seasonal celebrations that honor the six stages of creation as described in Zoroastrian cosmology. Each Gahambar is associated with a particular aspect of creation, such as the sky, water, earth, plants, animals, and humans. These festivals, spread throughout the year, invite Zoroastrians to give thanks for the elements that sustain life and to reflect on their role as stewards of the natural world. During Gahambars, Zoroastrians gather to share communal meals, offer prayers, and engage in acts of charity, reinforcing the connection between spiritual practice and the wellbeing of the community. The Gahambars are a reminder that the material world is not separate from the spiritual, but is an integral part of Ahura Mazda's creation that must be respected and cherished.

These seasonal festivals underscore the Zoroastrian belief in living in harmony with nature and recognizing the divine presence within all aspects of the world. By celebrating the cycles of the earth, Zoroastrians affirm their place within a universe that is alive with the presence of the divine. The festivals provide a structure for the year that is deeply intertwined with the natural rhythms of the earth, ensuring that spiritual practice is woven into the changing seasons. Through these observances, Zoroastrians are reminded that their actions—whether in honoring the changing seasons or sharing their blessings—have a direct impact on the balance between Asha and Druj, contributing to the ongoing struggle to maintain order and goodness in the world.

The celebrations of Nowruz, Mehregan, Yalda, and the Gahambars each offer unique opportunities for spiritual renewal and communal gathering, reflecting the enduring values of Zoroastrianism. They serve as living reminders of a tradition that celebrates the divine through the joy of life's cycles, encouraging the faithful to cultivate gratitude, seek purity, and engage in acts of kindness. As Zoroastrianism continues to adapt to modern life, these festivals remain a cornerstone of its practice, ensuring that the ancient connection between nature, community, and the divine remains vibrant and relevant in a changing world. Through each celebration, Zoroastrians reaffirm their dedication to the principles that have guided them for millennia, embracing the light that shines through the darkest nights and the hope that comes with each new dawn.

The vibrant cycle of Zoroastrian festivals is not just a way to mark the passage of time, but a deeply spiritual practice that weaves together community, memory, and cosmic alignment. Each festival is imbued with layers of ritual and meaning that reflect the core Zoroastrian values of Asha (truth and order) and the eternal battle against Druj (falsehood and chaos). Through these celebrations, Zoroastrians come together to connect with their ancient traditions, honor Ahura Mazda, and strengthen the bonds that unite their communities. This chapter delves deeper into the specific practices and rituals of these festivals, exploring how they are performed and the profound sense of continuity they create among Zoroastrians across the world.

One of the key rituals performed during Nowruz is the Farvardigan, or Muktad, a ten-day period leading up to the New Year dedicated to honoring the spirits of the deceased, known as Fravashis. During the Farvardigan, Zoroastrian families prepare their homes and temples to welcome these ancestral spirits, believing that the Fravashis return to offer their blessings and receive gratitude. Families set up small altars with fresh flowers, fruits, and sacred fire, reciting prayers to invoke the protection and guidance of the spirits. This act of remembrance emphasizes the Zoroastrian belief in the enduring presence of the spiritual world and the importance of respecting the connection between past and present. The Farvardigan is a time of reflection, where the living honor those who have come before them, recognizing that the strength of the community is built upon the legacy of those who have upheld Asha throughout the ages.

The rituals of Jashan ceremonies, which occur during various festivals, provide another window into the communal and devotional aspects of Zoroastrian celebrations. A Jashan is a prayer service conducted by Mobeds (priests) to bless the community, often performed to commemorate special occasions or to give thanks for the blessings of Ahura Mazda. During these ceremonies, priests recite verses from the Avesta, offer myazda (ritual offerings of fruits, milk, and sacred bread), and perform the ritual of Atash Niyayesh, where the sacred fire is revered with offerings and prayers. The congregation gathers around, participating through their presence and silent recitation, reinforcing a shared spiritual focus. The Jashan serves as a powerful reminder of the unity of the Zoroastrian community, where every individual plays a part in sustaining the spiritual health of the whole.

One particularly significant Jashan is the celebration of Khordad Sal, the birthday of the prophet Zarathustra. On this day, Zoroastrians gather in fire temples and community halls to remember the life and teachings of their prophet. The celebration includes prayers that recount Zarathustra's revelations and his message of good thoughts, good words, and good deeds. It is a time to renew one's commitment to living according to the principles of Asha, reflecting on the ways in which Zarathustra's teachings can guide modern life. Khordad Sal is not only a celebration of a historical figure but also a moment of spiritual introspection, where Zoroastrians are reminded of their role as followers of a tradition that seeks to bring light into the world.

During Mehregan, one of the unique practices involves the Haft Mewa, or the arrangement of seven fruits. This symbolic display is meant to honor the abundance provided by Mithra, the deity of light, loyalty, and friendship. Each fruit represents a different blessing, such as health, prosperity, and fertility. Families come together to enjoy the fruits, sharing in a meal that symbolizes both physical and spiritual nourishment. The act of sharing during Mehregan reflects the Zoroastrian commitment to charity and hospitality, emphasizing that true celebration involves giving to others and ensuring that the blessings of life are shared with all. The communal nature of Mehregan, like that of Nowruz, serves to strengthen the bonds between Zoroastrians, reminding them that their faith is both a personal journey and a collective experience.

The ritual practices associated with Tirgan, a summer festival dedicated to Tishtrya, the star that brings rain, further highlight the connection between Zoroastrian celebrations and the natural world. Tirgan is celebrated with rituals that involve splashing water, symbolizing the life-giving rains that Tishtrya brings to the earth. This festival is a joyful time, especially for children, who engage in playful water fights and dances. Zoroastrians believe that the waters of Tishtrya bring spiritual cleansing as well as physical renewal, aligning with their broader belief in the sacredness of natural elements. The playful spirit of Tirgan, combined with the reverence for water, illustrates the balance in Zoroastrianism between serious devotion and the celebration of life's simple joys. It is a festival where laughter and gratitude merge, honoring the cycles that sustain the earth.

Zartosht No Diso, the commemoration of the death of Zarathustra, provides a more somber yet deeply reflective contrast to the more festive holidays. It is a day for prayer, mourning, and contemplation of the teachings that Zarathustra left behind. During Zartosht No Diso, Zoroastrians visit fire temples to offer prayers for the prophet's soul and reflect on the moral and spiritual lessons he imparted. It is a time to consider the challenges of maintaining Asha in a world that often leans towards chaos and deceit, and to draw strength from the prophet's example. This day serves as a reminder of the continuity of the Zoroastrian tradition, encouraging the faithful to remain steadfast in their commitment to righteousness, even in the face of adversity.

The celebration of Navjote, or the initiation ceremony for young Zoroastrians, is another key ritual that often takes place around major festivals like Nowruz or Mehregan. During Navjote, children are welcomed into the Zoroastrian faith in a ceremony that involves the donning of the Sudreh (white undershirt) and Kusti (sacred cord). The ceremony is a communal event, bringing together family and friends to witness the child's entry into the religious community. As part of the ceremony, the child recites prayers and is taught the significance of maintaining purity and upholding the principles of Asha throughout their life. The Navjote ceremony symbolizes a moment of spiritual awakening, where the individual assumes their responsibility to the cosmic struggle between good and evil. By conducting this ceremony during festival times, families emphasize the connection between personal faith and the larger cycles of renewal and celebration that define Zoroastrian practice.

Across all these celebrations, the interplay of light and darkness, of purity and renewal, remains a central theme. Rituals like the lighting of oil lamps during Yalda or the kindling of the sacred fire during Jashan ceremonies serve as constant reminders of the Zoroastrian belief in the power of light to overcome even the deepest shadows. These acts of illumination, whether performed in temples or homes, reflect the timeless struggle of Asha against Druj, urging the faithful to kindle the flame of righteousness within themselves. The physical light, whether it burns brightly in a temple's fire altar or gently flickers on a family's Haft-Seen table, symbolizes the spiritual light that each Zoroastrian is called to nurture in their daily life.

In the modern world, Zoroastrian festivals have adapted to new cultural contexts, with communities finding ways to celebrate their traditions in diverse and globalized environments. While the settings may change, the essence of these festivals remains, providing continuity for Zoroastrians living far from the lands where these traditions first took root. Diaspora communities gather in homes, community centers, and adapted fire temples, creating spaces where the ancient prayers resonate with new voices. The shared experience of celebrating these festivals becomes a source of strength and identity, offering a way for Zoroastrians to stay connected to their roots while embracing their place in a diverse and changing world.

These celebrations are not only a means of preserving tradition but are also an affirmation of life, a way of embracing the divine presence in every moment of joy and reflection. They offer a reminder that Zoroastrianism is a living faith, one that finds expression in the cycles of nature, in the rhythm of daily life, and in the warmth of community. Through these rituals, Zoroastrians honor their past, celebrate their present, and look forward with hope, confident in the belief that as long as the light is tended, Asha will endure.

Chapter 13
Life After Death

The Zoroastrian view of life after death presents a vision of the cosmos where moral choices in life resonate far beyond the earthly realm, shaping the destiny of the soul in the afterlife. This belief system is rooted in the teachings of Zarathustra, who emphasized the importance of each individual's actions, thoughts, and words in determining their spiritual fate. For Zoroastrians, death is not seen as an end, but as a transition to a spiritual journey that reveals the consequences of one's earthly life. The concept of judgment after death reflects the broader Zoroastrian cosmology, where the forces of Asha (truth) and Druj (deception) continue their eternal struggle, with the human soul playing a crucial role in maintaining the balance between them.

Central to the Zoroastrian understanding of the afterlife is the Chinvat Bridge—the Bridge of Judgment. According to the Avesta and later Zoroastrian texts, when a person dies, their soul lingers near the body for three days and nights, during which time prayers are offered by the family and the community. These prayers, often recited by Mobeds (priests) and the deceased's loved ones, seek to comfort the soul on its journey and to invoke the protection of Ahura Mazda. The community's role in these prayers underscores the belief that death is not a solitary experience but a passage that involves the support and solidarity of those left behind.

On the fourth day, the soul is believed to reach the Chinvat Bridge, where it is judged based on the moral quality of its life on Earth. This bridge is described as a narrow path suspended over an abyss, symbolizing the razor-thin line between virtue and vice. Here, the soul encounters three spiritual entities: Mithra, the divine judge associated with truth and contracts; Sraosha, the guardian of prayers; and Rashnu, the deity of justice. Together, they weigh the soul's deeds using a divine scale, where the good deeds are measured against the bad. If the good deeds outweigh the bad, the soul finds the bridge broad and easy to cross, leading to the realms of light. However, if the bad deeds outweigh the good, the bridge becomes narrow and perilous, and the soul risks falling into the abyss below.

This judgment process reflects the Zoroastrian emphasis on moral responsibility and the idea that every thought, word, and action contributes to the cosmic struggle between good and evil. Unlike some religious traditions that focus on divine grace as the sole arbiter of salvation, Zoroastrianism places significant weight on the individual's choices and the ethical integrity of their life. This emphasis encourages followers to live with a sense of purpose, mindful of the impact of their actions on both their soul and the world around them.

The outcome of this judgment determines the soul's journey to one of three possible realms: Garōdmān, the House of Song (Paradise); Hamistagan, the intermediate place; or Duzakh, the House of Lies (Hell). Garōdmān is described as a realm filled with divine light, where the soul is reunited with Ahura Mazda and experiences eternal joy alongside other righteous spirits. It is a place of spiritual fulfillment, where the virtues cultivated in life continue to flourish, and the soul finds peace in the company of other followers of Asha. In this realm, the light of Ahura Mazda illuminates every aspect of existence, symbolizing the ultimate triumph of good over evil.

Hamistagan, the intermediate state, is for those souls whose good and bad deeds are evenly balanced. This state is neither one of bliss nor torment but rather a place of waiting, where the soul exists in a kind of spiritual suspension. In Zoroastrian tradition, Hamistagan represents the complexity of human morality, acknowledging that many lives contain a mixture of virtues and shortcomings. While in Hamistagan, the soul remains in a liminal state, reflecting on its life and awaiting the final renewal of the world, known as Frashokereti, when all souls will eventually be purified and reunited with Ahura Mazda. This intermediate realm emphasizes the belief in the potential for spiritual growth and redemption, even after death.

Duzakh, or the House of Lies, is reserved for those who have aligned themselves with Druj through acts of deceit, cruelty, and injustice. It is depicted as a dark and cold place, where souls endure suffering as a result of their moral failures. Unlike many depictions of Hell in other traditions, Zoroastrian Duzakh is not eternal; it is a place of purification rather than permanent punishment. The suffering experienced by the souls in Duzakh is understood as a consequence of their actions, a period where they confront the harm they have caused and the deviations from Asha. The existence of this realm serves as a stern reminder of the consequences of moral corruption but also underscores the Zoroastrian belief in eventual cosmic restoration, where even the darkest places will be transformed by the light of Ahura Mazda.

The journey of the soul through these realms highlights the Zoroastrian focus on individual agency and the responsibility to choose righteousness. Throughout life, Zoroastrians are encouraged to embody the principles of Humata, Hukhta, Hvarshta—Good Thoughts, Good Words, and Good Deeds—as a way of ensuring a favorable passage at the Chinvat Bridge. The teachings of Zarathustra emphasize that each person has the capacity to shape their spiritual destiny through their choices, reflecting a worldview where free will plays a central role. This belief in the power of choice inspires followers to engage actively in their communities, to support justice, and to care for the environment, recognizing that their actions have spiritual consequences that extend into the afterlife.

This understanding of life after death also profoundly influences Zoroastrian funerary practices, which are designed to respect the purity of the natural elements. According to tradition, the deceased's body is placed in a Dakhma, or Tower of Silence, where it is exposed to the elements and to carrion birds. This practice ensures that the body does not contaminate the sacred elements of earth, water, or fire. By returning the body to nature in this manner, Zoroastrians fulfill their duty to protect the purity of creation, even in death. While the soul embarks on its journey across the Chinvat Bridge, the body is released back into the cycle of nature, emphasizing the belief that physical life is part of a larger cosmic order.

The rituals surrounding death, including the prayers and purification rites performed by the Mobeds, reflect the Zoroastrian belief that the living can assist the soul in its journey. These practices ensure that the transition from the material to the spiritual realm is conducted with reverence and care, reinforcing the belief that death is a deeply spiritual process that connects the earthly realm with the divine. By engaging in these rites, Zoroastrians honor both the memory of the deceased and the cosmic order that guides all life.

The Zoroastrian view of life after death offers a vision where hope and justice are intertwined. It provides comfort to the living, offering the assurance that the efforts made in life to uphold Asha will be rewarded with reunion in the House of Song. At the same time, it serves as a call to ethical action, reminding believers that their choices shape not only their immediate world but also their eternal journey. In a tradition that places such value on the interplay of light and darkness, the path of the soul is seen as a continuation of the cosmic struggle, where every thought and deed contributes to the triumph of truth. This view inspires Zoroastrians to live with integrity and purpose, knowing that their legacy is not confined to the material world but is written into the very fabric of the universe.

As the journey of the soul progresses beyond the Chinvat Bridge, Zoroastrian eschatology reveals a rich tapestry of beliefs that illuminate the nature of the afterlife and the destiny that awaits each spirit. This chapter delves deeper into the realms of Paradise (Garōdmān), purgatory (Hamistagan), and the Zoroastrian concept of Hell (Duzakh), exploring how these concepts have evolved over time and their enduring impact on the ethical life of Zoroastrians. These teachings reflect the intricate relationship between cosmic order (Asha), moral responsibility, and the ultimate hope for universal restoration.

Garōdmān, often referred to as the House of Song, represents the ultimate destination for souls who have lived in accordance with Asha. This realm is described in the Avesta as a place of boundless light, joy, and spiritual fulfillment, where the soul is surrounded by the presence of other righteous spirits. Here, the divine radiance of Ahura Mazda illuminates every aspect of existence, offering a state of eternal peace and unity with the divine order. In Garōdmān, souls experience the bliss that comes from the realization of their highest potential, living in harmony with the values they upheld during their earthly lives. This vision of Paradise is not only a reward but also a continuation of the soul's journey toward perfection, where it can fully partake in the cosmic symphony of light and truth.

In Zoroastrian teachings, Garōdmān is more than a distant heavenly reward—it serves as an ethical goal that guides the actions of the faithful. The desire to reach the House of Song motivates Zoroastrians to live lives of integrity, kindness, and spiritual awareness. This emphasis on earning one's place in the afterlife through the cultivation of virtues highlights the Zoroastrian belief that every individual is an active participant in their spiritual destiny. The joy of Garōdmān is thus seen as the natural outcome of a life lived in alignment with the principles of Asha, where the soul's light grows brighter with every good thought, word, and deed.

In contrast, Duzakh, or the House of Lies, presents a vision of the afterlife that serves as a stark warning against the consequences of moral failure. This realm is depicted as dark, cold, and desolate, a place where the soul is confronted with the full weight of its alignment with Druj (falsehood). Unlike the fiery infernos of other religious traditions, Zoroastrian Hell is a place of spiritual desolation rather than physical torment. It is a state where the soul is isolated from the divine light, trapped in the darkness that it cultivated through deceit, cruelty, and betrayal of the values of Asha. The suffering experienced in Duzakh is not seen as eternal, however, but as a temporary state meant to purify the soul through the realization of its moral failings.

The concept of Duzakh underscores the Zoroastrian belief in the inherent goodness of creation and the possibility of redemption. Even in the depths of this shadowy realm, the soul retains the potential for transformation. This belief is central to the idea of Frashokereti, the final restoration of the world, when all souls—regardless of their initial fate—will be purified and reconciled with Ahura Mazda. The teachings of Zarathustra emphasize that no soul is beyond the reach of divine mercy, and that the eventual triumph of Asha over Druj will bring about the healing of all creation. This vision of hope offers solace to the faithful, reminding them that the struggle between good and evil, both in life and beyond, is ultimately oriented toward renewal and unity.

Hamistagan, the intermediate state, provides a nuanced view of the afterlife that acknowledges the complexity of human behavior. Here, souls who have lived lives of both virtue and vice dwell, experiencing neither the joys of Garōdmān nor the desolation of Duzakh. Hamistagan represents a state of reflection and spiritual stasis, where the soul contemplates its actions and awaits the cosmic renewal. It is a place where the balance of good and bad deeds is closely measured, offering the possibility for the soul to grow in understanding and align more fully with Asha over time. In this way, Hamistagan reflects the Zoroastrian belief that the journey toward spiritual growth does not end with physical death, but continues as the soul seeks to harmonize with the divine order.

The role of Frashokereti in Zoroastrian eschatology is particularly significant in understanding the ultimate fate of all souls. This concept, which describes the eventual renovation and purification of the world, envisions a time when the forces of Asha will fully prevail, erasing the influence of Druj and bringing about a perfect, immortal state for all creation. At this time, the souls in Hamistagan and Duzakh are believed to be cleansed of their impurities, emerging to join the righteous in the House of Song. The world itself will be transformed, with death and suffering abolished, and the physical realm elevated to a divine plane. This idea of a final transformation embodies the Zoroastrian hope for a future where justice, peace, and truth reign supreme, and where every soul finds its place within the restored order.

The belief in Frashokereti shapes the way Zoroastrians approach their earthly lives, instilling a sense of responsibility for the future of the world and the fate of all souls. It encourages the faithful to engage in acts that contribute to the betterment of the world, from charity and community service to environmental stewardship. By aligning their actions with the vision of a purified world, Zoroastrians participate in the ongoing process of creation, making choices that support the realization of a world filled with light and harmony. The idea that each person's deeds can influence the ultimate restoration of the cosmos underscores the profound interconnectedness between individual actions and the broader fate of the universe.

These beliefs about the afterlife also influence Zoroastrian funerary rites, which are designed to respect the spiritual journey of the deceased while maintaining the purity of the natural elements. The recitation of prayers during the days leading up to the soul's judgment is intended to provide guidance and support, ensuring that the transition from the earthly to the spiritual realm is as smooth as possible. These rituals, including the use of consecrated fire and the recitation of sacred verses, reinforce the belief that the soul remains part of the community, even as it embarks on its journey across the Chinvat Bridge.

In contemporary times, Zoroastrian communities continue to adapt these ancient beliefs and practices to fit modern contexts. For those who no longer observe the traditional use of Dakhmas, cremation or burial is conducted with a focus on maintaining the spiritual integrity of the rites, ensuring that the sacred elements remain respected. Despite these changes, the core teachings about the soul's journey, the significance of moral actions, and the hope for Frashokereti remain central to Zoroastrian faith. They offer a framework for understanding life and death that is deeply rooted in the belief that every life contributes to the divine plan, and that every soul is destined to find its place within the light of Ahura Mazda.

Zoroastrian views of the afterlife provide a powerful narrative that blends accountability with compassion, emphasizing the importance of ethical living while offering hope for ultimate redemption. The journey of the soul, from the trials of the Chinvat Bridge to the promise of Garōdmān and the cleansing fires of Frashokereti, is a reflection of the Zoroastrian vision of the cosmos as a dynamic space where each action reverberates through time and space. This vision encourages followers to live with a sense of purpose, knowing that their choices shape not only their own destiny but contribute to the greater cosmic struggle. Through their beliefs about life after death, Zoroastrians hold to the promise that, in the end, Asha will triumph, bringing light and order to every corner of creation.

Chapter 14
The Amesha Spentas

The Amesha Spentas, often translated as the "Beneficent Immortals," occupy a central role in Zoroastrian theology and cosmology, representing divine aspects of Ahura Mazda's creation. These seven spiritual entities are seen not merely as deities but as embodiments of the principles that govern the universe and maintain the cosmic order of Asha. Each Amesha Spenta holds dominion over a particular aspect of existence, guiding the faithful and helping to sustain the balance between good and evil in the world. Through their attributes and associations, the Amesha Spentas offer Zoroastrians a framework for understanding their relationship with the divine, with nature, and with their own spiritual development.

Ahura Mazda, the supreme deity in Zoroastrianism, is considered the source from which the Amesha Spentas emanate. They serve as extensions of his will, manifesting his qualities throughout creation and ensuring that Asha—truth, righteousness, and order—pervades the universe. The Amesha Spentas are not only venerated for their individual powers but are also deeply intertwined, forming a spiritual network that represents the interconnected nature of life. Zoroastrians understand these divine beings as guides who assist in the ongoing struggle against Druj, the forces of chaos and falsehood, by maintaining the integrity of creation.

Among the Amesha Spentas, Vohu Manah, which means "Good Mind," is considered fundamental. Vohu Manah represents the divine wisdom that inspires good thoughts and guides human beings towards moral and ethical decisions. This entity governs the mind and intellect, encouraging clarity, compassion, and understanding. Vohu Manah's influence is crucial in helping Zoroastrians discern between right and wrong, and in fostering a sense of empathy toward all living beings. This Amesha Spenta is also associated with animals, symbolizing the compassion and care that should be extended to all creatures. For Zoroastrians, cultivating Vohu Manah means developing a mindset that is aligned with the principles of Asha, allowing the individual to make choices that contribute to the greater good.

Next is Asha Vahishta, or "Best Truth," who embodies the very essence of Asha itself. Asha Vahishta is the guardian of truth, order, and the natural laws that govern the cosmos. This Amesha Spenta represents the divine order that keeps the universe in balance, ensuring that every aspect of creation functions in harmony with the will of Ahura Mazda. In Zoroastrian practices, Asha Vahishta is invoked in prayers and rituals that seek to maintain purity and righteousness, whether in personal conduct or in the community. Asha Vahishta's influence extends to the realm of fire, seen as the physical manifestation of truth and purity on earth. Fire, as a symbol of this divine being, is central to Zoroastrian worship, with fire temples serving as places where the light of Asha Vahishta is revered and maintained. Through this connection, Zoroastrians are reminded that to live truthfully is to live in alignment with the cosmic order that Asha Vahishta upholds.

Spenta Armaiti, or "Holy Devotion," represents the virtues of love, humility, and devotion to the divine. Spenta Armaiti is seen as the guardian of the earth, embodying the nurturing qualities that sustain life and provide for the needs of all beings. This Amesha Spenta teaches Zoroastrians the importance of living with a spirit of gratitude and respect for nature, recognizing that the earth is a sacred gift that requires careful stewardship. Spenta Armaiti's influence is evident in the Zoroastrian emphasis on environmental care and the ethical use of natural resources. Zoroastrians believe that by honoring the earth and treating it with reverence, they align themselves with the qualities of Spenta Armaiti, contributing to the preservation of Asha in the world.

Khshathra Vairya, or "Desirable Dominion," embodies the principles of strength, authority, and the just exercise of power. This Amesha Spenta is associated with the sky and metal, representing the strength needed to protect the world from the encroaching forces of chaos. Khshathra Vairya is invoked in the context of leadership and governance, where the emphasis is on using power wisely and fairly. This divine entity serves as a reminder that true authority comes from the responsibility to uphold justice and protect the vulnerable. For Zoroastrians, following the path of Khshathra Vairya means striving to be a force for good in the world, using their influence to support the values of fairness and integrity. Through this, they contribute to the establishment of a society that reflects the divine order that Khshathra Vairya represents.

Haurvatat and Ameretat, often considered twin entities, are associated with wholeness and immortality, respectively. Haurvatat, which means "Wholeness" or "Perfection," is the guardian of water, a sacred element in Zoroastrianism that symbolizes life, purity, and renewal. Haurvatat's influence encourages the faithful to seek balance and completeness in their spiritual lives, reflecting the natural harmony found in water's flow. Rituals involving water, such as ablutions and the consecration of sacred springs, honor Haurvatat's role in maintaining purity. Ameretat, meaning "Immortality," is associated with plants and eternal life, symbolizing the resilience and continuity of the soul beyond physical death. Ameretat's presence reminds Zoroastrians of the eternal nature of the soul and the promise of life that endures through cycles of growth and renewal. Together, Haurvatat and Ameretat inspire a vision of life that is both spiritually fulfilled and eternal, guiding the faithful toward a deeper connection with the divine.

Lastly, Spenta Mainyu, the "Holy Spirit," represents the creative and life-giving aspect of Ahura Mazda's essence. Spenta Mainyu is not considered separate from Ahura Mazda but rather as an extension of his creative energy, working to foster growth, goodness, and vitality throughout the cosmos. Spenta Mainyu embodies the forces that promote life, innovation, and positive change, countering the destructive tendencies of Angra Mainyu (the Destructive Spirit). The presence of Spenta Mainyu in the world is a reminder that creation itself is a sacred act, one that Zoroastrians are called to participate in through their own acts of creativity, care, and compassion. By aligning with Spenta Mainyu, Zoroastrians commit to nurturing life and opposing anything that threatens the harmony of creation.The interplay between the Amesha Spentas and their associations with natural elements like fire, water, earth, and plants reflects a worldview where every part of creation is seen as imbued with spiritual significance. For Zoroastrians, the Amesha Spentas serve as models of divine virtues that they strive to embody in their daily lives. Through rituals, prayers, and meditations on the qualities of each Amesha Spenta, the faithful seek to deepen their connection with these divine principles, ensuring that their actions reflect the higher ideals that sustain the cosmos.

By understanding the roles of the Amesha Spentas, Zoroastrians are reminded that their spiritual path is not walked alone; they are supported by these divine beings who represent the best qualities that humanity can aspire to. The relationship between the Amesha Spentas and the physical world encourages Zoroastrians to see their own lives as part of a larger, divine tapestry, where each act of kindness, each truth spoken, and each moment of devotion contributes to the ongoing maintenance of Asha. As guides and protectors, the Amesha Spentas provide both a blueprint for living and a source of spiritual strength, helping Zoroastrians navigate the complexities of life with wisdom, devotion, and a commitment to the eternal struggle against chaos and falsehood.

The significance of the Amesha Spentas in Zoroastrian spirituality extends beyond their symbolic roles, as they are woven into the fabric of Zoroastrian worship, ethics, and daily life. Each of the Amesha Spentas offers a path for the faithful to connect with Ahura Mazda's divine order through specific practices, prayers, and meditations. This chapter delves into the deeper attributes of each Amesha Spenta, exploring how they are invoked in ritual, their presence in sacred texts, and their influence on the moral and spiritual guidance of Zoroastrians.

Vohu Manah (Good Mind) is especially central to Zoroastrian prayer and meditation practices. The Gathas, the hymns attributed to Zarathustra, often invoke Vohu Manah as a guide for understanding divine wisdom and making decisions aligned with Asha. In reciting these ancient verses, Zoroastrians seek to cultivate clarity and insight, using their minds to discern the paths that lead to righteousness. Vohu Manah's association with the intellect means that it is considered essential for achieving a deeper comprehension of spiritual truths. During rituals, the faithful reflect on how their thoughts shape their actions, seeking the influence of Vohu Manah to maintain a mindset that is compassionate, thoughtful, and true. In this way, the good mind is not just an abstract ideal but a daily practice, guiding Zoroastrians to act with empathy toward all living beings.

In Zoroastrian temples, Asha Vahishta (Best Truth) is often symbolized through the ever-burning sacred fire, known as Atar. The fire represents the presence of Asha Vahishta, reminding worshippers of the purity and integrity that this Amesha Spenta embodies. The constant flame serves as a visual meditation on the eternal nature of truth, which, like fire, must be tended and preserved. Zoroastrians offer sandalwood and other offerings to the fire, invoking Asha Vahishta to bless their prayers and maintain the spiritual purity of their intentions. This connection between fire and truth underscores the belief that living a life in harmony with Asha is akin to keeping a flame alive within oneself, warding off the darkness of deceit and falsehood. Asha Vahishta inspires the faithful to strive for honesty in all aspects of their lives, seeing every act of truthfulness as a contribution to the divine order that sustains the universe.

Spenta Armaiti (Holy Devotion) holds a special place in the Zoroastrian relationship with the earth, and rituals honoring this Amesha Spenta often include prayers of gratitude for the bounty of nature. In agricultural communities, farmers may offer thanks to Spenta Armaiti before planting or harvesting, acknowledging the Amesha Spenta's role in nurturing the soil and sustaining life. During the celebration of festivals such as Mehregan and the Gahambars, Zoroastrians give thanks for the fruits of the earth, seeking the blessings of Spenta Armaiti to ensure that the land remains fertile and productive. These practices reflect a broader ethical commitment to the care of the earth, seeing nature as a sacred trust that must be protected. By aligning their actions with the spirit of Spenta Armaiti, Zoroastrians emphasize the importance of humility, patience, and respect for the natural world, recognizing that devotion to the divine is expressed through stewardship of creation.

Khshathra Vairya (Desirable Dominion) is invoked in times when strength and justice are needed. Zoroastrians look to this Amesha Spenta for guidance in leadership roles, whether within the family, community, or larger society. Khshathra Vairya's association with metals—symbols of durability and resilience—serves as a reminder that true power is not about domination but about providing stability and protection for those under one's care. In traditional prayers, Zoroastrians ask for the strength of Khshathra Vairya to uphold justice, to defend against oppression, and to be a source of positive influence. This focus on just dominion reinforces the idea that every Zoroastrian has a role in maintaining social harmony, ensuring that their actions contribute to a world where fairness and integrity prevail. Khshathra Vairya challenges the faithful to reflect on how they use their authority, urging them to wield power with a sense of responsibility and to be protectors of the vulnerable.

Haurvatat (Wholeness) and Ameretat (Immortality) together offer a vision of spiritual and physical well-being that is central to Zoroastrian life. The concept of Haurvatat is often invoked during purification rituals, such as those involving Zam (water) to cleanse both body and spirit. These rituals, which include the Padyab (ritual washing) and other ablutions, are performed not only for physical cleanliness but also as acts of spiritual alignment with Haurvatat's qualities of completeness and harmony. In seeking Haurvatat's blessing, Zoroastrians aim to achieve a balanced life, where health, well-being, and spiritual awareness come together. Ameretat, on the other hand, is invoked in prayers for the eternal journey of the soul. This Amesha Spenta is closely associated with the hope of the soul's survival beyond death, offering the promise of a life that transcends the material realm. The duality of Haurvatat and Ameretat serves as a reminder that wholeness and immortality are intertwined, with the care for one's spiritual and physical self leading to an existence that endures through time.

In daily life, Zoroastrians incorporate the principles of these Amesha Spentas through the practice of the Kusti ritual. This prayerful act, performed multiple times a day, involves the unwinding and retying of the Kusti (a sacred cord worn around the waist) while reciting prayers that invoke the virtues of the Amesha Spentas. Each time the Kusti is tied, the worshipper reaffirms their commitment to living in accordance with Asha, aligning their mind, body, and spirit with the cosmic order that the Amesha Spentas embody. This ritual, though simple in practice, serves as a powerful reminder of the presence of these divine entities in every aspect of life, encouraging the faithful to maintain a constant awareness of their spiritual responsibilities.

The connection between the Amesha Spentas and the natural world extends to the sacred landscapes of Zoroastrian practice. Fire temples, rivers, mountains, and even certain plants are seen as manifestations of the divine order that the Amesha Spentas uphold. Pilgrimages to sacred sites, such as the Atash Behram (highest grade fire temples) or the springs and rivers associated with Haurvatat, offer Zoroastrians a chance to deepen their connection with these spiritual entities. At these sites, prayers and offerings are made to honor the Amesha Spentas, seeking their guidance and strength. These pilgrimages, though physical in nature, are also journeys of the spirit, where the faithful seek to realign themselves with the forces that shape the universe.

In the Zoroastrian diaspora, where communities are often separated from the physical landscapes of ancient Persia, the invocation of the Amesha Spentas takes on new forms. Modern Zoroastrians find ways to adapt their rituals and prayers to contemporary settings, ensuring that the presence of these divine beings remains a vital part of their spiritual lives. Whether in urban temples or home altars, the qualities of the Amesha Spentas are evoked through prayers that seek wisdom, truth, strength, devotion, wholeness, and the promise of a spiritual journey that transcends the bounds of time. The Amesha Spentas remain timeless guides, offering Zoroastrians a pathway to spiritual fulfillment that is as relevant today as it was in ancient times.

The Amesha Spentas, in their roles as divine manifestations of Ahura Mazda's will, provide a bridge between the material and the spiritual, helping Zoroastrians navigate the challenges of life with a sense of purpose and direction. They remind the faithful that every aspect of existence, from the thoughts of the mind to the care of the earth, is part of a greater cosmic order that requires constant attention and respect. Through their prayers and rituals, Zoroastrians seek the presence of these divine beings in their lives, drawing strength from their timeless qualities. The Amesha Spentas represent the ideal toward which the faithful strive, serving as enduring symbols of the values that have defined Zoroastrianism for millennia: wisdom, truth, devotion, justice, balance, immortality, and the sacred spirit of creation.

Chapter 15
Light and Darkness

The interplay between light and darkness is a central theme in Zoroastrianism, representing the eternal struggle between good and evil, truth and falsehood, Asha (order) and Druj (chaos). This dualistic framework underpins not only the Zoroastrian understanding of the universe but also shapes the spiritual and ethical perspectives of its followers. Light, associated with Ahura Mazda, symbolizes truth, knowledge, and the divine essence that illuminates the path of righteousness. Darkness, on the other hand, is linked with Angra Mainyu, representing deceit, ignorance, and the forces that seek to disrupt the divine order.

In the teachings of Zarathustra, light is more than just a physical phenomenon; it is a manifestation of spiritual purity. Ahura Mazda is often described as the Light of Lights, whose radiance sustains the cosmos. The imagery of light in Zoroastrian texts serves as a metaphor for divine wisdom and the moral clarity that guides the faithful. It is through the illumination of Ahura Mazda's light that followers can discern the right path, making choices that align with Asha. This association with light is vividly present in the Zoroastrian practice of keeping sacred fires burning in temples, symbolizing the eternal presence of the divine.

The concept of light in Zoroastrianism is not confined to temples but extends to the daily practices of the faithful. Morning prayers, known as Havan Gah, are offered at dawn when the first rays of sunlight pierce through the darkness. This ritual act acknowledges the victory of light over darkness, mirroring the cosmic battle between Ahura Mazda and Angra Mainyu. The faithful recite invocations that praise the sun as a creation of Ahura Mazda, reflecting on the power of light to dispel ignorance and bring warmth and life to the world. This reverence for light is a reminder that each day brings a renewed opportunity to choose righteousness, to turn toward the light of truth, and to act in accordance with the values that uphold the cosmic order.

The association between light and good extends to the ethical framework of Zoroastrianism. Just as light is considered pure and life-giving, so too are the thoughts, words, and deeds that reflect the principles of Asha. Zoroastrians believe that each virtuous act contributes to the spread of light in the world, helping to combat the shadows cast by Druj. This dualistic worldview emphasizes that while darkness and evil exist, they are not equal to the power of light. Instead, darkness is viewed as an absence of light, a void that can be filled through acts of goodness and the illumination of divine wisdom. This perspective shapes the way Zoroastrians approach their moral responsibilities, encouraging them to become beacons of light in their communities and in their daily lives.

Darkness, in contrast, represents the destructive impulses embodied by Angra Mainyu. This entity is not just a figure of evil but symbolizes the chaotic forces that threaten to unravel the harmony of creation. Angra Mainyu's influence is seen in acts of deceit, violence, and all that seeks to disrupt the order established by Ahura Mazda. In Zoroastrian cosmology, the struggle between light and darkness is not merely an abstract battle; it is a dynamic tension that manifests in every aspect of life. The presence of darkness challenges the faithful to remain vigilant, to resist the temptations of falsehood, and to align their actions with the light of Asha.

This dualistic vision is particularly evident in the Zoroastrian understanding of the human soul's journey. Upon death, the soul is believed to cross the Chinvat Bridge, a passage where the forces of light and darkness contend for the soul's ultimate fate. Those who have lived in alignment with Asha, embodying the principles of truth and goodness, find the bridge wide and easy to cross, leading them toward the light of Garōdmān. For those whose lives have been dominated by deceit and chaos, the bridge becomes narrow, leading them into the darkness of Duzakh. This vivid imagery reinforces the importance of choosing light over darkness throughout one's life, as each action contributes to the soul's path in the afterlife.

Yet, despite the sharp contrasts between light and darkness, Zoroastrianism teaches that the struggle between these forces has a hopeful resolution. The vision of Frashokereti, the ultimate renewal of the world, foresees a time when the power of light will fully overcome darkness. In this future age, Angra Mainyu's influence will be nullified, and all creation will be bathed in the divine radiance of Ahura Mazda. This eschatological promise inspires Zoroastrians to engage actively in the fight against falsehood, believing that their efforts contribute to the eventual triumph of Asha. It is a message of hope, suggesting that darkness, while formidable, is ultimately transient, destined to give way to the eternal light.

The symbolism of light and darkness also permeates Zoroastrian art and literature, where metaphors of illumination and shadow are used to explore the moral and spiritual dimensions of life. In poetic verses, the struggle of the human soul is often likened to a battle between light-filled thoughts and dark temptations, with the outcome determined by the choices one makes. Ancient texts such as the Yashts and the Yasna contain hymns that celebrate the brilliance of Ahura Mazda's creation, urging the faithful to seek the clarity of mind and spirit that comes from embracing the light. These literary traditions continue to inspire Zoroastrian thought, serving as a reminder that the journey toward spiritual enlightenment is a lifelong endeavor.

The practice of lighting oil lamps during religious ceremonies is another way in which Zoroastrians express their reverence for light. These lamps, placed before images of Ahura Mazda or the sacred fire, symbolize the desire for the soul to be illuminated by divine wisdom. The soft glow of the lamps creates a space where the faithful can reflect on the presence of the divine in their lives, allowing the light to guide their prayers and meditations. This act of kindling light is seen as a small yet meaningful way of participating in the cosmic struggle, an affirmation of faith in the power of light to transform and uplift.

Zoroastrian festivals like Nowruz, the Persian New Year, also incorporate themes of light and renewal. Celebrated during the vernal equinox, Nowruz marks the triumph of spring over winter, light over darkness, and new life over dormancy. During this time, Zoroastrians decorate their homes with candles and lamps, symbolizing the light of hope that accompanies the new year. It is a time for families to gather, to reflect on the past, and to welcome the blessings of Ahura Mazda for the year to come. The light of Nowruz is a metaphor for the renewal of both the world and the soul, encouraging the faithful to begin anew with a commitment to the values of Asha.

The Zoroastrian view of light and darkness is not merely an ancient cosmology but a lens through which followers perceive their place in the world. It encourages a life lived with intention, where each choice is an opportunity to spread light or to succumb to shadow. By embracing the teachings of Zarathustra, Zoroastrians find guidance in the light that shines from Ahura Mazda, using it to navigate the complexities of existence and to find purpose in the timeless struggle for truth and order. Through their reverence for light and their vigilance against darkness, they honor a tradition that has taught them to see the world not only as it is but as it could be—a place where the light of Asha burns brightly, guiding all toward a future of peace and harmony.

In Zoroastrianism, the dualistic themes of light and darkness go beyond mere metaphors, deeply influencing the rituals, symbols, and philosophy that shape the daily lives of the faithful. The interplay between these opposing forces is not only a cosmic narrative but also a personal journey, wherein each believer navigates their own internal struggles between virtue and vice, truth and falsehood. This chapter delves into the practical expressions of this dualism in Zoroastrian rituals, the deeper interpretation of light and darkness in sacred texts, and their significance in shaping the Zoroastrian ethical framework.

One of the most profound expressions of light in Zoroastrian ritual is the reverence for fire, an element that embodies the presence of Ahura Mazda's divine light on Earth. The fire altar, found in temples and homes alike, serves as a focal point for prayer, meditation, and communal gatherings. This sacred flame, kept burning perpetually in Atash Behram (Fire of Victory) temples, represents the eternal battle against the encroaching darkness of ignorance and evil. The flame's purity is meticulously maintained by Mobeds (Zoroastrian priests), who ensure that the sacred fire remains untainted, symbolizing the unbroken connection between the divine and the material world. Through rituals like the Yasna and the recitation of Avestan hymns before the fire, the faithful seek to strengthen their inner light, allowing the warmth and clarity of the flame to inspire their actions and thoughts.

In Zoroastrian prayer, the invocation of light is more than a physical gesture; it is a call for spiritual enlightenment. Prayers such as the Ashem Vohu and Yatha Ahu Vairyo emphasize the desire for the soul to be aligned with Asha, the divine truth that guides all creation. These prayers are traditionally recited at specific times of day, corresponding with the cycles of the sun— dawn, midday, and sunset—when the presence of light is most perceptible. Each time, the act of turning toward a source of light, whether it is the rising sun or the temple flame, symbolizes a renewal of the commitment to Asha. The faithful seek to fill their inner lives with the radiance of truth, using the metaphor of light as a guide to combat the darker impulses of doubt, anger, and despair.

Zoroastrian rituals also emphasize the role of the Kusti, a sacred cord that represents the binding of the self to the light of Ahura Mazda. As part of daily prayers, Zoroastrians untie and retie the Kusti while facing a source of light, be it the sun or a sacred fire. This act symbolizes the purification of the soul and the reaffirmation of the individual's dedication to walking in the light. The Kusti serves as a reminder that the struggle between light and darkness is not just an external battle but an ongoing inner discipline. Each time it is tied, it signifies a moment of reflection on the nature of one's thoughts, words, and deeds, urging the practitioner to cast away any shadows of falsehood and to embrace clarity and truth.

The presence of light as a central theme is also deeply embedded in Zoroastrian mythology and cosmology. The Bundahishn, a Zoroastrian creation text, describes the origins of the universe as a manifestation of light and purity brought forth by Ahura Mazda. This divine light faced immediate opposition from Angra Mainyu, who emerged from the darkness with the intent to destroy and corrupt creation. According to this narrative, the initial clash between light and darkness set the stage for an enduring cosmic struggle, with the material world serving as the battleground. The role of humans, as described in the Bundahishn, is to choose the side of light, becoming allies of Ahura Mazda by adhering to the principles of Asha. This cosmic perspective reinforces the importance of every individual's actions, as each choice contributes to the balance between order and chaos, between illumination and shadow.

The Zoroastrian vision of the afterlife is similarly shaped by the dichotomy of light and darkness. The Chinvat Bridge, which the soul crosses after death, is illuminated by the light of one's good deeds and darkened by the weight of one's misdeeds. Those who have lived in accordance with the light of Asha find the bridge welcoming, their path guided by the radiance of their virtuous life. Conversely, those who have aligned themselves with deceit and chaos encounter the bridge as a treacherous passage, shrouded in darkness. This vivid imagery serves as a moral compass for the living, reminding them that their actions directly influence their spiritual journey and ultimate fate. The vision of a soul journeying toward the light or falling into darkness emphasizes the Zoroastrian belief in personal accountability and the transformative power of spiritual alignment.

Beyond the ritualistic and eschatological aspects, the symbolism of light and darkness profoundly shapes the Zoroastrian approach to community and social ethics. The concept of Hamazor, which means unity and strength through shared purpose, is seen as a collective effort to foster light in the world. Zoroastrians believe that by coming together in acts of charity, kindness, and communal worship, they can amplify the light of Asha and push back against the darkness that seeks to isolate and divide. This communal pursuit of light is evident in traditions such as Jashan ceremonies, where the community gathers to offer prayers for the well-being of the world and to strengthen their bonds with each other. During such gatherings, the fire at the center symbolizes their shared commitment to maintaining the spiritual light within their homes, communities, and the broader world.

In artistic expressions, the themes of light and darkness often manifest in Zoroastrian iconography, architecture, and even literature. The Faravahar, a prominent Zoroastrian symbol, represents the human soul's aspiration toward light and higher truths. Its wings, often depicted with rays or feathers that resemble sunlight, signify the spiritual journey toward enlightenment and the rejection of the shadows of ignorance. Similarly, fire temples are designed to capture natural light, with open spaces that allow sunlight to enter, blending the sacred flames within with the light from the heavens. This architectural choice serves as a reminder of the ever-present divine light that Zoroastrians strive to emulate.

Zoroastrian literature, from the poetic verses of the Gathas to modern interpretations, continues to explore the themes of light and darkness, offering timeless reflections on the human condition. Writers often draw parallels between the natural world and spiritual truths, using the cycle of day and night as a metaphor for the soul's quest for wisdom. For example, dawn is seen as a symbol of spiritual awakening, a time when the soul rises from the darkness of ignorance into the clarity of understanding. Night, while associated with rest and reflection, is also a reminder of the ever-present danger of drifting away from the path of light. Through these literary works, the Zoroastrian tradition maintains a rich dialogue between the physical and the spiritual, reminding the faithful of the continuous choice between embracing the light or surrendering to the shadows.

In modern times, the relevance of these ancient themes continues to guide Zoroastrians as they navigate the complexities of a changing world. The metaphor of light and darkness offers a framework for addressing ethical dilemmas, from questions of justice and honesty to the challenges of cultural preservation in the diaspora. The emphasis on light as a source of hope and renewal resonates with contemporary concerns about the future, encouraging Zoroastrians to remain steadfast in their commitment to truth and goodness, even in the face of adversity. It also inspires a sense of responsibility toward the environment, as the preservation of nature's light and purity is seen as part of maintaining the cosmic balance.

The struggle between light and darkness, though ancient, is never static. It evolves with each generation, finding new expressions in the prayers, rituals, and moral choices of the faithful. As Zoroastrians light the sacred fire or recite ancient hymns, they participate in a tradition that has long seen the world as a space where light must be kindled, protected, and shared. This chapter, then, is not just a recounting of symbols and rituals but an invitation to understand how the Zoroastrian faith offers a vision of life as a journey toward the light—a path where every step taken in truth, every moment of clarity, and every act of kindness adds to the brightness that holds back the darkness. Through this vision, Zoroastrians continue to find meaning and purpose, drawing strength from the belief that, ultimately, the light will prevail.

Chapter 16
Influence on Other Religions

Zoroastrianism, as one of the world's oldest monotheistic religions, has had a profound and enduring influence on the development of later religious traditions, particularly those that emerged in the broader Near Eastern and Western traditions. This chapter explores the intricate ways in which Zoroastrian concepts and beliefs interacted with and shaped the theological frameworks of Judaism, Christianity, and Islam. The exchange of ideas between these religions created threads that wove Zoroastrian themes into the broader tapestry of monotheistic thought.

In ancient Persia, Zoroastrianism's rise coincided with the expansion of the Achaemenid Empire, which, at its height, stretched across a vast territory, including regions inhabited by the Jewish people. When the Achaemenids, under Cyrus the Great, conquered Babylon in 539 BCE, they ended the Babylonian captivity of the Jews, allowing them to return to Jerusalem and rebuild their temple. This historical moment is more than a political event; it marks the beginning of a significant cultural and religious exchange between Zoroastrians and the Jewish exiles. Cyrus himself is even depicted positively in the Hebrew Bible, celebrated as a liberator and a servant of God.

Zoroastrianism's influence on Judaism is often discussed in the context of eschatological ideas, such as the concepts of an afterlife, resurrection, and the final judgment of souls. Before the Persian influence, Jewish scriptures contained limited references to these ideas, focusing more on a collective identity and the promises made to the people of Israel. However, during the period of Persian rule, Jewish thought began to incorporate ideas reminiscent of Zoroastrian beliefs—such as the resurrection of the dead and the concept of a final judgment where good would be rewarded and evil punished. These ideas bear a striking resemblance to Zoroastrian teachings about Frashokereti (the renewal of the world) and the judgment of souls on the Chinvat Bridge. It suggests that Zoroastrianism contributed to shaping the Jewish apocalyptic vision that later influenced Christian eschatology.

The dualistic elements of Zoroastrianism, particularly the cosmic struggle between Ahura Mazda and Angra Mainyu, also left their mark on early Jewish thought, which began to grapple more explicitly with the presence of evil in the world. The evolution of the figure of Satan in Jewish literature, particularly during the Second Temple period, mirrors some aspects of Angra Mainyu, representing a more defined adversarial force against divine order. While Judaism ultimately developed a monotheistic framework that diverges from the Zoroastrian dualistic cosmology, the notion of a spiritual battle between forces of good and evil became more pronounced during and after the Persian influence.

Christianity, emerging from a Jewish context, inherited many of these ideas, further amplifying the eschatological and dualistic themes that had been influenced by Zoroastrian thought. The concept of a messianic savior, present in Zoroastrianism through the figure of the Saoshyant, finds a parallel in the Christian idea of Christ as the redeemer who will return to vanquish evil and restore divine order. The Zoroastrian vision of a final renovation of the world, in which all souls are purified and reconciled with Ahura Mazda, shares conceptual space with the Christian promise of a new heaven and a new earth following the Last Judgment.

Additionally, the imagery of light and darkness, central to Zoroastrian teachings, resonates throughout the New Testament. For example, the Gospel of John presents Jesus as "the light of the world," a phrase that echoes the Zoroastrian association of Ahura Mazda with the divine light that dispels darkness. Early Christian texts often draw upon metaphors of light overcoming darkness, a theme deeply rooted in the Zoroastrian worldview of cosmic struggle. These parallels suggest that Zoroastrianism's emphasis on the metaphysical battle between light and dark helped shape the symbolic language of Christian theology.

Islam, too, absorbed certain Zoroastrian elements during its early development in the context of the Sassanian Empire, where Zoroastrianism was the dominant religion. The Islamic concept of the Day of Judgment, where each soul is held accountable for their deeds, bears similarities to Zoroastrian eschatological beliefs. In both religions, there is a bridge that souls must cross—Sirat in Islam and Chinvat in Zoroastrianism—symbolizing the path to the afterlife, with the righteous proceeding to paradise and the wicked falling into torment. Though these concepts developed independently within the Islamic tradition, the cultural and theological exchange between Zoroastrians and early Muslims may have contributed to shaping such parallel ideas.

Furthermore, the Zoroastrian practice of daily prayer rituals, the significance of purity, and the ethical focus on community well-being have resonances in Islamic practices. The emphasis on cleanliness, ritual purity, and the structured times for prayer in Islam can be seen as reflecting some of the ritualistic disciplines of Zoroastrianism. This continuity of spiritual practices across cultures highlights how religions evolve by integrating aspects of neighboring traditions while preserving their core beliefs.

Beyond theological parallels, Zoroastrianism also contributed to the philosophical currents that influenced later monotheistic thought. In the cosmopolitan environment of the Sassanian Empire, where scholars from various religious and cultural backgrounds exchanged ideas, Zoroastrian theological discussions interacted with Greek, Jewish, and Christian philosophical traditions. Concepts such as the nature of the soul, the importance of free will, and the cosmic struggle for order versus chaos became part of a shared discourse that enriched the intellectual heritage of the Near East. These discussions laid the groundwork for medieval Islamic philosophy, which sought to harmonize reason with religious belief, often drawing upon earlier Zoroastrian metaphysics and ethical reasoning.

The influence of Zoroastrianism on other religions is not a simple matter of direct borrowing but rather a complex process of cultural interaction and mutual influence. As Zoroastrianism engaged with the diverse religious landscape of the ancient world, its ideas spread through trade, migration, and the expansion of empires, finding new expressions in the evolving beliefs of other traditions. This blending of religious thought reflects the dynamism of spiritual traditions as they adapt to new contexts, enriching their narratives while preserving their distinct identities.

Yet, Zoroastrianism also retained its unique identity amidst these interactions, maintaining a clear vision of its own cosmic drama and ethical imperatives. The Zoroastrian emphasis on personal responsibility, the moral imperative to choose the path of Asha, and the belief in an ultimate victory of good over evil continue to distinguish it, even as it contributed to the spiritual heritage of other faiths. Its role in shaping religious thought across the ancient world speaks to the enduring power of its teachings and their capacity to inspire reflection on the nature of the divine and the human journey.

Zoroastrianism's contributions to the development of religious thought underscore its place as a foundational pillar in the history of spirituality. Its influence on Judaism, Christianity, and Islam highlights how shared themes—such as the battle between good and evil, the hope for a savior, and the pursuit of divine truth—transcend specific doctrines, connecting humanity in its search for meaning and purpose. As we explore these connections, we gain a deeper appreciation of the ways in which Zoroastrianism helped to shape the spiritual contours of the world, leaving an indelible mark on the religious landscape that continues to resonate through the centuries.

The influence of Zoroastrianism on other religious traditions is a subject of rich academic debate, with scholars examining the intricate web of ideas that flowed between cultures and religions throughout history. This chapter delves deeper into the scholarly discussions about how Zoroastrian beliefs may have been adapted or reinterpreted in the religious texts of Judaism, Christianity, and Islam, exploring the nuances of these interactions and the profound impact they had on theological and philosophical thought.

One of the central points of scholarly focus is the concept of the messiah, a savior figure who plays a crucial role in the eschatological vision of Zoroastrianism and is paralleled in both Jewish and Christian traditions. The Zoroastrian notion of the Saoshyant—a future savior who will come at the end of time to defeat evil and restore the world—shares similarities with the Jewish concept of the Mashiach and the Christian vision of the second coming of Christ. While the exact nature of these figures differs across the religions, the underlying theme of a divinely ordained redeemer who brings about a final cosmic renewal suggests a shared lineage of thought.

In the Jewish apocalyptic texts of the Second Temple period, the expectation of a messiah who would restore justice and peace echoes the role of the Saoshyant in Zoroastrianism. The transformation of messianic expectations in Judaism during and after the Persian influence marks a significant shift from earlier beliefs, which focused more on earthly kingship and the restoration of Israel. Scholars have noted that the dualistic framework of a battle between good and evil, central to Zoroastrian eschatology, may have helped shape Jewish apocalyptic literature, such as the Book of Daniel and the Dead Sea Scrolls. These texts emphasize the coming of a messianic era and the final judgment, reflecting a worldview that sees history as a battleground between divine and malevolent forces.

In Christianity, the influence of Zoroastrian eschatology can be seen in the New Testament's depiction of the end times, particularly in the Book of Revelation. The imagery of a final battle between forces of light and darkness, and the ultimate triumph of good over evil, resonates with Zoroastrian concepts of cosmic conflict and renewal. The promise of a new heaven and a new earth, a world cleansed of suffering and corruption, aligns with the Zoroastrian vision of Frashokereti, where the world is restored to its original purity and harmony. This parallel is not a direct borrowing but suggests that early Christian writers were engaged in a broader religious discourse that included Zoroastrian ideas about the end of the world.

Moreover, the figure of Satan in Christian thought, as the embodiment of evil and opposition to God, has been compared to Angra Mainyu, the destructive spirit in Zoroastrianism. While the Christian Satan is not equivalent to Angra Mainyu, both represent a profound challenge to divine order, leading to a struggle that encompasses both the spiritual realm and human history. The development of Christian demonology, with its emphasis on the fall of rebellious angels and the ultimate defeat of demonic forces, may have been influenced by Zoroastrian dualism, which emphasizes the cosmic battle between good and evil as a central aspect of existence.

In the Islamic tradition, the influence of Zoroastrianism is more subtle but can be discerned in discussions about the nature of the afterlife and the process of judgment. Islamic teachings about the Day of Judgment, where every soul is assessed for their deeds and sent either to paradise or hell, share conceptual similarities with Zoroastrian beliefs about the Chinvat Bridge. In both religions, this moment of reckoning is not just a moral evaluation but a fundamental cosmic event that reinforces the triumph of divine justice. The Qur'an's descriptions of the afterlife, with vivid imagery of gardens for the righteous and fiery pits for the wicked, reflect a dualistic vision of the cosmos that is reminiscent of Zoroastrian eschatological ideas.

Additionally, the Islamic concept of a final savior, known as the Mahdi, who will emerge in the end times to restore justice, has been discussed in relation to the Zoroastrian Saoshyant. While the origins of the Mahdi concept are rooted in early Islamic thought, the broader cultural context of the Sassanian Empire, where Zoroastrianism was the state religion, may have provided a framework for such messianic expectations. The Mahdi and the Saoshyant both symbolize a hope for a divine intervention that will bring an end to the age of suffering and inaugurate a new era of divine order.

Beyond theological parallels, Zoroastrianism also influenced philosophical discussions in the Islamic world, especially during the early centuries of the Islamic caliphates when scholars of diverse backgrounds gathered in cities like Baghdad and Gondeshapur. The House of Wisdom in Baghdad became a melting pot of Greek, Persian, Indian, and Zoroastrian ideas, where scholars debated metaphysics, ethics, and cosmology. The Zoroastrian emphasis on free will and the moral responsibility of individuals to choose between good and evil found resonance in Islamic philosophical thought. Figures like Avicenna (Ibn Sina) and Al-Farabi engaged with these ideas, blending them with Greek philosophy and Islamic teachings to create a rich intellectual tradition that considered the nature of the soul, the existence of evil, and the role of divine providence.

In addition, the themes of light and darkness, so prominent in Zoroastrian symbolism, continued to influence Islamic mystical traditions. Sufi writings, which often employ metaphors of light to describe divine knowledge and spiritual awakening, reflect a continuity of thought that stretches back to Zoroastrian concepts of divine illumination. The poetry of Rumi, for example, frequently uses the imagery of light as a symbol of divine presence and spiritual clarity, echoing ancient Zoroastrian reverence for light as a manifestation of Ahura Mazda's truth. While Sufi mysticism developed within the framework of Islamic monotheism, it absorbed and transformed elements from the broader spiritual traditions that predated Islam, including Zoroastrianism.

The interaction between Zoroastrianism and other religious traditions thus represents a complex tapestry of influence, adaptation, and reinterpretation. It is not merely a one-way transmission of ideas but a dynamic process where Zoroastrian concepts were integrated into the theological frameworks of Judaism, Christianity, and Islam, even as these religions developed their own unique identities. This blending of ideas across cultural and religious boundaries highlights the fluidity of ancient thought and the shared concerns that have shaped human spirituality—questions about the nature of good and evil, the destiny of the soul, and the ultimate fate of the world.

Zoroastrianism's influence on these religions also underscores the interconnectedness of the ancient world, where trade routes, migrations, and imperial conquests facilitated the exchange of not only goods but also ideas. The Persian Empire served as a bridge between East and West, a place where religious traditions could meet, interact, and transform. The impact of Zoroastrian thought on monotheistic traditions remains a testament to the way in which ancient wisdom can leave a lasting legacy, shaping the spiritual and ethical landscapes of humanity for centuries to come.

This deeper exploration into the academic perspectives on Zoroastrian influence helps us appreciate the enduring relevance of this ancient religion, not as a relic of the past but as a vibrant participant in the shaping of religious thought. It invites us to reflect on how Zoroastrianism's vision of cosmic order, moral responsibility, and the ultimate triumph of good continues to echo in the stories, beliefs, and hopes that define much of the world's spiritual heritage. Through these connections, Zoroastrianism remains a silent yet ever-present force in the ongoing dialogue between humanity's greatest spiritual traditions.

Chapter 17
Fire Temples

The Fire Temples, or Atashkadeh, hold a central place in the practice and spirituality of Zoroastrianism. More than mere places of worship, they serve as sacred spaces where the divine presence of Ahura Mazda is manifested through the eternal flame. These temples have become symbols of Zoroastrian identity and continuity, preserving rituals and traditions that date back thousands of years. In this chapter, we explore the architectural, spiritual, and cultural significance of these temples, as well as their role in fostering a sense of community among Zoroastrians throughout history.

The architecture of a Zoroastrian fire temple is simple yet profound, designed to focus attention on the sacred fire, which represents light, purity, and the divine essence of Ahura Mazda. The structure is typically oriented to allow natural light to illuminate the inner sanctum where the fire burns, creating a harmonious blend of natural and divine illumination. Many fire temples are built with domes or skylights above the Atashgah (altar of the fire), allowing sunlight to enter during the day, symbolizing the unity between the celestial and terrestrial light.

At the heart of each temple is the sacred fire, categorized into three main types based on their level of sanctity. The highest is the Atash Behram (Fire of Victory), which requires the consecration of fire from sixteen different sources, including lightning and household fires, making it the most revered. The Atash Adaran and Atash Dadgah follow, with each serving different levels of communal and personal worship. The Atash Behram represents the pinnacle of ritual purity and is housed in temples of great significance, where it is tended continuously by priests to ensure that it remains pure and unextinguished.

The ritual maintenance of the sacred fire involves strict procedures, emphasizing the Zoroastrian focus on purity and spiritual discipline. Only ordained priests, known as Mobeds, are allowed to approach the fire directly, and they do so only after performing ablutions and donning ritual clothing, such as the white padan (mouth-covering cloth) to prevent their breath from contaminating the flames. This meticulous care underscores the belief that the fire is a living connection to the divine, embodying the spiritual energy that sustains creation. Through daily offerings of sandalwood and frankincense, the fire is not just sustained but spiritually nourished, symbolizing the Zoroastrian commitment to fostering light and life.

For Zoroastrians, the fire temple is more than a place of worship—it is a space where communal identity is cultivated and maintained. The temple serves as a gathering point for religious festivals, rites of passage, and communal prayers, such as during the Jashan ceremonies, which celebrate the creation and offer thanks to Ahura Mazda for the blessings of life. These gatherings strengthen the bonds among community members, providing a sense of continuity with their ancestors and a shared commitment to preserving their ancient traditions. Through the collective experience of prayer before the sacred flame, Zoroastrians reaffirm their dedication to the principles of Asha and the struggle against Druj.

The spiritual importance of fire temples also extends to the personal lives of Zoroastrians. Many visit the temples regularly to pray and to seek guidance, standing before the flames and reciting the Avestan hymns that have been passed down through generations. For individuals, the fire represents a constant source of inspiration and a reminder of the inner light that guides one's thoughts, words, and actions. It is believed that the presence of the sacred fire helps to purify the mind and spirit, aligning worshippers more closely with the divine order that Ahura Mazda has established in the universe.

Historically, fire temples played a crucial role in maintaining Zoroastrian identity during periods of political upheaval and cultural change. During the Sassanian Empire, Zoroastrianism was the state religion, and the construction of fire temples symbolized the unity of the empire under the divine guidance of Ahura Mazda. The Atash Behram temples, in particular, were not only centers of religious activity but also symbols of royal authority and cultural continuity, their flames representing the light of Ahura Mazda guiding the realm. However, with the advent of the Islamic conquest, many Zoroastrian temples were destroyed or repurposed, and the faithful were forced to protect their sacred fires in secret or relocate them to more secure regions.

One such example is the Atash Behram in Yazd, Iran, which has survived for centuries as a beacon of Zoroastrian faith in a region where the religion became a minority. In places like Yazd, Zoroastrians preserved their practices under challenging conditions, maintaining their temples as quiet sanctuaries of light amidst a changing cultural and religious landscape. These temples became safe havens for rituals, education, and the passing down of sacred knowledge, ensuring that the Zoroastrian tradition remained intact even during times of persecution.

In the diaspora, fire temples have also adapted to new environments, carrying with them the essence of Zoroastrian spiritual life while responding to the practical realities of migration. Communities in India, particularly the Parsis, have established fire temples that continue to be vibrant centers of religious life. In India, cities like Mumbai and Surat became hubs for Zoroastrian refugees after the Islamic conquest of Persia, where they built new Atash Behrams and Adarans. These temples served not only as places of worship but as social centers that helped the community maintain their unique identity amidst a vastly different cultural landscape.

In recent years, as the Zoroastrian diaspora has spread further across the world, from North America to Australia, fire temples have emerged in new contexts, adapting to modernity while preserving their core traditions. These new temples often blend traditional Persian and Indian architectural elements with modern design, creating spaces that are accessible to Zoroastrians living in urban environments far from the lands of their ancestors. Despite these changes, the essential role of the fire—its ritual care, its symbolism, and its spiritual presence—remains unchanged, providing continuity for the Zoroastrian faith in the modern world.

Fire temples also hold an important cultural dimension for Zoroastrians, serving as a focal point for educating younger generations about their heritage. Classes on the Gathas, Zoroastrian history, and the meaning of rituals are often held within the walls of these temples, where the younger members of the community learn the significance of their ancient customs and the values that underpin their faith. This educational role ensures that the flame of knowledge, like the sacred fire, is passed down unbroken, allowing each new generation to find their place within the continuum of Zoroastrian tradition.

The significance of fire temples, therefore, extends beyond their physical structures; they embody the spiritual heart of Zoroastrianism, a living symbol of a faith that sees the world as a cosmic struggle between light and darkness. The flames that burn within these temples are not just material phenomena—they are considered reflections of Ahura Mazda's divine essence, guiding the faithful toward righteousness and illuminating the path of Asha. In every prayer offered before the fire, in every ritual act of tending the flame, Zoroastrians connect with a tradition that has endured through millennia, a tradition that holds steadfast to the belief that light, in all its forms, is the truest expression of the divine.

Through the resilience of fire temples and their enduring presence in Zoroastrian life, the ancient wisdom of Zarathustra continues to burn brightly, offering a timeless message of hope, purity, and the eternal power of light. The next chapter will further explore the practices and ceremonies within these sacred spaces, delving into the rituals that have been preserved and adapted through the centuries, revealing the profound connection between the sacred fire and the lived experience of Zoroastrian faith.

In the dim glow of the eternal flame, the rituals and ceremonies conducted within the Zoroastrian fire temples unfold, forming a bridge between the ancient past and the present. These rituals are not only a means of connecting with Ahura Mazda but also a way to reinforce the cosmic order of Asha, renewing the bond between the divine and the material world. This chapter delves into the specific practices and ceremonies that take place within fire temples, revealing the layers of meaning embedded in each gesture, prayer, and offering, as well as their importance in preserving the spiritual essence of Zoroastrianism.

Central to the spiritual life within a fire temple is the Yasna ceremony, a complex liturgical ritual that embodies the core principles of Zoroastrian worship. The Yasna, meaning "worship" or "sacrifice," is performed by Mobeds (priests) and involves the recitation of verses from the Avesta, the Zoroastrian sacred texts. This ritual is conducted before the sacred fire, where libations of haoma, a sacred drink made from the ephedra plant, are offered. The Yasna is not only an act of veneration but a re-enactment of the cosmic order, reflecting the struggle between Asha and Druj. Each recitation and offering made during the Yasna is intended to align the physical world with the spiritual realms, reinforcing the power of Asha over chaos.

A key component of the Yasna is the preparation and offering of haoma, which holds deep symbolic significance. Haoma is believed to possess divine properties, capable of purifying both body and spirit. The priests chant ancient hymns as they pound the plant, mixing it with water and milk, before presenting it to the sacred fire. This act represents the eternal cycle of life, death, and rebirth, as well as the nourishment of the divine flame that sustains creation. The ritualized preparation of haoma underscores the Zoroastrian belief in the interconnectedness of all things, where the elements of earth, water, and fire come together to honor the divine.

Alongside the Yasna, another significant ritual is the Afrinagan, a prayer of blessing that is performed for various occasions, such as births, marriages, and the remembrance of the deceased. The Afrinagan involves the lighting of candles and the offering of fruits and flowers before the sacred fire, accompanied by the chanting of prayers that invoke blessings upon individuals and the community. This ceremony emphasizes the Zoroastrian values of generosity and gratitude, seeking the favor of Ahura Mazda for prosperity, happiness, and protection from the influences of evil. It is a moment when the community gathers to reinforce their bonds with one another and to celebrate the harmony between the human and the divine.

The daily maintenance of the sacred fire itself is a deeply ritualistic practice, requiring the utmost care and reverence. The Mobeds cleanse the altar and the surrounding space, ensuring that the fire remains unpolluted by the impurities of the material world. They add sandalwood and frankincense to the flames, which not only nourish the fire but also carry the prayers of the faithful upward, towards the realm of Ahura Mazda. This process is seen as an act of devotion, a means of maintaining the purity that lies at the heart of Zoroastrian ethics. It symbolizes the eternal struggle to keep the inner light of the soul burning brightly, untainted by the darkness of falsehood and disorder.

Weddings in the Zoroastrian tradition, known as Navjote for initiations or simply Nikah for marriages, often include special ceremonies conducted within the fire temples, where the couple is blessed before the sacred fire. During these rituals, the couple sits before the flames, which represent the presence of Ahura Mazda as a witness to their union. The priests chant prayers that emphasize the importance of living according to Asha, guiding the couple toward a life of mutual respect, love, and spiritual growth. This act of commitment before the fire signifies the promise to uphold truth and to contribute to the cosmic order through their partnership.

The Jashan ceremony is another integral part of life within the fire temple, celebrating significant life events or marking communal occasions like the Zoroastrian New Year, Nowruz. During a Jashan, the Mobeds perform rituals of thanksgiving and invoke blessings upon the participants and the community. The ceremony includes the arrangement of myazd—offerings of bread, milk, fruits, and flowers—before the sacred fire. These offerings represent the bounties of creation, a recognition of Ahura Mazda's generosity, and a reminder of humanity's role as stewards of the earth. The collective recitation of prayers during the Jashan fosters a sense of unity, reminding the faithful of their shared purpose in upholding the values of their ancient faith.

Beyond these formal rituals, fire temples also serve as spaces for meditation and personal prayer, where individuals come to reflect on their inner lives and seek guidance. The sacred fire, with its constant warmth and light, offers a space for contemplation, where the flickering flames become a symbol of the divine spark within each soul. It is in these quiet moments that Zoroastrians find solace, drawing strength from the presence of Ahura Mazda and renewing their resolve to live in accordance with the principles of Asha.

The adaptability of fire temple rituals has also allowed them to remain relevant in the Zoroastrian diaspora, where temples have emerged in places far from their origins in Persia. Communities in India, particularly among the Parsis, have maintained these traditions with great fidelity, while also adapting certain practices to their new environments. In Mumbai, for instance, the Atash Behrams and Agiyaris (lesser fire temples) serve as centers of both spiritual life and cultural preservation, ensuring that the flame of Zoroastrian identity continues to burn brightly even in a foreign land.

In more recent years, as Zoroastrian communities have settled in places like North America, Europe, and Australia, new fire temples have been established, providing spaces where the ancient rituals can be performed even in a modern context. These temples are often built with a blend of traditional and contemporary architecture, reflecting the community's commitment to preserving their heritage while embracing the realities of their new homes. The rituals, while performed in a new setting, retain their timeless essence, maintaining the connection to Ahura Mazda and the teachings of Zarathustra.

The role of fire temples in modern Zoroastrian life also extends to the preservation of religious education. Within their walls, Mobeds teach the next generation about the Gathas, the moral teachings of Zoroastrianism, and the proper conduct of rituals. This educational role is crucial in a time when the Zoroastrian community faces the challenges of a shrinking population and the pressures of assimilation. Through instruction in the fire temples, young Zoroastrians learn the importance of the sacred flame not only as a symbol but as a living practice that connects them to their ancestors and their faith.

Fire temples, with their enduring flames, remain a potent symbol of the Zoroastrian worldview—a reminder of the eternal struggle to maintain purity, truth, and light in a world that often confronts darkness. The rituals performed within these sacred spaces reinforce the communal bonds and individual commitments that sustain the Zoroastrian tradition, ensuring that the flame of faith is passed from generation to generation, unbroken and undimmed. As the faithful gather before the fire, they are reminded of their role in the cosmic drama, as guardians of the light and as stewards of the divine order that Zarathustra proclaimed.

These rituals, ancient yet alive, continue to shape the daily life and spiritual experience of Zoroastrians across the world. They stand as a testament to a religion that has weathered the storms of history while holding fast to the symbols and practices that define its essence. In the quiet glow of the fire temple, amidst the prayers and offerings, Zoroastrians find a space where time stands still, and the ancient wisdom of their faith continues to speak, guiding them toward a future where the light of Asha can shine ever more brightly.

Chapter 18
Priests

In the heart of Zoroastrian tradition, where the fire burns with undying light, the role of the Mobeds—the Zoroastrian priests—stands as a beacon of spiritual continuity and guidance. Throughout history, these religious figures have been the guardians of the sacred flame, ensuring that the teachings of Zarathustra are not only preserved but practiced with reverence. Their responsibilities extend beyond mere ritual performance; they are the stewards of the spiritual and moral life of the Zoroastrian community, upholding the core tenets of Asha and the wisdom embedded within the Avesta.

The path to becoming a Mobed is one of dedication, beginning with the early instruction of young boys born into priestly families. This journey is not merely academic; it is an immersion into the spiritual essence of Zoroastrianism. Young initiates, often starting their training at the age of seven or eight, are taught the recitation of the Gathas—the hymns believed to be composed by Zarathustra himself. Memorizing these verses is seen as a way to internalize the divine wisdom they carry. Alongside these teachings, they learn the rituals, the intricate movements and recitations required for ceremonies like the Yasna and Vendidad.

The training of a Mobed also includes a deep understanding of the symbolic meanings of rituals, such as the preparation of haoma and the maintenance of the Atash Behram, the highest grade of sacred fire. This education ensures that each action performed by the Mobed during rituals is infused with a conscious awareness of its significance. The relationship between a Mobed and the sacred fire is profound; he serves as the caretaker, ensuring that the flames remain pure and are not extinguished, a responsibility that symbolizes the eternal struggle to keep Asha alive in the world.

The hierarchy among Zoroastrian priests reflects the depth of their knowledge and experience. At the foundational level are the Ervads, who conduct basic rituals and offer daily prayers. With time and additional training, an Ervad may advance to become a Mobed, a role that allows them to perform more complex ceremonies, such as weddings and initiations. At the pinnacle of this structure is the Dastur, a high priest responsible for guiding the spiritual direction of the community and offering interpretations of the sacred texts. Dasturs hold the authority to preside over important communal rituals and serve as intermediaries between the divine will of Ahura Mazda and the daily lives of the faithful.

This hierarchical structure is not only about authority but also about the transmission of wisdom from one generation to the next. The older Mobeds mentor the younger, passing down not only the precise methods of ritual but also the nuances of understanding the Avesta's teachings. This relationship between mentor and apprentice is a vital aspect of preserving the depth of Zoroastrian spiritual practice, ensuring that the continuity of tradition remains unbroken even as the world changes around them.

The life of a Mobed is deeply intertwined with the cycles of nature and the rhythms of communal life. They are present at the most crucial moments in a Zoroastrian's life—from birth and initiation to marriage and death. At each of these life stages, the Mobed performs rituals that are meant to sanctify the events and align them with the cosmic order. For instance, the Navjote, or initiation ceremony, marks a young Zoroastrian's entry into the faith. Here, the Mobed guides the initiate in donning the Sudreh (a sacred shirt) and Kusti (a sacred girdle), symbols of the commitment to uphold Asha. Through this ritual, the Mobed plays a central role in binding the individual to the spiritual lineage of Zoroastrianism.

Beyond their ritualistic duties, Mobeds are often sought after for their counsel, offering guidance on moral and ethical dilemmas faced by their communities. Their role as advisors reflects their deep understanding of the Zoroastrian cosmological vision, where every action has a spiritual consequence. This advisory role becomes particularly significant when addressing contemporary issues that may not have direct precedents in the ancient texts. Mobeds interpret the principles of Asha and Druj, helping the faithful to navigate the complexities of modern life while remaining true to their spiritual heritage.

In the contemporary era, the role of Mobeds has evolved in response to the challenges facing the Zoroastrian community, such as the dwindling number of adherents and the pressures of assimilation into different cultures. In diaspora communities, particularly among the Parsis of India and Zoroastrians in Western countries, Mobeds have taken on additional roles as cultural ambassadors, working to preserve Zoroastrian identity amidst the diverse influences of global society. This requires a balance—maintaining the integrity of ancient rituals while making them accessible to a younger generation that may not speak the traditional languages of the Avesta.

Mobeds in the diaspora often find themselves bridging the gap between ancient traditions and modern expectations. This can involve translating prayers into local languages or adapting ceremonies to suit the schedules and lifestyles of those living far from the heartlands of Persia. For example, while the daily fire rituals might be condensed in some communities due to the practicalities of modern life, the spiritual essence of these practices is upheld. This adaptability is a testament to the resilience of the Zoroastrian faith and the creativity of its spiritual leaders in maintaining the flame.

In addition to their spiritual and cultural duties, Mobeds are tasked with the stewardship of Zoroastrian places of worship, ensuring that fire temples remain centers of community life. They oversee not only the maintenance of the sacred fire but also the upkeep of the temple grounds, ensuring that these spaces remain places of purity and reflection. The fire temples become venues for community gatherings, religious festivals, and educational programs, where Mobeds play a central role in fostering a sense of unity and continuity among the faithful.

The path of a Mobed is not one of material reward; it is a vocation that demands humility and a deep sense of duty to the divine. Many Mobeds, especially those serving in smaller diaspora communities, balance their religious responsibilities with secular occupations, finding ways to support their families while remaining dedicated to their spiritual calling. This dual life requires a delicate balancing act, where the demands of the material world must be met without losing sight of the spiritual ideals that guide their lives.

As the custodians of one of the world's oldest continuous religious traditions, Mobeds carry a legacy that stretches back to the teachings of Zarathustra himself. They are not just performers of rituals; they are the keepers of a spiritual flame that has burned through millennia, a flame that has survived the upheavals of empires and the shifting tides of belief. Their role is a reminder that the essence of Zoroastrianism lies not only in its ancient texts or its grand temples but in the daily acts of devotion and service that keep the spirit of Asha alive in the world.

In a world where the continuity of small religious communities faces many challenges, the Mobeds' dedication to their sacred duty stands as a testament to the enduring power of faith. They embody the ideals of Zoroastrianism, striving to live by the principles of Humata (Good Thoughts), Hukhta (Good Words), and Hvarshta (Good Deeds), setting an example for the community they serve. Through their unwavering commitment, the Mobeds ensure that the ancient call to live in harmony with the divine order continues to echo through the corridors of time, guiding the Zoroastrian faithful in their pursuit of a life illuminated by the light of Asha.

The role of Mobeds in Zoroastrianism is deeply intertwined with both the spiritual and cultural dimensions of the faith, shaping not only the religious practices but also the identity of the Zoroastrian community. As they guide rituals and uphold the teachings of Zarathustra, Mobeds become central figures in the continuity of traditions that date back millennia. Beyond their foundational duties, the complexity and breadth of their responsibilities extend into the realms of ritual purity, community bonding, and the preservation of sacred knowledge.

At the core of a Mobed's duties are the rituals that define key moments in the lives of the faithful. From the solemnity of funeral rites to the celebratory essence of weddings, these ceremonies are not merely cultural markers but moments of spiritual transition. Funerary rites, for instance, are highly structured, aiming to assist the soul in crossing the Chinvat Bridge. These rituals include prayers and specific actions designed to protect the soul from evil influences during its passage. Through these practices, Mobeds ensure that the sacred order of Asha remains intact, even in the face of death.

One of the central rituals performed by Mobeds is the Yasna, an elaborate liturgy that includes the preparation of haoma, a sacred plant whose juice is used in the ritual. The Yasna is more than a prayer; it is an invocation that calls upon Ahura Mazda and the Amesha Spentas, weaving a connection between the physical and spiritual worlds. During the Yasna, the Mobed recites passages from the Avesta, which, when spoken in their ancient language, are believed to hold transformative power. This ritual serves to reaffirm the community's alignment with cosmic truth, and it is a reminder of the eternal struggle between Asha (order) and Druj (chaos).

In addition to the Yasna, Mobeds conduct the Vendidad ceremony, a purification rite that protects the community from physical and spiritual impurities. This ritual is especially significant in reinforcing the importance of purity, a theme that runs deep in Zoroastrianism. During the Vendidad, specific passages are recited to cleanse spaces and individuals from defilement, symbolizing the Zoroastrian emphasis on maintaining a pure environment as a reflection of inner spiritual purity. The ceremony also highlights the Mobed's role as a mediator, someone who bridges the material and spiritual worlds, ensuring that the cosmic order remains undisturbed.

The preservation of ritual knowledge is another critical aspect of a Mobed's role. Much of the Avesta's sacred content has been transmitted orally through generations, and Mobeds play a key role in this tradition. They are trained in the precise intonations and rhythms of the Avesta's chants, a practice that requires years of dedication. This oral transmission ensures that the power of the original recitations, believed to have been revealed by Zarathustra, remains potent. Even as the written text of the Avesta serves as a reference, it is the spoken word, passed from teacher to student, that preserves the mystical essence of the teachings.

The role of Mobeds extends beyond religious rituals into the communal and educational life of Zoroastrians. In regions where Zoroastrianism is a minority religion, Mobeds often become educators, teaching the youth about their heritage, the meanings behind rituals, and the ethical framework of the faith. In this capacity, they serve as mentors, helping to instill a sense of identity and continuity in the younger generation. They explain the significance of daily prayers, the symbolism behind wearing the Sudreh and Kusti, and the importance of living in harmony with Asha.

This mentorship is particularly important in the context of the Zoroastrian diaspora, where young Zoroastrians may face challenges in maintaining their religious identity amidst a multicultural environment. The Mobed's ability to connect ancient teachings with contemporary life helps to bridge the generational gap, ensuring that the younger members of the community see the relevance of their heritage. By adapting the wisdom of Zarathustra to modern dilemmas—be they ethical challenges or questions about personal conduct—Mobeds keep the teachings of the Avesta alive and resonant.

Mobeds also play a vital role during Zoroastrian festivals, such as Nowruz (Persian New Year) and the Gahanbars, which are seasonal festivals celebrating different aspects of creation. During these gatherings, Mobeds lead the community in prayers and rituals that honor the cycles of nature and reaffirm the bond between humanity and the divine. The lighting of the sacred fire during these festivals symbolizes the triumph of light over darkness, a central theme in Zoroastrian cosmology. Through their leadership in these ceremonies, Mobeds help to sustain the communal spirit and ensure that the sacred rhythms of Zoroastrian life are maintained.

Another dimension of the Mobed's work involves pastoral care, particularly in guiding individuals through spiritual struggles and moral decisions. Zoroastrianism places a high value on free will, with each individual responsible for choosing between Asha and Druj. Mobeds act as spiritual guides, helping their followers navigate these choices. They offer counsel in times of difficulty, helping Zoroastrians understand how their actions align with or diverge from the principles of Asha. This advisory role often involves interpreting ancient texts in ways that can provide clarity in the context of modern issues, such as ethical business practices or questions about environmental stewardship.

Despite the vital role they play, the life of a Mobed is not without its challenges. In regions where the Zoroastrian population is small, there are few new initiates entering the priesthood. This has led to an aging population of Mobeds, and the question of succession has become increasingly urgent. In response, some communities have begun initiatives to encourage young Zoroastrians to consider the path of the Mobed, emphasizing the importance of keeping their spiritual heritage alive. Programs have emerged that blend traditional training with modern educational methods, aiming to make the life of a Mobed accessible and appealing to a new generation.

Furthermore, the responsibilities of Mobeds in diaspora communities often include efforts to educate the broader public about Zoroastrianism. They participate in interfaith dialogues, offering insights into Zoroastrian beliefs and practices to those unfamiliar with this ancient faith. Through lectures, temple tours, and public discussions, Mobeds become ambassadors of Zoroastrian wisdom, dispelling misconceptions and highlighting the enduring values of their tradition. This role is especially important in fostering a deeper understanding of Zoroastrianism among non-Zoroastrians, contributing to a more inclusive view of the world's religious landscape.

Mobeds also face the challenge of maintaining the purity of rituals while adapting to the realities of contemporary life. For example, the strict rules regarding the use of natural elements in rituals—such as the need for fresh, flowing water—can be difficult to observe in urban environments. Some Mobeds have adapted these practices by finding symbolic alternatives that remain true to the spirit of the traditions, showing that the essence of the rituals can be preserved even when the details are modified. This adaptability ensures that Zoroastrianism remains a living faith, capable of thriving in diverse contexts without losing its core values.

Yet, even with the pressures of modernity, the central mission of the Mobed remains unchanged: to be a guardian of the sacred flame, a transmitter of ancient wisdom, and a guide for those seeking to live in alignment with Asha. The Mobed's role as a spiritual custodian is a testament to the resilience of Zoroastrianism, which has withstood centuries of change and challenge. Through their dedication, Mobeds keep alive the timeless message of Zarathustra, reminding the community of their place within the cosmic struggle between order and chaos.

As Zoroastrianism faces the challenges of the present and looks toward the future, the Mobeds' steadfast devotion to their sacred duties offers a source of continuity and hope. Their rituals bind the community to the past, while their guidance helps it navigate the uncertainties of the modern world. In every prayer they recite, in every flame they tend, Mobeds embody the enduring spirit of a faith that, against all odds, has continued to illuminate the path of righteousness for over three thousand years.

Chapter 19
Zarathustra in Oral Traditions and Legends

The figure of Zarathustra, shrouded in both historical fact and myth, has been a central character in the spiritual consciousness of Zoroastrian communities for centuries. Beyond the foundational texts of the Avesta, the stories surrounding Zarathustra's life have been passed down through generations, becoming rich oral traditions that blend mystical elements with cultural narratives. These tales serve not only as a means of preserving the past but also as a source of inspiration and identity for Zoroastrians facing the challenges of modernity.

One of the most intriguing aspects of Zarathustra's story is his birth, which is surrounded by miraculous signs that indicate his divine mission. According to oral traditions, the moment of his birth was marked by a supernatural glow that illuminated the room, signaling that a unique prophet had arrived in the world. It is said that evil forces, aware of the threat he posed to their dominion, sought to eliminate Zarathustra even as a child. However, every attempt to harm him failed, as divine protection enveloped the future prophet. These stories not only emphasize his special status but also align with the Zoroastrian theme of the eternal struggle between good and evil, even before he could speak his first words.

As Zarathustra grew, legends describe his early life as one marked by wisdom and curiosity, setting him apart from his peers. He is often depicted as a child with a profound connection to the natural world, able to perceive the divine presence in the elements of fire, water, earth, and air. Such stories portray him as a seeker of truth long before his divine revelation, suggesting that his path as a prophet was woven into the fabric of his being from an early age. This narrative, deeply rooted in oral tradition, serves as a reminder that the spiritual journey of a prophet is not merely a moment of enlightenment but a lifetime of preparation and introspection.

One of the pivotal moments in these stories is Zarathustra's encounter with Ahura Mazda, the supreme deity. The encounter is said to have taken place on a riverbank, where Zarathustra entered a trance-like state and beheld a vision of Ahura Mazda, surrounded by the Amesha Spentas. It was here that he received the divine mandate to spread the message of Asha (truth) and to combat the lies and chaos represented by Angra Mainyu. This event is more than just a moment of revelation; in oral traditions, it is described as a cosmic event, where time seemed to stand still, and the future course of humanity was altered. This mystical encounter is often recounted during religious gatherings, serving as a cornerstone of Zoroastrian identity and a symbol of the power of divine truth.

The early resistance that Zarathustra faced from the rulers and priests of his time is another theme that features prominently in these oral accounts. According to tradition, Zarathustra's teachings were initially met with hostility, as they challenged the established religious practices and the power structures that benefited from them. He was imprisoned and faced trials designed to discredit his message. Yet, through divine intervention and his unwavering commitment to truth, Zarathustra overcame these obstacles. His triumph is celebrated in stories where natural elements come to his aid, such as the account of a miraculous flood that freed him from his chains. These narratives highlight the resilience of the prophet and the ultimate victory of divine justice, reinforcing the Zoroastrian belief in the power of righteousness.

A key part of the oral traditions involves Zarathustra's interaction with King Vishtaspa, who would become his most influential convert and patron. According to legend, Zarathustra's entry into the court of Vishtaspa was met with skepticism, as rival priests tried to undermine him. To prove the truth of his teachings, Zarathustra performed a series of miracles, including healing the king's beloved horse, which had been struck down by an unknown affliction. The restoration of the horse's health was seen as a sign of Ahura Mazda's favor, leading King Vishtaspa to accept Zarathustra's teachings and declare Zoroastrianism the state religion. This moment is often recounted with a sense of triumph, symbolizing the power of faith to overcome doubt and opposition.

These legends serve a crucial role in preserving the cultural memory of Zoroastrians, particularly in times of adversity. During periods of persecution, such as the Islamic conquest of Persia, these stories became a source of resilience, reminding the community of their origins and the divine favor that had guided their prophet. As Zoroastrian communities dispersed and adapted to new lands, these tales were carried with them, evolving with each telling but always retaining the essence of Zarathustra's mission. They became a way to keep the spirit of Zoroastrianism alive, even when practicing the faith openly was fraught with danger.

In these stories, Zarathustra is not only a prophet but also a symbol of the eternal struggle against ignorance and deceit. His teachings, passed down through sacred texts, are given life and vibrancy through the narratives that surround them. The tales of his encounters with supernatural beings, the battles he fought against sorcery, and his debates with those who opposed him all serve to illustrate the challenges faced by those who seek to uphold truth in a world filled with deception. These accounts portray Zarathustra as a figure who embodies the qualities that Zoroastrians aspire to: courage, wisdom, and an unwavering commitment to the path of Asha.

Oral traditions have also played a role in filling the gaps left by the loss of many Zoroastrian texts over the centuries. Stories that were never written down, or that may have been lost in the turmoil of historical upheavals, survived through storytelling. Families would gather during festivals like Nowruz and recount the life of Zarathustra, ensuring that even in the absence of written records, the essence of his message would endure. In this way, the oral traditions surrounding Zarathustra act as a living archive of Zoroastrian values, shaping the identity of the faithful across generations.

These stories also reveal the diverse interpretations of Zarathustra's legacy across different Zoroastrian communities. In some versions, he is portrayed as a mystic who could communicate with nature, while in others, he is depicted as a wise philosopher whose logic and reason were unassailable. Each interpretation adds a layer of richness to the Zoroastrian tapestry, showing how the essence of Zarathustra's teachings has been adapted to resonate with different cultural and historical contexts. This adaptability has allowed Zoroastrianism to maintain its core message while embracing the unique expressions of faith found within its diverse followers.

The reverence for Zarathustra in these traditions is profound, yet it is coupled with a recognition of his humanity. Stories often depict moments of doubt or loneliness during his mission, times when he questioned whether his efforts would succeed. In these narratives, Zarathustra is comforted by visions of Ahura Mazda or signs that reaffirm the righteousness of his path. This dual portrayal—both as a divinely guided prophet and a man who faced the struggles of life—makes Zarathustra's story deeply relatable. It reminds the faithful that even the greatest spiritual leaders must grapple with doubt, and that perseverance in the face of adversity is itself a path to divine truth.

The oral traditions and legends of Zarathustra, passed down through centuries, form an integral part of the spiritual heritage of Zoroastrians. They weave together the mystical and the historical, offering a narrative that transcends time. Through these stories, the memory of Zarathustra is not confined to the pages of ancient scriptures but lives on in the spoken word, in the shared experiences of communities, and in the hearts of those who continue to seek the light of Asha in their own lives. These narratives serve as a bridge between the ancient and the present, ensuring that Zarathustra's teachings remain a guiding star in the ever-changing night sky of human experience.

As the tales of Zarathustra passed through generations, they evolved with each telling, adapting to the cultural and spiritual needs of Zoroastrian communities. These stories, while rooted in ancient times, have a fluidity that allowed them to integrate local influences and interpretations, providing a rich tapestry of legends that reveal the diverse ways in which Zoroastrians have connected with their prophet. In this evolution, the figure of Zarathustra became more than a distant spiritual leader—he became a symbol of resilience and hope, embodying qualities that resonate with the faithful across different epochs and landscapes.

A central theme in these stories is the transformation of Zarathustra from a solitary seeker of truth into a revered prophet whose teachings reshaped an entire culture. In the more mystical traditions, Zarathustra is seen as possessing a deep understanding of the cosmic forces that govern the universe, able to perceive the subtle interplay between light and darkness. It is said that he could communicate with nature, and that the elements themselves—fire, water, earth, and air—responded to his presence. In these accounts, Zarathustra's connection with Ahura Mazda allowed him to see beyond the material world, into the realms where the divine battle between Asha (truth) and Druj (lie) played out on a grander scale.

These mystical tales often emphasize the extraordinary nature of Zarathustra's life, painting a portrait of a prophet who was not merely chosen by the divine but who actively shaped his own destiny through acts of courage and insight. One popular narrative recounts his encounter with demonic beings sent by Angra Mainyu, the spirit of chaos, to deter him from his mission. According to tradition, Zarathustra faced these entities with unwavering conviction, using sacred chants and prayers to banish them. The imagery of this struggle, of light confronting darkness in its most tangible form, resonates deeply with Zoroastrian followers. It serves as a metaphor for the everyday battles they face against falsehoods and temptations, affirming that the path of righteousness requires both strength and steadfastness.

As these legends spread, they also absorbed the cultural contexts of the regions where Zoroastrians settled, especially during periods of migration. For instance, among the Parsi communities in India, the tales of Zarathustra took on new dimensions, blending with local folklore and gaining a distinctive regional flavor. In these versions, Zarathustra's wisdom is often compared to the teachings of other ancient sages, creating a dialogue between Zoroastrianism and the spiritual traditions of the Indian subcontinent. This syncretism is evident in the way Zarathustra's story is told during festivals like Nowruz, where elements of Zoroastrian cosmology are celebrated alongside the changing of seasons, emphasizing renewal and the eternal cycle of life.

The adaptation of these legends is not limited to religious or spiritual contexts. They have also found their way into Persian literature and poetry, where the figure of Zarathustra is often invoked as a symbol of spiritual purity and philosophical depth. The works of poets like Ferdowsi in the Shahnameh and the writings of medieval mystics weave Zarathustra's story into the broader cultural narrative of Persia, blending history with myth. In this literary tradition, Zarathustra becomes a symbol of the Iranian spirit—eternally struggling against adversity, seeking knowledge, and preserving the ancient wisdom of the land. Such portrayals helped to maintain a sense of continuity with pre-Islamic Persian culture, providing a touchstone for identity during times of cultural upheaval.

Yet, even as these stories grew and transformed, they maintained a core message: Zarathustra's unwavering dedication to the truth and his vision of a world where Asha prevails over Druj. In some narratives, his struggles are seen as a precursor to the challenges that Zoroastrian communities would face in later centuries, as they contended with the rise of new empires and religions that reshaped the Middle East. The endurance of these stories through times of persecution and displacement illustrates the power of oral tradition to sustain a community's spirit, even when their physical presence in a land becomes tenuous. The tales of Zarathustra's trials thus mirror the experiences of his followers, creating a powerful sense of shared history and fate.

These stories also contain a profound pedagogical aspect, serving as a means of transmitting ethical and philosophical lessons to younger generations. Parents would tell their children stories of Zarathustra's wisdom and his encounters with both celestial and terrestrial challenges, emphasizing the virtues of honesty, humility, and courage. Through these narratives, complex theological concepts were made accessible, teaching the values of good thoughts, good words, and good deeds in a way that was relatable and engaging. Even as the stories took on the characteristics of myth, they retained a didactic purpose, ensuring that the principles of Zoroastrianism would remain relevant to each new generation.

The flexibility of these legends has also allowed them to adapt to the challenges of modernity. As Zoroastrian communities have spread across the globe, settling in places as diverse as North America, Europe, and Australia, the stories of Zarathustra have been retold in new forms. Contemporary Zoroastrians continue to gather during community events and retell the tales of their prophet, using them as a way to connect with their heritage while adapting the themes to modern struggles—be it the quest for identity in a multicultural world or the challenge of sustaining ancient traditions in a rapidly changing society.

In recent years, some Zoroastrians have turned to media such as film, theater, and digital storytelling to keep the spirit of these legends alive. These new interpretations often explore Zarathustra's relevance to contemporary issues, like environmental stewardship and the ethical use of technology, reflecting the evolving concerns of the community. Yet, even in these modern retellings, the essence of the original stories remains: the vision of a world where truth triumphs over falsehood, where each individual's choices contribute to the cosmic balance between good and evil. These adaptations demonstrate the enduring power of Zarathustra's story to inspire and guide, transcending the boundaries of time and place.

Despite the changes in their form and context, the stories of Zarathustra continue to hold a special place in the collective memory of Zoroastrians. They serve as a reminder that their faith is not only a matter of doctrine and ritual but also a living narrative, woven into the very fabric of their identity. Through the telling and retelling of these tales, the Zoroastrian community finds a sense of continuity with their past, even as they look toward the future. Zarathustra's story is thus not merely a relic of history but a vibrant, evolving tradition that remains a source of strength and inspiration.

The legacy of these oral traditions also offers a broader insight into the power of storytelling within human cultures. Through myth and legend, communities are able to preserve the essence of their beliefs, adapt to new realities, and find meaning in their struggles. Zarathustra's legends have accomplished this across millennia, helping to keep the Zoroastrian faith alive through periods of prosperity and persecution alike. The stories that began on the windswept plains of ancient Persia have journeyed across continents, carried in the hearts of those who refuse to let their light fade.

In the end, the legends of Zarathustra are a testament to the resilience of the Zoroastrian spirit. They reflect a profound understanding that the search for truth is a journey without end, and that each generation must find its own way to carry the flame forward. Through these stories, Zarathustra remains a companion to the faithful, guiding them through the darkness with the promise of a brighter dawn, where Asha shines ever clearer, and the world moves closer to the divine order envisioned so long ago by a prophet on the banks of a sacred river.

Chapter 20
The End Times

Among the most profound and enigmatic aspects of Zoroastrianism is its vision of the end times—a narrative that intertwines cosmic battles, divine renewal, and the promise of a world transformed. At the heart of Zoroastrian eschatology lies the prophecy of a great restoration, known as Frashokereti, where the universe is purified, evil is vanquished, and order is re-established according to the divine will of Ahura Mazda. It is a vision that holds both hope and solemnity, as it promises not only a glorious new world but also the trials and tribulations that must precede it.

Central to this belief is the arrival of the Saoshyant, a savior figure prophesied to lead humanity through the final struggle against the forces of Angra Mainyu. According to Zoroastrian tradition, the Saoshyant will emerge in a time of great turmoil, a period when chaos and falsehood seem to dominate the earth. This figure is not merely a warrior but a spiritual guide, tasked with uniting the righteous and awakening humanity to the principles of Asha—truth and order. In many ways, the Saoshyant is seen as the fulfillment of Zarathustra's teachings, embodying the same divine mission to combat evil and bring enlightenment.

The imagery of the end times in Zoroastrianism is vivid, portraying a cosmic upheaval where the material and spiritual realms converge in a final battle. The ancient texts describe this period as one where the earth itself seems to tremble, where natural disasters and celestial signs herald the approach of the ultimate conflict. It is said that the rivers will swell, the sun and moon will grow dim, and the very fabric of reality will be tested as the opposing forces of Asha and Druj clash in their last, desperate struggle. Yet amidst this chaos, the faithful are called to remain steadfast, for it is their adherence to truth and righteousness that will help to tip the scales in favor of the divine.

The role of Ahura Mazda during this eschatological period is depicted as that of a cosmic judge and orchestrator of the final judgment. Through the revelations imparted to Zarathustra and preserved in the Avesta, the Zoroastrian faithful understand that Ahura Mazda's justice is not arbitrary but is based on the accumulated deeds of each soul. As the end approaches, all human actions, thoughts, and intentions are weighed, and the fate of every soul hangs in the balance. This judgment occurs at the Chinvat Bridge, a passage that each soul must cross after death, with the righteous finding it a broad and easy path, while the wicked encounter a perilous crossing, leading them to realms of suffering.

It is through this lens that the Zoroastrian concept of salvation is understood—not as a matter of blind faith, but as a consequence of one's moral choices throughout life. The arrival of the Saoshyant and the unfolding of the end times serve as a reminder that the cosmic struggle between good and evil is mirrored in the daily actions of individuals. Each choice to embrace Asha contributes to the ultimate triumph over Angra Mainyu, reinforcing the Zoroastrian emphasis on personal responsibility and the power of free will.

The Saoshyant's role is to catalyze this global awakening, summoning the scattered remnants of the faithful to join in the fight against the darkness. Legends describe this figure performing miraculous acts, such as resurrecting the dead and healing the earth from the scars of destruction wrought by Angra Mainyu's followers. The resurrection, a pivotal moment in Zoroastrian eschatology, is believed to restore all souls to their physical bodies, allowing them to partake in the final renewal. This vision offers a profound sense of hope, suggesting that no soul is beyond redemption and that all will have the opportunity to align themselves with Ahura Mazda's divine order.

The purification of the world, known as Frashokereti, is depicted as a transformative event where the material and spiritual realms are fused in perfect harmony. In this renewed world, suffering and falsehood have no place, as the elements themselves—fire, water, earth, and air—are purified from the taint of Druj. It is a vision of a world where every being, from the smallest creature to the greatest mountain, sings in unison the praise of Ahura Mazda. The faithful are reassured that their struggles and sacrifices in this life are not in vain, for they contribute to the creation of this ideal state.

The transition to this perfected world, however, is not without trials. The texts speak of a river of molten metal that will flow across the earth, a test that all souls must endure. For the righteous, this river is described as a warm, purifying bath, while for the wicked, it is a searing punishment, a final reckoning for their alignment with falsehood and chaos. This imagery serves to emphasize the Zoroastrian belief in cosmic justice, where the consequences of one's life choices are experienced directly in the transition to the new world.

As the final battle concludes, Angra Mainyu and his demonic forces are bound and cast into the depths of non-existence, where they can no longer disrupt the harmony of creation. In some interpretations, this act is seen as a return to the primordial state of order, a restoration of the world to the way Ahura Mazda intended before the corruption of evil. The new era that follows is characterized by peace, prosperity, and an unbroken connection between the divine and the earthly realms. Humanity, united under the teachings of Zarathustra and the guidance of the Saoshyant, enters an age where suffering, deception, and death are but distant memories.

The Zoroastrian vision of the end times is not merely a prophecy but a framework that shapes the ethical and spiritual life of the faithful. It teaches that every action in the present has cosmic significance, that each moment of moral choice is a step toward or away from the realization of a divine reality. The narrative of the Saoshyant and the coming renewal inspires believers to strive for purity of thought and deed, knowing that their efforts contribute to a greater cosmic victory. It serves as a call to vigilance, reminding the faithful that while the battle between Asha and Druj is ancient, its conclusion remains unfinished, and each soul has a role to play in bringing it to a just end.

The hope embedded in Zoroastrian eschatology resonates particularly in times of hardship, offering a vision of ultimate justice when worldly justice seems elusive. For those who have faced persecution or displacement, the story of the end times provides a powerful reassurance that their faithfulness is not forgotten, and that a brighter era awaits beyond the trials of this world. It is this promise of renewal that has allowed Zoroastrianism to endure through centuries of adversity, as a beacon guiding its followers through the darkest of times.

As Zoroastrian communities contemplate their place in the modern world, the ancient teachings about the end times continue to hold relevance. They challenge believers to consider what it means to live in alignment with Asha in an age of rapid change and uncertainty. The Saoshyant's message—that a better world is possible if humanity chooses to strive for it—remains a source of inspiration, even as the faithful grapple with the complexities of contemporary life.

In the unfolding drama of creation and renewal, Zoroastrianism's vision of the end times serves as a reminder that the struggle for truth and righteousness is timeless, stretching from the dawn of creation to the last days of existence. The promise of Frashokereti, of a world restored to divine order, continues to echo in the hearts of those who seek the light of Ahura Mazda, offering a timeless assurance that, no matter how long the night, the dawn will come, bringing with it the fulfillment of all that is good.

The Zoroastrian vision of the end times continues with a deeper exploration of the final judgment and the transformation that awaits both the living and the dead. In this cosmic narrative, the fate of every soul is intertwined with the grand destiny of the universe itself, revealing the intimate link between individual deeds and the overarching struggle between good and evil. The final judgment, or the crossing of the Chinvat Bridge, is a moment of ultimate reckoning, where the weight of one's actions and choices is measured with unerring precision. Ahura Mazda, alongside divine entities like Mithra, presides over this moment, guiding souls toward their deserved outcomes.

The Chinvat Bridge serves as a metaphysical threshold between the material world and the spiritual realms. For those whose lives aligned with Asha—truth, righteousness, and divine order—the crossing is said to be smooth, leading them into realms of light and joy. The Avesta describes this experience with poetic imagery, where the soul is greeted by its Daena, a spiritual counterpart that takes the form of a beautiful maiden, embodying the virtues cultivated during the individual's life. This journey leads to Garōdmān, the House of Song, where the righteous dwell in eternal communion with Ahura Mazda.

In contrast, those who strayed from the path of Asha and embraced Druj—falsehood, deception, and chaos—find the crossing perilous. As they attempt to traverse the Chinvat Bridge, it narrows beneath their feet, transforming into a blade-like passage that plunges them into a chasm of darkness. For these souls, the Daena appears as a frightening, disfigured figure, a manifestation of the negative deeds accumulated during their earthly existence. They are drawn into a realm of suffering, known as Duzakh or the Zoroastrian hell, where they experience the consequences of their actions in a purgatorial state. However, even this state is not eternal, as Zoroastrianism holds the belief in the possibility of ultimate purification through Frashokereti.

The concept of Frashokereti, or the "making wonderful," is central to the eschatological hope of Zoroastrianism. This cosmic event signifies the restoration of creation to its original, uncorrupted state. The Saoshyant, alongside other spiritual leaders, plays a crucial role in this renewal process, leading a final battle against the remnants of Angra Mainyu's influence. This is not a mere physical confrontation but a spiritual struggle where the forces of light and truth strive to cleanse the universe of lingering evil. It is a process that transcends time, culminating in the ultimate victory of good and the dissolution of all forms of suffering.

During Frashokereti, the fire of judgment is kindled across the earth, a symbol of divine purification. The molten river, which flows over the earth, burns away impurities, refining both the physical world and the spiritual essence of all beings. For the righteous, this fire is a caress, a warm embrace that solidifies their connection to Asha. For the wicked, it is a searing trial, forcing a confrontation with the consequences of their choices. Yet, in Zoroastrian thought, even this suffering serves a redemptive purpose, as it prepares all souls for the final unity with the divine order.

In the midst of this purification, the Saoshyant is said to perform the resurrection of the dead, bringing all souls back into their bodies to experience the world's renewal firsthand. This moment is portrayed as a reunion of the living and the departed, where families and communities come together once more, sharing in the joy of a world reborn. The earth is described as being reshaped into a place of perfect balance, where the elements—earth, water, fire, and air—exist in their purest forms, free from the corruption of Angra Mainyu's influence.

With the defeat of Angra Mainyu, time itself is transformed. The concept of time as an endless cycle of creation and destruction gives way to a new era of unchanging bliss. This period, often referred to as the "New Time," is marked by the cessation of all forms of decay and death. In this age, the world no longer suffers from the passage of time; instead, it exists in a state of eternal spring, where nature flourishes and all beings live in harmony. Ahura Mazda's presence is fully realized, permeating every aspect of existence, and the distinction between the material and spiritual realms dissolves into unity.

This vision of an eternal, harmonious world is not only a theological concept but also a profound ethical guide for Zoroastrians. It reinforces the importance of contributing to this eventual renewal through daily actions, aligning with Asha and resisting the temptations of Druj. The promise of Frashokereti serves as a reminder that every small act of goodness, every choice toward truth, is a step toward the world's final transformation. It inspires believers to live as agents of cosmic change, knowing that their efforts are part of a divine narrative that stretches beyond their lifetime.

Zoroastrian teachings about the end times also emphasize the communal nature of this eschatological hope. The renewal of the world is not a solitary experience but a collective journey. As communities gather in anticipation of Frashokereti, they reflect on the stories of ancient heroes and martyrs who resisted the encroachments of darkness. This shared memory strengthens their resolve, linking their present struggles to the larger saga of the cosmos. Festivals such as Nowruz, which marks the Persian New Year, become moments to celebrate not only the renewal of nature but also the promise of a future where all creation will be restored.

Yet, within this cosmic vision lies a deeply personal dimension. The journey toward the end times is ultimately a path that each individual must walk. The teachings about the Saoshyant and Frashokereti challenge every believer to confront their own inner struggles, to discern where they stand between Asha and Druj. The notion that the Saoshyant could arise from any person of true conviction serves as a call to action, urging each follower to strive for moral excellence and spiritual insight. It is a message that transcends the boundaries of time, resonating with those who seek meaning in an ever-changing world.

In a modern context, the Zoroastrian vision of the end times offers a counter-narrative to despair and nihilism. It proposes that the challenges of the present, no matter how overwhelming, are but a prelude to a deeper transformation. It is a call to persevere through adversity, to see beyond the surface of events and recognize the hidden workings of divine justice. For many Zoroastrians today, these teachings provide a spiritual anchor amidst the uncertainties of diaspora and the shifting tides of global change.

The enduring power of this vision lies in its ability to balance the gravity of the cosmic struggle with a message of hope. It does not shy away from acknowledging the reality of suffering, yet it insists that this suffering is not without purpose. Through the lens of Frashokereti, pain and loss become part of a process of refinement, leading toward a future where all things find their rightful place in the order of Asha. This belief in a final reconciliation between good and evil, where even the most stubborn forces of chaos are ultimately subdued, offers a sense of closure to the long and arduous journey of existence.

As the teachings of the end times continue to shape Zoroastrian practice, they remind believers that the story of creation is still unfolding. The final chapters have yet to be written, and each individual has a role to play in determining how the narrative reaches its conclusion. The promise of a world renewed by Frashokereti is not a distant fantasy but a living tradition, passed down through the centuries, waiting to be realized through the actions of the faithful. It is a call to remain vigilant, to nurture the sacred flame of Ahura Mazda's wisdom, and to prepare for the dawn of a new age where darkness will be no more.

In this way, the Zoroastrian vision of the end times remains a profound testament to the resilience of the human spirit, a declaration that, despite the trials of history, hope endures. It invites all who hear its message to look beyond the present moment, to see the divine patterns woven into the fabric of reality, and to trust that, in the end, light will triumph.

Chapter 21
Ritual Chants

In Zoroastrianism, the sacred chants and hymns that form part of its ritual practices are more than mere words; they are bridges that connect the earthly realm with the divine. Each sound, each intonation, carries a spiritual potency, believed to resonate with the cosmic order established by Ahura Mazda. Central among these is the Yasna, a liturgical chant that serves as a cornerstone of Zoroastrian worship. It is a profound prayer that invokes the elements, the spirits, and the divine beings that oversee the world's order. The Yasna is not just a recitation but a ritual performance, where the spoken word becomes a tool for invoking spiritual energies and fostering harmony between the material and spiritual worlds.

The chants of Zoroastrianism, traditionally sung in Avestan, the ancient liturgical language, are believed to carry an intrinsic power. In these invocations, every syllable is considered a vibrational force that interacts with the unseen realms, guiding the practitioner's mind into alignment with Asha. This tradition has been preserved across centuries through the precise transmission from teacher to disciple, emphasizing the importance of accuracy in pronunciation and melody. The ancient Mobeds, or priests, dedicate years to mastering these recitations, understanding that their role as custodians of these chants is crucial for maintaining the link between humanity and the divine.

The Yasna ceremony itself is an intricate ritual that requires concentration and discipline. Conducted around a central fire, the ceremony involves the preparation of haoma, a sacred plant considered to have spiritual properties. As the priest chants the sacred verses, the haoma is consecrated and offered to the fire, symbolizing a bridge between the physical elements and the spiritual light of Ahura Mazda. Through this process, the ritual chants purify the space, creating a spiritual haven where the divine presence can be felt. This act of chanting not only consecrates the offerings but also purifies the hearts of those participating, renewing their connection to Asha.

In addition to the Yasna, other chants such as the Gathas hold a special place in Zoroastrian worship. The Gathas are believed to be the very words of Zarathustra himself, and their recitation is considered a form of communion with the prophet's teachings. These hymns reflect Zarathustra's vision of a world governed by the principles of truth, righteousness, and justice, and their melody is said to carry the essence of his spiritual revelations. The Gathas are not merely recited; they are experienced, with each verse offering layers of meaning that unfold through the rhythmic cadence of the chant. For the Zoroastrian faithful, the act of chanting the Gathas is a way to internalize the prophet's wisdom, allowing it to guide their daily actions.

Chanting, in Zoroastrianism, is often performed collectively, turning individual devotion into a communal act of worship. In fire temples, the voices of the community rise together, weaving a tapestry of sound that is believed to cleanse the environment of negative energies. This communal aspect reinforces the bonds between members of the Zoroastrian community, creating a shared space of spiritual refuge. The chants serve as a reminder of the collective responsibility to uphold Asha and resist the influences of Druj, fostering a sense of unity that transcends the individual.

The power of sound in Zoroastrian rituals is deeply connected to the concept of Manthra, a term referring to a sacred utterance or prayer that embodies spiritual power. Manthra is not only about the words themselves but the intention behind them, the inner state of the practitioner as they speak. It is said that a properly spoken Manthra can invoke divine blessings, offering protection against the chaos of Angra Mainyu. In this sense, the act of chanting becomes an act of creation, shaping reality through the spoken word and aligning the practitioner's spirit with the cosmic order.

The connection between chanting and nature is also emphasized in Zoroastrian practice. Many of the hymns honor the natural elements—water, earth, air, and fire—recognizing them as sacred manifestations of Ahura Mazda's creation. These chants are believed to maintain the harmony between human beings and the natural world, ensuring that each element remains in balance. The reverence shown to these elements through sacred chants highlights the Zoroastrian commitment to preserving the natural world, an integral part of their spiritual duty.

Through the ages, Zoroastrian chants have adapted to the cultural and geographical contexts of the diaspora. In India, among the Parsi community, the chanting tradition has been preserved with a meticulous devotion, ensuring that the ancient melodies continue to resonate in fire temples far from their Persian origins. This adaptation is not merely about preservation but also about resilience, a way for the Zoroastrian community to maintain their identity in a world that has changed drastically since the time of Zarathustra. The chants become a living link to the past, a means of carrying forward the essence of Zoroastrian spirituality into the present.

The chants also play a role in rites of passage, marking significant moments in the life of a Zoroastrian. From the initiation ceremony of the Navjote, where a child is welcomed into the faith, to the solemn recitations that accompany a soul's journey beyond the Chinvat Bridge, these chants provide comfort, guidance, and a sense of continuity. They remind the community that each individual life is part of a greater spiritual journey, interconnected with the cosmic struggle between Asha and Druj.

As Zoroastrianism navigates the complexities of the modern world, the role of ritual chanting continues to evolve. The preservation of these ancient melodies in a time of rapid change is seen as a sacred duty, a testament to the resilience of Zoroastrian culture. Yet, beyond preservation, there is a recognition that the chants must remain relevant, offering spiritual nourishment to new generations who seek meaning in a fast-paced world. The challenge lies in balancing the need to keep these traditions intact with the desire to make them accessible to a globalized community of believers.

In a time when many young Zoroastrians grow up far from the temples of Iran and India, efforts to teach these chants have embraced new methods. Recordings of the Yasna and Gathas are shared online, reaching those who cannot attend rituals in person. Workshops and gatherings around the world focus on teaching the correct pronunciation and understanding of the Manthras, ensuring that the spiritual depth of the chants is not lost in translation. These efforts reflect a broader commitment to keeping the flame of Zoroastrianism alive, ensuring that the sacred sounds that once echoed through ancient fire temples continue to resonate in the hearts of the faithful.

Thus, the tradition of Zoroastrian ritual chants remains a vital thread in the tapestry of the faith, connecting the modern practitioner to a lineage that stretches back to the dawn of time. It is a reminder that in a world of constant change, some things endure—like the power of a sacred word, spoken with devotion, rising like incense toward the eternal light of Ahura Mazda.

The role of ritual chanting in Zoroastrianism is woven into the fabric of spiritual life, extending beyond mere recitation into the realm of deep metaphysical resonance. Every chant carries with it the weight of tradition, a thread that links each generation back to the ancient practices first inspired by Zarathustra's teachings. While the Yasna and the Gathas are central, other chants—each with its own melody and intonation—serve specific roles within the spiritual framework of Zoroastrian rituals. These chants hold the power to consecrate, to purify, and to call forth the divine presence during moments of prayer and meditation.

Among these are the Niyash and the Yashts, prayers that pay homage to the divine spirits associated with natural elements and celestial beings. Each chant is an invocation, a call to the divine energies that govern creation. The Niyash, for example, is sung to honor the sun, the moon, and the waters—acknowledging their life-giving powers and their place within the cosmic order. Through these chants, Zoroastrians express gratitude and reverence for the divine gifts of nature, reaffirming their role as stewards of Ahura Mazda's creation. The melodic patterns of the Niyash echo the rhythms of the natural world, creating a sense of unity between the worshipper and the divine.

The Yashts, on the other hand, are more intricate hymns dedicated to individual divinities, such as Mithra, the guardian of covenants, or Anahita, the goddess of waters. Each Yasht is a tapestry of ancient mythological narratives, praises, and invocations, blending the poetic with the mystical. When chanted during special ceremonies, the Yashts are believed to invoke the favor of these spiritual entities, offering protection, blessings, and guidance. The cadences of the Yashts, with their varying tempos and intonations, create a dynamic spiritual atmosphere, elevating the mind to contemplate the divine mysteries.

The art of chanting in Zoroastrianism is as much about the correct pronunciation and rhythm as it is about the inner state of the reciter. The spiritual disposition, or the purity of heart, is considered essential for the efficacy of the chants. In this, the ancient practice of maintaining spiritual discipline before entering the fire temple or participating in ceremonies is of utmost importance. Mobeds, the custodians of these traditions, undergo rigorous training not only to master the complex melodies but also to cultivate an inner alignment with Asha, the truth and order that they seek to manifest through each word uttered. Their voices carry a resonance that is believed to be capable of bridging the temporal with the eternal.

The transmission of these chanting techniques from teacher to disciple has historically been a process of deep mentorship, where the focus is not just on learning but on embodying the spiritual principles that the chants represent. In this tradition, the act of listening is as important as the act of reciting. It is through listening to the voice of an experienced

Mobed that the subtleties of each chant are absorbed, allowing the initiate to capture the full depth of the ritual. This oral tradition emphasizes that sacred knowledge is best passed through experience rather than mere textual study.

In Zoroastrian communities around the world, the preservation of chanting has faced challenges, especially in the modern era where many families live far from the traditional centers of worship. In response, there has been a growing effort to document these chants through recordings, ensuring that the younger generation can access and learn these sacred melodies even if they are far from a fire temple. Online platforms have become repositories of these ancient practices, where recordings of the Yasna, Yashts, and other chants are shared, bridging the gap between tradition and modernity.

This adaptation of ancient chants into digital media is a reflection of the evolving nature of Zoroastrian worship, where tradition and technology meet. These recordings, often accompanied by explanations of their meanings and spiritual significance, help younger Zoroastrians connect with their heritage in a way that aligns with contemporary life. In the diaspora, where Zoroastrians are spread across continents, this has been a crucial means of maintaining a sense of community, despite geographical distances. For many, listening to these chants becomes a way to reconnect with the roots of their faith, to hear the same words that echoed in the ancient temples of Persia.

Yet, the digitization of chanting traditions also brings with it questions of authenticity and fidelity. The delicate balance between preserving the ancient intonations and adapting to the contexts of new generations requires careful consideration. Mobeds and community leaders often debate the best ways to maintain the integrity of these chants while ensuring their accessibility to those who may never step inside a fire temple. This conversation is part of a larger dialogue within Zoroastrianism about the preservation of tradition in a changing world, where the desire for spiritual connection must coexist with the realities of modern life.

Despite these challenges, the heart of chanting remains unchanged—a practice meant to uplift, to purify, and to connect the soul with the divine. Even in the quiet solitude of a home, far from the presence of a Mobed, a Zoroastrian can chant the simple words of the Ashem Vohu or the Yatha Ahu Vairyo, two of the most ancient and powerful mantras of the faith. These short invocations distill the essence of Zoroastrian philosophy, focusing on truth, righteousness, and the eternal struggle to align oneself with Asha. For many Zoroastrians, the repetition of these mantras is a daily reminder of their spiritual path, a moment to center themselves amid the distractions of everyday life.

The power of chanting extends into rites of passage, moments that mark the stages of life for Zoroastrians. The Navjote ceremony, a young Zoroastrian's initiation into the faith, is accompanied by the chanting of sacred verses, a ritual that symbolizes the passing of spiritual knowledge from one generation to the next. Similarly, during marriage ceremonies, chants bless the union and call upon divine protection for the couple's journey together. In the final rites, when a Zoroastrian passes on, the sacred chants guide the soul towards the Chinvat Bridge, offering comfort to the bereaved and ensuring that the departed is accompanied by the sacred words of their faith.

The impact of chanting goes beyond the spiritual to touch the communal and cultural aspects of Zoroastrian life. At festivals such as Nowruz, the Persian New Year, the chants fill the air with a sense of renewal and hope. During these gatherings, the act of chanting together reinforces the bonds between community members, turning the simple act of recitation into a powerful collective experience. It is in these moments that the full depth of Zoroastrian ritual becomes evident—a faith that is as much about the communal experience of the divine as it is about the individual's journey towards spiritual enlightenment.

As Zoroastrian communities continue to adapt to a globalized world, the tradition of chanting serves as a reminder of their enduring connection to the ancient wisdom of Zarathustra. It is a way of keeping alive the spiritual insights that have been passed down through millennia, ensuring that they do not fade into the echoes of history. Instead, these chants continue to resonate—sometimes in the ancient fire temples of Iran, sometimes in the small gatherings of diaspora communities, and sometimes through the digital speakers of those learning their ancestral prayers anew.

In every form, the chant remains a testament to the living spirit of Zoroastrianism, an unbroken line of sound that reaches back to the dawn of the faith and extends forward into the unknown future. It embodies the Zoroastrian belief that the spoken word holds power, a power that can shape, transform, and uplift both the individual and the world. Through this enduring tradition, the sacred chants of Zoroastrianism offer a path to connection—a reminder that within each voice lies the potential to touch the eternal light of Ahura Mazda.

Chapter 22
The Diaspora

The story of the Zoroastrian diaspora is a tale of endurance, adaptation, and cultural preservation. As the Arab conquest reshaped the Persian landscape, many Zoroastrians faced profound changes to their social, religious, and political status. Yet, even in the face of adversity, the faith and cultural traditions of this ancient community found ways to survive, eventually taking root in new lands. This chapter delves into the journeys that led Zoroastrians beyond the borders of Persia, their struggles to maintain their beliefs in foreign environments, and the creation of new communities that would ensure the continuity of their spiritual heritage.

The initial waves of Zoroastrian migration began shortly after the Islamic conquest of Persia in the 7th century. As the new rulers imposed restrictions on religious practices and Zoroastrians faced increasing pressure to convert, a significant number of believers sought refuge in regions where they could preserve their customs. Many fled to the mountainous areas of northern Iran, where pockets of Zoroastrian practice endured for centuries. Others journeyed further, embarking on the perilous sea routes that led them to the western coasts of India, where they eventually established a thriving community known as the Parsis.

The Parsi migration is one of the most significant chapters in the history of the Zoroastrian diaspora. Arriving in Gujarat around the 8th or 9th century, the Parsis negotiated with local rulers for the right to practice their faith freely. A well-known legend tells of the Parsi priests meeting a local king, who, upon being offered a vessel filled to the brim with milk, was told that their presence would be like adding sugar to milk—enhancing but not overwhelming. This metaphorical assurance symbolized the Parsis' commitment to integrating into their new homeland while preserving their distinct religious identity. Over time, the Parsis built fire temples, established communities, and became an integral part of the cultural fabric of India.

The move to India allowed Zoroastrianism to flourish in a new context, away from the pressures faced in Iran. However, the Parsis also encountered the challenge of adapting their customs to fit into a predominantly Hindu and Muslim society. This adaptation required careful negotiation between maintaining the core tenets of their faith and embracing the new cultural environment. They preserved the essential elements of Zoroastrian rituals, from the sacred fire to the Navjote ceremony, while adapting certain practices to align with their new surroundings. The result was a vibrant Parsi culture that maintained its religious distinctiveness while contributing to the broader Indian society through philanthropy, education, and trade.

The challenges of the diaspora extended beyond religious practices to the preservation of language and tradition. The Parsi community made efforts to retain the use of Avestan and Pahlavi, the ancient languages of their scriptures, within their religious context, even as Gujarati and other regional languages became the common tongue of daily life. This linguistic duality became a hallmark of the community's cultural resilience, symbolizing their link to a distant homeland and their commitment to maintaining a spiritual lineage that spanned millennia.

Meanwhile, in Iran, Zoroastrian communities continued to face discrimination and economic hardships under successive Muslim dynasties. Yet, small Zoroastrian populations managed to survive in cities like Yazd and Kerman, regions known for their enduring devotion to the old faith. Here, they kept alive the ancient customs in secrecy, protecting their fire temples and gathering for rituals under the constant shadow of persecution. These communities, although diminished, served as a living connection to the Zoroastrian past of Persia, preserving traditions that would later inspire a sense of pride and revival among Zoroastrians around the world.

The 19th and 20th centuries brought new shifts as Zoroastrian communities in both Iran and India sought to re-establish connections with one another and with the broader world. This period saw increased interactions between the Parsis and the Zoroastrians of Iran, with the Parsis often offering financial assistance to their Iranian counterparts. These exchanges were more than acts of charity—they were efforts to rebuild a sense of unity among Zoroastrians separated by time, geography, and historical circumstances. Such interactions helped reinforce a shared identity, reminding the communities of their common heritage and the universal teachings of Zarathustra.

The modern era also brought new migrations, as economic opportunities and political upheavals led Zoroastrians to settle in Western countries, including the United States, Canada, the United Kingdom, and Australia. These newer diaspora communities found themselves in yet another phase of adaptation, integrating into Western society while striving to pass on their traditions to the next generation. For many, the move to the West represented a chance to escape the lingering prejudices they faced in Iran or to find new opportunities for education and professional growth.

The dispersion of Zoroastrians into various parts of the world presented both opportunities and challenges. In cities like Los Angeles, Toronto, and London, Zoroastrians formed new associations and built cultural centers to maintain their community spirit. These centers became places of gathering, where families could celebrate Nowruz together, young members could learn about their heritage, and elders could pass down the stories of their ancestors. At the same time, the pressures of assimilation and the smaller size of these communities made it increasingly difficult to keep younger generations engaged in the faith.

In the Western diaspora, Zoroastrians often face the delicate balance between embracing the freedom to practice their religion openly and the risk of losing younger generations to the secular influences of their new homelands. Many families find themselves navigating questions of identity, trying to preserve the core principles of their faith while ensuring that their children feel a sense of belonging in their broader social context. The result is a dynamic and evolving understanding of what it means to be Zoroastrian in the 21st century—one that draws from ancient teachings while engaging with the realities of a globalized world.

The story of the Zoroastrian diaspora is also a narrative of cultural exchange. In each new environment, Zoroastrians have contributed to the societies they inhabit, from the influential business and philanthropic endeavors of the Parsis in India to the academic and cultural contributions of Zoroastrians in the West. These communities have become living examples of the Zoroastrian principles of Asha and Vohu Manah, bringing order, truth, and good intentions into their interactions with others. Their emphasis on education, charity, and integrity has earned Zoroastrians a reputation for being industrious and principled members of society, no matter where they have settled.

Yet, with each generation, the challenge of maintaining Zoroastrian identity becomes more pressing. Community leaders and elders are deeply aware of the need to keep the ancient fire burning—not just in the literal sense of the sacred flames in their temples, but as a symbol of the enduring spiritual light of Ahura Mazda. This challenge has inspired many to develop new approaches, from online platforms where young Zoroastrians can connect and learn about their faith, to initiatives that promote intercultural understanding and awareness of Zoroastrian history and philosophy.

The resilience of the Zoroastrian diaspora is ultimately a testament to the enduring strength of a faith that has weathered centuries of change. It reflects the adaptability of a community that has carried the ancient wisdom of Zarathustra across oceans and borders, preserving it through countless transformations. Each generation of the diaspora, whether in Iran, India, or far-flung corners of the West, has faced the question of what it means to be a Zoroastrian in their time—and each has found ways to answer it, keeping alive the spirit of their ancient tradition while embracing the opportunities of the world around them.

The persistence of the Zoroastrian diaspora is marked not only by adaptation but by a continuous effort to weave their ancient faith into the fabric of new homelands. As the community spread across India, the West, and beyond, the challenges of sustaining their cultural and religious heritage evolved. Each new context required a delicate balance—retaining the essence of their beliefs while navigating modernity, embracing new identities without losing the core values taught by Zarathustra. This chapter delves deeper into the contributions, cultural adaptations, and identity struggles of Zoroastrian diaspora communities, exploring their ongoing efforts to maintain a connection with their past.

In India, the Parsi community became a significant part of the social and economic landscape, contributing notably to industry, education, and the arts. Pioneers like Jamsetji Tata and Dadabhai Naoroji were instrumental in shaping modern India's industrial and political ethos, yet their contributions were always deeply intertwined with their Zoroastrian values. Their philanthropy, driven by the principle of "Hvarshta" (good deeds), left a lasting legacy in the form of educational institutions, hospitals, and cultural foundations that continue to serve society. The Parsis' emphasis on charity and social welfare became a hallmark of their identity in India, reflecting the Zoroastrian tenet of promoting the welfare of all creation.

This spirit of giving and community service, however, was accompanied by an internal tension—the desire to maintain a distinct identity amidst the wider Indian society. As intermarriage and assimilation into broader cultural practices increased, the community faced debates over what it meant to be authentically Parsi. These discussions often revolved around issues like the preservation of rituals, the use of Avestan in religious ceremonies, and adherence to traditional dress and customs. The question of who could be considered Zoroastrian or Parsi, especially in cases of mixed heritage, sparked passionate debates, revealing the deep-seated concerns over the dilution of their ancient traditions.

In Iran, the struggles of the remaining Zoroastrian communities took on a different character. Under the shadow of centuries-long marginalization, they found themselves striving to maintain their customs with limited resources. In the face of cultural pressures, Zoroastrians in Yazd, Kerman, and Tehran endeavored to keep alive their religious practices, safeguarding the sacred fires and gathering for communal rituals, even as many faced social isolation. The post-revolutionary period in Iran, with its focus on Islamic values, brought renewed challenges, but it also sparked a sense of pride and solidarity among Zoroastrians determined to protect their identity. In recent decades, there has been a revival of cultural pride, with Zoroastrians in Iran emphasizing the preservation of historical sites and increasing efforts to educate the youth about their heritage.

As Zoroastrian communities established themselves in the West, they found new avenues to express their identity and share their rich heritage with others. In cities like New York, London, and Toronto, Zoroastrian associations and cultural centers have become focal points for community life. Here, Zoroastrians gather to celebrate traditional festivals like Nowruz and Gahambars, organize youth camps, and engage in interfaith dialogues that introduce others to the wisdom of Zarathustra. These efforts are not merely about preserving rituals—they represent a broader mission to keep the Zoroastrian values of truth, righteousness, and harmony relevant in a globalized world.

The Zoroastrian diaspora's engagement with modern technology has been pivotal in their efforts to preserve and disseminate their heritage. Social media platforms, online prayer gatherings, and digital archives have enabled members of the faith to stay connected across continents. This digital presence has allowed for a reimagining of community, one that transcends geographical borders and fosters a sense of unity among Zoroastrians worldwide. Young Zoroastrians, particularly those born in Western countries, have used these tools to explore their identity, seeking a balance between their heritage and their place in multicultural societies. For many, this connection to their roots has taken the form of exploring ancient texts, learning Avestan chants, and participating in discussions on how Zoroastrian values can address contemporary challenges like environmental sustainability and social justice.

The experience of the Zoroastrian diaspora has also been shaped by the contributions of influential figures who have acted as cultural bridges. Scholars, writers, and leaders within the diaspora have worked to interpret Zoroastrian teachings in ways that resonate with modern audiences. Their writings and public engagements have highlighted the timeless relevance of Zoroastrian concepts like Asha (truth and order) and Spenta Mainyu (the spirit of creativity and growth). By framing Zoroastrianism as a tradition that values individual choice, environmental stewardship, and the pursuit of knowledge, these thought leaders have helped the diaspora to see their faith not just as an ancient legacy but as a philosophy with profound implications for modern life.

Yet, even with these advancements, the Zoroastrian diaspora remains acutely aware of the demographic challenges facing their community. The global Zoroastrian population is small, and with each passing generation, the question of continuity becomes more pressing. Birth rates within the community are low, and the rules around intermarriage have led to further reductions in numbers. This has spurred a variety of initiatives aimed at community-building and engagement. Programs like youth leadership camps, Zoroastrian student associations, and intercultural workshops have emerged as means to foster a sense of belonging among younger members. These programs emphasize the idea that while the rituals and practices of Zoroastrianism are ancient, the way they are lived can evolve to meet the needs of a changing world.

For many Zoroastrians in the diaspora, the preservation of their faith is also a matter of safeguarding their cultural memory. This includes efforts to document the history of their migration, the struggles faced in their new homelands, and the contributions they have made to various societies. Such documentation serves not only as a historical record but as a source of inspiration, reminding younger generations of the resilience and adaptability of their ancestors. Projects like oral history recordings and community archives have been crucial in capturing the diverse experiences of Zoroastrians, ensuring that their story remains accessible to future generations.

The challenges of the diaspora, while daunting, have also sparked a sense of renewal within the community. In recent years, there has been a movement towards reinterpreting Zoroastrianism in a way that speaks to contemporary values and global challenges. This includes a focus on environmental ethics, which resonates with the ecological crises of today. The Zoroastrian emphasis on preserving nature, respecting the purity of the elements, and living in harmony with the earth has found new relevance, inspiring younger generations to view their faith as a guide for environmental activism.

This renewal is also evident in the growing interest among scholars and the general public in the history and teachings of Zoroastrianism. The community's openness to sharing their heritage through cultural festivals, public lectures, and academic collaborations has helped to elevate the profile of Zoroastrianism on the world stage. By emphasizing the universal themes of their faith—such as the battle between good and evil, the power of individual choice, and the pursuit of truth—Zoroastrians have positioned their ancient tradition as a source of wisdom that speaks to the shared human experience.

In the modern landscape, the Zoroastrian diaspora embodies a living paradox: a small community carrying forward an ancient tradition while engaging with the complexities of global modernity. Their story is not merely about survival but about the active creation of a future where the teachings of Zarathustra continue to inspire. Through their cultural resilience, their commitment to education and community, and their willingness to adapt without losing sight of their spiritual roots,

Zoroastrians around the world have found ways to keep their traditions alive, offering a testament to the enduring power of faith and cultural memory.

Thus, the diaspora represents a continuation of a journey that began with Zarathustra's revelations in ancient Persia—a journey that has crossed seas and spanned continents, yet remains deeply rooted in the timeless principles of Asha and Vohu Manah. For the Zoroastrian community, the future holds both uncertainty and promise, and in each corner of the world where a sacred fire burns, the story of resilience and hope continues to unfold.

Chapter 23
The Islamic Conquest of Persia

The seventh-century Islamic conquest of Persia brought profound changes to the cultural and religious landscape of the region, marking a turning point in the history of Zoroastrianism. As Arab forces advanced, they encountered a land deeply rooted in the ancient teachings of Zarathustra, where Zoroastrian fire temples dotted the landscape, and the Avesta served as the guiding light for both spiritual and daily life. Yet, with the arrival of the new Islamic rulers, the social order was irrevocably altered, and Zoroastrianism faced its most significant challenge.

In the beginning, the conquest was marked by resistance and conflict, as Persian forces, led by the Sasanian Empire, struggled to defend their territories. Despite their efforts, the Sasanian Empire eventually crumbled, overwhelmed by the military might and strategic acumen of the Arab armies. The fall of Ctesiphon, the Sasanian capital, symbolized the end of an era for Zoroastrians, as it paved the way for Islamic rule over Persia. The defeat did not only signify a political shift; it marked the beginning of a transformation in the religious life of the region.

The initial aftermath of the conquest was characterized by a period of tolerance, where Zoroastrians were granted the status of dhimmis—non-Muslims who could continue practicing their religion under Islamic rule in exchange for paying the jizya, a special tax. However, the imposition of this tax placed an economic burden on Zoroastrian communities, leading many to face the difficult choice between conversion to Islam or enduring economic hardship. For some, conversion offered a path to social mobility and relief from the taxes, but for others, it was a sacrifice of their most deeply held beliefs.

As the new Islamic rulers consolidated their power, they implemented changes that affected the fabric of Zoroastrian community life. The influence of Zoroastrianism began to wane as mosques replaced fire temples, and Arabic gradually supplanted Middle Persian as the language of administration and scholarship. The loss of the Sasanian court, which had been a staunch supporter of Zoroastrianism, left the community without a central patron to uphold their traditions. Zoroastrian priests, the Mobeds, faced increasing difficulty in maintaining their sacred fires and passing down the teachings of the Avesta to new generations.

Yet, despite these pressures, Zoroastrianism did not disappear. Communities in rural areas and in regions like Yazd and Kerman became refuges for the faithful. In these remote areas, Zoroastrians sought to preserve their customs in secret, away from the watchful eyes of the new rulers. Families would gather in their homes to whisper prayers, recite verses from the Avesta, and share the stories of their ancestors who had followed Zarathustra's path. The fire temples that remained became not only places of worship but symbols of resistance and identity, where the sacred flames represented a continuous link to their heritage and the divine presence of Ahura Mazda.

In this new context, Zoroastrian communities had to adapt their practices to survive. The rituals once performed openly in the grand temples of the Sasanian Empire were now conducted with discretion. Celebrations of Nowruz, which had long been a public event marking the renewal of life, became quieter affairs, but they retained their significance as a time to reflect on the resilience of their faith. The sacred duty to preserve the purity of fire, water, and earth took on new meaning, as Zoroastrians sought to maintain the integrity of their beliefs even under the shadow of a dominant culture that sought to reshape their world.

The adaptation to this new reality also brought shifts in the Zoroastrian understanding of their place in the universe. The teachings of Asha (cosmic order) and the eternal struggle against Druj (chaos) acquired a deeper resonance as Zoroastrians interpreted their changing circumstances as part of this cosmic battle. The survival of their community amidst adversity was seen as a manifestation of their role as guardians of Asha, a commitment to uphold truth and righteousness despite the challenges imposed by the new social order. This belief became a source of strength, guiding Zoroastrians through periods of uncertainty and loss.

The challenges of preserving Zoroastrianism under Islamic rule extended beyond religious practices to everyday life. Zoroastrians found themselves marginalized, limited in their opportunities for education, trade, and public life. Many faced discrimination and social ostracism, which further reinforced the sense of being a community apart. This sense of isolation led to a tighter communal bond among Zoroastrians, as they leaned on each other for support, forging a strong collective identity that helped them endure the centuries of change and upheaval that followed.

Over time, as more Persians converted to Islam, the Zoroastrian population dwindled, and the knowledge of their ancient texts and traditions became increasingly endangered. The loss of manuscripts and oral traditions during this period posed a severe threat to the preservation of Zoroastrian heritage. Yet, through the dedication of a few faithful Mobeds and scholars, efforts were made to compile and preserve what remained of the sacred texts. The Pahlavi literature, which recorded much of the Zoroastrian theological and philosophical thought, became a crucial source of knowledge, acting as a bridge between the ancient pre-Islamic past and the future of the faith.

The Islamic conquest of Persia was not just a story of decline for Zoroastrianism; it was a testament to the resilience and adaptability of a community determined to retain its spiritual identity. In the midst of political and social transformation, Zoroastrians maintained their connection to the ancient teachings of Zarathustra, adapting their practices to the realities of their new environment while never abandoning the core principles of their faith. Through perseverance, they managed to keep the essence of their beliefs alive, ensuring that the flame of their tradition would continue to burn, even if more dimly than before.

This chapter explores the complex dynamics of this period, reflecting on the strategies of survival and adaptation that Zoroastrians employed as they navigated a world transformed by new rulers and new ideologies. It sheds light on the experiences of those who chose to remain true to their ancient path despite the challenges, and on how their resilience became a foundation for the Zoroastrian communities that would continue to endure, both in Persia and beyond its borders.

The Islamic conquest, therefore, serves as a pivotal moment in the history of Zoroastrianism—not only as a time of loss but as a crucible in which the community's identity was reshaped and reaffirmed. It set the stage for the migration of Zoroastrians to new lands, such as India, where they would become known as Parsis, and for the emergence of a diaspora that would carry their beliefs into the future. It is a story of struggle, of adaptation, and above all, of an enduring commitment to the ideals of Asha and the teachings of Zarathustra, even when faced with the formidable tide of history.

The aftermath of the Islamic conquest of Persia left deep marks on the Zoroastrian community, transforming their religious practices, cultural identity, and societal roles. This chapter delves further into the resilience and survival strategies of Zoroastrians during the long period of Islamic rule, highlighting how their traditions were preserved, adapted, and sometimes concealed as they navigated a challenging and often hostile environment.

As Islamic influence solidified throughout Persia, the conditions for Zoroastrians grew increasingly difficult. While the initial conquest allowed some religious freedom through the status of dhimmi, later periods saw heightened pressure to conform to the Islamic norms of the new rulers. Zoroastrians, being a minority in a predominantly Muslim society, faced not only economic burdens like the jizya tax but also social stigma and restrictions. Their religious practices, which had once flourished openly in grand fire temples, were now conducted discreetly to avoid persecution or interference from authorities.

Despite these challenges, the Zoroastrian community remained committed to the core tenets of their faith, holding on to the essence of their rituals and beliefs. A key aspect of this preservation was the role of the Mobeds, or Zoroastrian priests, who became not only spiritual leaders but also guardians of knowledge. They meticulously memorized and transmitted the verses of the Avesta, maintaining the oral tradition even as the written texts became scarcer and were often hidden to prevent confiscation or destruction by those who saw them as relics of a superseded religion.

In secluded communities, far from the political centers of the Islamic caliphates, Zoroastrians found a measure of safety to continue their practices. Towns like Yazd and Kerman became bastions of Zoroastrian culture, where the rituals of the Yasna and prayers to Ahura Mazda could still be heard. These enclaves served as sanctuaries where the fire temples were preserved, albeit with much less grandeur than in the days of the Sasanian Empire. The sacred fires, symbols of the divine presence, continued to burn, becoming potent symbols of Zoroastrian endurance.

In these times of adversity, Zoroastrian theology evolved to reflect the community's experiences. The concept of Asha (order, truth) and its eternal struggle against Druj (chaos, falsehood) gained new layers of meaning, as Zoroastrians interpreted their social and political marginalization as part of a cosmic struggle. This perspective provided a source of resilience, as the community saw itself as the upholders of truth in a world increasingly dominated by other beliefs. This view also fostered a sense of spiritual isolation but reinforced the community's resolve to preserve their unique identity.

The adaptation of rituals to new conditions was a crucial element in the continuity of Zoroastrianism. While public celebrations like Nowruz were curtailed, many families continued to mark these occasions within the privacy of their homes, passing down customs to the younger generations. The Gahambars—seasonal festivals that celebrated the creation of elements like water, earth, and fire—remained central to the Zoroastrian calendar, albeit with simpler rites. These celebrations served as moments of communal solidarity, where stories of Zarathustra and the ancient kings of Persia were retold, keeping alive the memory of their heritage.

The secrecy surrounding Zoroastrian practices extended to the study of religious texts. The Pahlavi scriptures, written in a language no longer widely spoken, became both a repository of ancient wisdom and a tool for keeping religious knowledge hidden from those outside the community. Texts like the Denkard and Bundahishn, which provided theological commentary and cosmological insights, were copied and studied in quiet corners, ensuring that the teachings of Zarathustra would not be lost to time. The Zoroastrian community's emphasis on education, even in this constrained context, helped maintain a connection to their spiritual roots.

As Zoroastrians adapted to their new circumstances, their interactions with the Islamic culture around them led to subtle changes in their practices. Some Zoroastrian customs absorbed influences from Persian Islamic traditions, blending elements while maintaining their distinct theological framework. This blending was not a sign of surrender but a strategy of survival, allowing Zoroastrians to navigate their dual identity as Persian subjects of an Islamic caliphate and as followers of an ancient faith. Yet, they remained vigilant in preserving the fundamental aspects of their religion, such as the reverence for fire, the recitation of ancient prayers, and the ethical principles of Good Thoughts, Good Words, and Good Deeds.

The continued existence of Zoroastrianism during this period also depended on its ability to adapt to the changing social and economic structures. Many Zoroastrians turned to trades and crafts, often working as artisans, weavers, and merchants—occupations that allowed them to operate somewhat independently from the mainstream economic activities dominated by Muslim guilds. Through these roles, they were able to maintain a degree of economic stability, ensuring that their community could support the upkeep of remaining fire temples and the education of future generations in Zoroastrian doctrine.

The challenges of the Islamic era also spurred migration, leading some Zoroastrians to seek refuge beyond the borders of Persia. This movement, especially towards India, laid the groundwork for the emergence of the Parsi community, which would become a vibrant center of Zoroastrian life in the centuries to come. However, those who remained in Persia continued to uphold their traditions, despite the pressures of assimilation. The story of their perseverance is a testament to their deep-rooted commitment to the teachings of Zarathustra and their hope for a time when their faith could once again flourish openly.

The survival of Zoroastrianism in the face of the Islamic conquest illustrates a complex interplay between adaptation and resistance. Zoroastrians in Persia did not passively accept their diminished status; instead, they found ways to negotiate their place within a transformed society. They held on to their traditions, even as they adapted to new realities, ensuring that the core of their beliefs could endure through the centuries. Their resilience allowed Zoroastrianism to persist, even in a world where their ancient temples and sacred texts seemed on the verge of vanishing.

This chapter highlights how, through these subtle forms of resistance, the Zoroastrian community preserved its spiritual essence and laid the groundwork for future revitalization efforts. The strategies they employed—ranging from clandestine worship to the reinterpretation of their struggles as part of a larger cosmic narrative—demonstrate the enduring power of faith and identity in the face of profound cultural upheaval. While the Islamic conquest fundamentally reshaped the landscape of Persia, it did not extinguish the flame of Zoroastrian belief, which continued to burn, offering a beacon of hope and continuity to those who still followed the path of Zarathustra.

Chapter 24
The Philosophy of Free Will

In the Zoroastrian worldview, the concept of free will is fundamental, shaping the spiritual and ethical landscape in which every individual navigates their existence. Unlike deterministic traditions, Zoroastrianism places a profound emphasis on the power of choice, seeing it as a divine gift bestowed by Ahura Mazda. This chapter delves into how the teachings of Zarathustra articulate this principle and the way it intertwines with the cosmic struggle between Asha (order, truth) and Druj (chaos, falsehood).

From the earliest passages of the Gathas, Zarathustra's hymns within the Avesta, the theme of free will emerges as a defining aspect of humanity's relationship with the divine. Zarathustra's message is clear: each person has the capacity to choose between good and evil, and this choice is not only a privilege but a sacred duty. The world, as envisioned by Zoroastrian teachings, is a battleground where human choices tip the scales in favor of either order or chaos, aligning with the forces of light or darkness.

Central to this philosophy is the role of human beings as moral agents within the grand cosmic order. Ahura Mazda, as the supreme deity, created a world where the battle between truth and falsehood is ever-present. Yet, he did not dictate the outcome; rather, he entrusted each soul with the responsibility to choose. This idea contrasts with other ancient beliefs that often placed fate in the hands of capricious gods or predetermined cosmic forces. In Zoroastrianism, humans are seen as co-creators of their destiny, capable of shaping their fate through thoughts, words, and actions.

This belief in the moral agency of individuals is encapsulated in the triad "Humata, Hukhta, Hvarshta"—Good Thoughts, Good Words, Good Deeds. This guiding principle emphasizes that every thought, every word spoken, and every action taken has consequences, not only for the individual but for the world at large. Choosing to act in accordance with Asha, therefore, is not merely a personal moral choice but a contribution to the maintenance of cosmic order. Conversely, succumbing to Druj is seen as aiding the forces of darkness, contributing to the imbalance in the universe.

The notion of free will is also closely linked to the Zoroastrian understanding of reward and punishment after death. The crossing of the Chinvat Bridge, where the soul is judged, is not a mere test of adherence to religious laws, but an evaluation of the sum total of choices made throughout life. It is here that the weight of one's decisions determines whether the soul ascends to the House of Song (Heaven) or falls into the abyss of darkness. The bridge, narrow for the wicked and wide for the righteous, symbolizes the clarity or confusion of a life lived in truth or falsehood.

Yet, the doctrine of free will in Zoroastrianism is not framed as a source of anxiety or burden. Instead, it is an empowering message, offering hope that even the smallest act of goodness contributes to the triumph of light over darkness. Zarathustra's teachings celebrate the potential within each individual to effect change, both in their inner world and the broader cosmic struggle. The belief that every action matters reinforces a sense of purpose and agency, guiding Zoroastrians to see themselves as active participants in the divine plan rather than passive recipients of fate.

This sense of agency extends beyond the individual to the collective responsibilities of the community. Zoroastrianism emphasizes that the faithful, by coming together in acts of worship, charity, and the upkeep of fire temples, strengthen Asha collectively. The community's role is to encourage each member to make choices that reflect the values of truth, purity, and harmony with the natural world, which is also considered an embodiment of divine order. This shared responsibility cultivates a culture where the freedom to choose is balanced by the understanding that each choice ripples through the fabric of the universe.

Ahura Mazda's role in this framework is not that of a distant or punitive god but of a compassionate creator who desires a partnership with his creation. The divine wisdom of Mazda offers guidance, through the sacred texts and the teachings of the Mobeds, but it does not dictate. Instead, it invites individuals to exercise their free will wisely, to align themselves with the divine order, and to become warriors of light in the ongoing battle against Angra Mainyu's deception. This perspective positions Ahura Mazda as a figure who respects human autonomy, offering support through spiritual insight while allowing each soul to carve its path.

The struggle between Asha and Druj is not only external but deeply internal, a battle waged in the heart and mind of every follower. Zoroastrian teachings often liken this to the tending of a sacred fire within each person. Just as the flames in the fire temples require care and vigilance to remain pure and bright, so too must individuals guard their thoughts and desires against the encroaching darkness. Free will is the tool with which the Zoroastrian faithful keep their inner fire alive, burning away falsehood and kindling the light of truth.

Through this understanding of free will, Zoroastrianism presents a profound moral philosophy that intertwines individual choices with the cosmic order. It teaches that each decision, no matter how small, contributes to the balance of the universe. This philosophy stands as a call to action, urging each person to recognize their capacity to shape the world around them, to see every moment as an opportunity to affirm life, truth, and the enduring presence of light amidst the shadows.

As the chapter explores, the emphasis on free will in Zoroastrian thought has not only shaped its followers' worldview but has also resonated with broader philosophical traditions that seek to understand the nature of human choice and responsibility. This engagement with the concept of free will provides a foundation for the next chapter, which will delve deeper into the tensions between freedom and destiny within Zoroastrian philosophy, exploring how these ideas continue to evolve in modern interpretations of the faith.

The interplay between free will and destiny within Zoroastrian thought offers a rich tapestry of philosophical contemplation. At the heart of this exploration lies a tension: the inherent freedom granted to humans by Ahura Mazda and the grand vision of a world shaped by cosmic forces. This chapter delves into how Zoroastrianism has navigated this tension, reflecting on ancient teachings, debates among scholars, and the modern interpretations that keep these ideas relevant today.

One of the central debates within Zoroastrian philosophy concerns the boundaries of human freedom in the context of a divinely orchestrated cosmic plan. While Zoroastrian teachings elevate the capacity of individuals to choose their path, they also assert that Ahura Mazda, the wise creator, has foreseen the ultimate victory of light over darkness. This seeming paradox— where human actions are free yet the outcome of the cosmic struggle is preordained—has inspired generations of Zoroastrian thinkers to reflect on the nature of destiny.

In Zoroastrian thought, the concept of Frashokereti, the renewal of the world, stands as the endpoint of this divine plan. It is a time when all of creation is purified and restored to a state of harmony under Ahura Mazda's rule. Yet, the path to this renewal is not a simple unfolding of fate. It is envisioned as a journey that requires the active participation of humanity. The faithful are called to align their will with the principles of Asha, to combat the forces of Druj, and to strive toward this divine future through their everyday choices.

Zarathustra's teachings suggest that while Frashokereti is inevitable, the role that each individual plays in the process is not. The scriptures emphasize that the timing and nature of this renewal depend on the cumulative moral choices made by humans. The divine will is thus not coercive; rather, it invites cooperation, offering a destiny that humanity must choose to embrace. It is through this voluntary alignment with Asha that Zoroastrians participate in the divine plan, hastening the triumph of good.

Throughout the centuries, Zoroastrian scholars have sought to articulate this balance between predestination and free will. Some have likened it to a gardener tending a garden. Ahura Mazda, as the divine gardener, sets the conditions—sun, soil, rain—allowing the plants to grow, yet it is the choice of each seed, the effort of each plant, that determines how it thrives. Humans, then, are like seeds in the garden of the world, growing according to their choices, even as the divine gardener watches over the larger unfolding of seasons.

This analogy also extends to the concept of the Chinvat Bridge, which connects the earthly realm to the spiritual world. The judgment that souls face upon crossing the bridge reflects the sum of their freely chosen actions. Yet, even here, Zoroastrian teachings hold space for divine mercy—a recognition that while humans are bound by their choices, Ahura Mazda's wisdom transcends human understanding, allowing for a balance between justice and compassion. This perspective has been a point of comfort for many Zoroastrians, offering hope that even when human choices falter, the divine vision remains one of ultimate restoration.

In contemporary interpretations of Zoroastrianism, the emphasis on free will continues to resonate, especially as the faith encounters modern ideas about autonomy, ethics, and personal responsibility. Today's Zoroastrians often reflect on how their ancient tradition addresses issues like environmental stewardship, social justice, and individual rights. The message that each person's choices can impact the broader world aligns with contemporary movements that advocate for active citizenship and ethical living.

For many modern Zoroastrians, the struggle between Asha and Druj is interpreted not only as a metaphysical battle but as a call to address tangible issues like climate change, social inequality, and the preservation of cultural heritage. The concept of free will empowers believers to see themselves as agents of change, echoing Zarathustra's ancient call to choose the path of truth and righteousness. This dynamic engagement with the world allows Zoroastrianism to maintain a relevant voice in global ethical conversations, highlighting the enduring significance of its teachings on freedom and responsibility.

Yet, this modern emphasis on autonomy also raises new questions. How does one maintain a sense of individual freedom while acknowledging the weight of a tradition that speaks of cosmic destiny? How do the principles of Zoroastrianism adapt to a world where many see fate as less divine and more shaped by socio-political forces? These questions mirror the internal dialogues that have long shaped Zoroastrian communities, fostering a living tradition that evolves while remaining rooted in its core values.

The modern Zoroastrian experience reflects a desire to harmonize personal agency with the communal pursuit of Asha. In diaspora communities, where adaptation to new cultural contexts is often necessary, the emphasis on free will becomes a source of strength. It allows Zoroastrians to navigate the challenges of maintaining identity while integrating into diverse societies, encouraging them to make choices that honor both their heritage and the realities of their new homes.

For younger generations of Zoroastrians, the philosophical reflections on free will become a bridge between tradition and modernity. They find in the teachings of Zarathustra a validation of their desire for a meaningful life, where their actions have significance beyond the individual and resonate with the broader cosmic narrative. The idea that each person's choices contribute to the unfolding of a divine plan provides a sense of purpose in a world that often feels uncertain and fragmented.

This chapter's exploration of free will within Zoroastrianism, both in its ancient roots and modern interpretations, underscores the dynamic interplay between human agency and divine wisdom. It is a philosophy that encourages both humility and empowerment, asking the faithful to recognize their limitations while embracing their power to shape the world. This duality, where free will and divine destiny coexist, forms a cornerstone of Zoroastrian identity, inviting believers to walk a path that is both self-directed and aligned with the eternal truths of Asha.

As we transition from this philosophical terrain, the narrative moves toward the broader cultural impact of Zoroastrianism on Persian society. The next chapter will begin to trace how these spiritual principles of free will, order, and cosmic struggle have left their mark on the art, architecture, and literature of Persia, revealing the indelible legacy of Zoroastrian thought in the cultural fabric of the region. Through this journey, we will see how Zoroastrian values have transcended religious boundaries, shaping a cultural heritage that continues to inspire the world today.

Chapter 25
Influence on Persian Culture

The threads of Zoroastrianism are woven deeply into the rich tapestry of Persian culture. From the grand architecture of ancient palaces to the intricate poetry that echoes through the ages, the influence of this ancient faith has shaped the cultural identity of Persia in profound ways. To trace this impact is to follow the shadow of Zarathustra's teachings across centuries, observing how the values of Asha, the cosmic struggle against Druj, and the reverence for the divine find expression in the arts, societal structures, and even the unspoken values that define Persian life.

At the heart of this cultural influence lies the Zoroastrian emphasis on duality—the eternal interplay between light and darkness, good and evil. This concept is not just a theological construct; it has inspired the symbolism found in the visual arts of Persia. In ancient Persian reliefs and architectural motifs, the theme of the struggle between order and chaos often emerges. The image of the Faravahar, with its winged form representing the human soul's journey towards divine truth, is a motif that has endured in Persian iconography, symbolizing the connection between the earthly and the spiritual.

In the architecture of ancient Persia, the Zoroastrian reverence for natural elements like fire and water becomes evident. The fire temples, with their sacred flames, served not only as places of worship but as centers of community and cultural cohesion. Their design reflects the Zoroastrian principle that fire, as a symbol of purity, must be sheltered from the elements yet remain a visible link to Ahura Mazda. This focus on protecting the sacred while allowing its light to shine outwardly mirrors the values of balance and respect that permeate Persian society. Even in modern Iran, remnants of these ancient temples and their influence can be seen in the architectural design of public and private spaces, where the balance of form and function carries echoes of these ancient principles.

Zoroastrianism's influence extends beyond stone and structure; it sings through the poetry and literature of Persia. The works of classical Persian poets, like Ferdowsi's Shahnameh—the epic of Persian kings—carry threads of Zoroastrian cosmology and moral values. Ferdowsi, writing long after Zoroastrianism had ceased to be the state religion, drew upon the ancient myths and stories of Zoroastrian heroes and battles between light and dark. His verses, woven with the imagery of divine justice and the eternal struggle against deception, echo the moral imperatives that Zarathustra preached. Through such works, Zoroastrian ideals of courage, truth, and the fight for justice were preserved and celebrated, even as Persia's religious landscape transformed.

The celebration of festivals like Nowruz, the Persian New Year, also reveals a Zoroastrian heritage that predates Islam by millennia. Nowruz, rooted in Zoroastrian cosmology, marks the rebirth of nature and the triumph of light over darkness with the arrival of spring. Though embraced by many different cultural and religious groups today, the festival's Zoroastrian roots are evident in the rituals that accompany it—rituals that honor the elements, light candles, and focus on renewal and purification. This celebration is not only a time of joy but a reflection of the ancient belief in the cyclical nature of existence, where each renewal is a chance to align more closely with Asha.

In the realm of governance, the ancient Persian concept of kingship was heavily influenced by Zoroastrian ideals. The notion of the Shahanshah, or "King of Kings," was intertwined with the idea that a ruler must embody the principles of Asha. A just king was expected to be a reflection of divine order on earth, ruling with wisdom and fairness as a servant of Ahura Mazda. This belief shaped the Persian imperial ideology, from the Achaemenid

Empire to the Sassanian dynasty, where kings often portrayed themselves as chosen by Ahura Mazda, fighting against the forces of chaos. The rock carvings and inscriptions from these eras, such as those at Persepolis, bear witness to this spiritual dimension of rulership, where earthly power is seen as an extension of cosmic harmony.

The influence of Zoroastrianism also manifests in the everyday cultural practices of Persian society, particularly in the respect for cleanliness and the emphasis on truth-telling, which were central tenets of Zarathustra's teachings. Practices like the use of incense for purification in homes, the observance of rituals to honor the elements, and the importance placed on speaking truthfully reflect a continuity of Zoroastrian values that have subtly persisted through generations, even as the religious context of Persia has evolved. These values have shaped social norms, fostering a culture that values honor, hospitality, and the ethical responsibilities of the individual toward their community.

Even the traditional Persian garden, known as paradise or pairi-daeza, draws upon Zoroastrian symbolism. These gardens were designed to represent the ideal of a heavenly order on earth—an oasis of harmony, where water flows freely and plants grow in lush abundance, reflecting the divine creation as envisioned by Ahura Mazda. The garden's enclosed space symbolized the struggle to maintain order and beauty against the encroaching chaos of the desert, much like the spiritual battle against Druj. This aesthetic of harmony with nature remains a cherished element in Persian art and architecture, influencing everything from urban design to the layout of family courtyards.

Moreover, the cultural impact of Zoroastrianism can be seen in Persian music, which, much like the ancient ritual chants, often seeks to bridge the material and spiritual worlds. Traditional melodies carry an echo of the invocations to Ahura Mazda, celebrating themes of nature, love, and the eternal dance between light and darkness. Music has served as a vessel for the transmission of Zoroastrian themes, offering a subtle but enduring reminder of the ancient worldview that once guided the people of Persia.

As we explore these layers of influence, it becomes clear that Zoroastrianism has left an indelible mark on the Persian cultural landscape. It shaped a vision of the world that is at once mystical and practical, where the cosmic and the mundane are intertwined. This influence endures, not only in the stone remnants of ancient temples or the words of revered poets but in the very rhythm of life in modern Iran, where the ancient echoes of Zarathustra's teachings can still be heard, even amidst the changes brought by time.

The next chapter will continue this exploration, delving deeper into how Zoroastrianism influenced the intellectual and artistic currents of classical Persian literature and philosophy, and how the echoes of this ancient faith continue to shape modern Iranian identity. As we move forward, the narrative will reveal the enduring legacy of Zoroastrian thought, tracing how it has woven its way into the cultural and intellectual heart of Persia, shaping a heritage that transcends religious boundaries and time.

The echoes of Zoroastrian thought extend beyond physical monuments and historical structures, resonating deeply within the intellectual and artistic traditions of classical Persian literature. This influence is more than a vestige of ancient beliefs; it is a current that shaped the philosophical and poetic imagination of Persia, lending a unique depth to its literary legacy. Persian poets, philosophers, and scholars drew upon Zoroastrian themes, exploring the mysteries of existence, the nature of good and evil, and the cosmic order through the lens of Zarathustra's ancient teachings.

In the poetry of Rumi, Hafez, and Saadi, the dualism that defines Zoroastrian cosmology—light and darkness, truth (Asha) and deceit (Druj)—finds a renewed expression, even as these poets wrote within the context of Islamic Persia. Their verses, filled with metaphors of light as a divine truth that illuminates the soul and darkness as a veil of ignorance, carry an underlying sense of the eternal struggle that Zoroastrianism articulated centuries before. The imagery of fire as a symbol of spiritual purity, and the soul's yearning for reunion with a higher light, echoes Zoroastrian rituals where fire is the medium through which the divine manifests. This subtle continuity shows how Zoroastrian ideas permeated Persian thought, shaping a spiritual landscape that is rich with layers of meaning.

The concept of divine order, central to Zoroastrianism, also permeates Persian philosophy. Thinkers such as Avicenna (Ibn Sina) and Suhrawardi engaged deeply with the idea of an ordered universe, drawing from both ancient Zoroastrian cosmology and the newer philosophical traditions that mingled in Persia. Suhrawardi's philosophy of illumination, for instance, is steeped in the metaphor of light as a symbol of knowledge and divine truth. While Suhrawardi was working within an Islamic framework, his emphasis on the light's emanation from a central source bears a striking resemblance to Zoroastrian concepts of Ahura Mazda as the light of creation, a presence that pervades and gives order to the cosmos.

In classical Persian literature, epic narratives like Shahnameh serve as more than mere chronicles of kings and heroes; they are a testament to the Zoroastrian worldview's influence on the ethos of kingship and leadership. The legendary figures of Rustam and other heroes are depicted not only as warriors but as defenders of Asha, striving to maintain justice and balance in the world. Ferdowsi, in weaving these ancient tales, ensured that the Zoroastrian sense of moral responsibility—where the struggle against chaos is a divine duty—remained a core part of Persian identity. Through his epic, the ancient stories of creation, the battle between good and evil, and the teachings of Zarathustra continued to resonate with Persian readers long after the official fall of Zoroastrianism as the state religion.

This influence is not limited to literature and philosophy; it extends into the social codes and ethics that have shaped Persian culture over the millennia. Concepts of mehr (love, friendship) and dad (justice) that underpin Persian ethics reflect Zoroastrian ideals, emphasizing the importance of community harmony, charity, and social justice. These values, derived from the teachings of Zarathustra, are embedded in the way Persian society has traditionally approached hospitality and mutual respect, creating a culture that values the interconnectedness of all life.

As Persian culture evolved, it continued to blend and reinterpret these Zoroastrian elements with new influences, creating a uniquely syncretic identity. For instance, the Persian mystic traditions often depict the soul's journey as a path toward the light—a quest for the inner flame that mirrors Zoroastrian notions of the divine spark within every individual. This journey is seen as a return to the primal unity, echoing Zoroastrian ideas of the soul's responsibility to align with Asha and reject the temptations of Druj. Even as Persian mysticism took on Islamic forms, the Zoroastrian focus on light, fire, and inner purification remained a foundational layer within the spiritual narratives of the time.

The influence of Zoroastrianism in shaping the Persian language is another testament to its lasting legacy. Many terms and idioms in the Persian language that refer to concepts of truth, order, and purity trace their origins back to Zoroastrian theological vocabulary. Words like Asha (truth, righteousness) have evolved but retain their resonance, subtly guiding the moral framework within which Persian society discusses virtue and ethics. Even expressions used in daily life, such as blessings or references to the natural elements, carry echoes of Zoroastrian reverence for the world's physical and spiritual dimensions.

The continuity of Zoroastrian elements in Persian culture has also played a role in shaping modern Iranian identity, especially in the way Iranians see themselves as guardians of an ancient heritage that predates Islam. In modern Iran, Zoroastrian festivals like Nowruz are celebrated not only for their cultural significance but as a symbol of continuity, a reminder of a past where Persian kings ruled with divine mandate under the principles of Asha. These festivals have become a point of pride and a marker of cultural identity, emphasizing a deep connection to the land's pre-Islamic roots. This sense of cultural continuity is evident in the pride many Iranians take in the ancient ruins of Persepolis and the reverence with which they regard figures like Cyrus the Great, whose rule was shaped by Zoroastrian ideals of justice and righteousness.

In the diaspora, too, Zoroastrian symbols and values continue to serve as a bridge between past and present, offering a source of identity for those who seek to maintain a connection with their heritage. Persian communities around the world have drawn upon Zoroastrian concepts as they navigate life in new lands, using these ancient teachings as a moral compass and a link to their cultural roots. This has allowed Zoroastrianism to maintain its relevance, not as a static belief system, but as a living tradition that adapts and evolves.

The philosophical and cultural synthesis that emerged in Persia has created a legacy where Zoroastrianism, though no longer the dominant faith, continues to shape the spiritual and intellectual landscape. It is a legacy where ancient teachings blend seamlessly with newer traditions, where the echoes of Zarathustra's words resonate in the chants of poets, the designs of gardens, and the meditations of philosophers. It is a legacy that persists in the way Persian culture values the balance between the material and spiritual worlds, between action and reflection, between the quest for knowledge and the pursuit of inner truth.

In this way, Zoroastrianism has proven to be more than a chapter in the history of Persia; it is a thread that runs through the entire fabric of Iranian culture, a constant that endures amidst change. It has left an indelible mark on the artistic and intellectual expressions of Persian civilization, influencing the ways in which Iranians see themselves and their place in the world. This profound cultural imprint remains a testament to the enduring wisdom of Zarathustra, whose teachings continue to illuminate the Persian spirit, guiding it toward a vision of the world where light and truth are forever pursued.

The next chapters will explore the Zoroastrian perspective on nature, environmental ethics, and the profound connection between spiritual duty and the natural world, highlighting how ancient principles continue to offer insights for modern ecological consciousness. As we turn our gaze towards these teachings, we will uncover the ways in which the respect for creation, central to Zoroastrian thought, aligns with contemporary efforts to honor and protect the environment.

Chapter 26
Environmental Ethics

In Zoroastrianism, nature is not merely a backdrop for human existence—it is an integral part of the cosmic order, a reflection of Ahura Mazda's divine creation. This ancient faith views the world as a sacred space, where every element, from the smallest drop of water to the towering mountains, is imbued with spiritual significance. The earth, sky, water, plants, and fire are all considered sacred, and Zoroastrians hold a deep responsibility to protect these elements, recognizing their role as stewards of creation.

The reverence for nature in Zoroastrian teachings stems from the understanding that the physical world is a manifestation of Asha, the principle of truth, order, and righteousness. Asha governs not only human morality but the very laws of nature, aligning the cycles of the seasons, the growth of crops, and the flow of rivers with a divine purpose. The world is seen as a battlefield where the forces of order, represented by Asha, must continually be upheld against the chaos of Druj, or falsehood. In this context, caring for the environment is not just an ethical choice—it is a spiritual duty, an act of devotion that upholds the cosmic balance.

Central to Zoroastrian environmental ethics is the concept of Khvarenah, or divine glory, which is believed to be present in all aspects of creation. This sacred energy infuses the natural world, making it a source of spiritual nourishment for humanity. When Zoroastrians tend to a garden, protect a water source, or care for animals, they are engaging in acts that honor the divine presence in the world around them. This perspective encourages a harmonious relationship between humans and their environment, fostering a sense of interconnectedness where the well-being of nature is directly linked to the well-being of the soul.

Water, for instance, holds a particularly esteemed place within Zoroastrian cosmology. It is revered as a purifier and a symbol of life, representing the flow of Ahura Mazda's blessings. The ancient practice of Ab-Zohr, a ritual offering to water, highlights the deep respect Zoroastrians have for this element. In regions of Persia where water scarcity has always been a challenge, this reverence translated into careful management of water resources. The construction of qanats—underground irrigation systems—by Zoroastrian communities in ancient times reflects a desire to use natural resources sustainably, ensuring that this precious element is preserved for future generations.

Similarly, the earth is seen as a living entity that must be protected from contamination and defilement. Zoroastrian scriptures, such as the Vendidad, contain instructions on how to treat the earth with respect, emphasizing that it should not be polluted by waste or harmful practices. The disposal of bodies, for example, is handled through the use of dakhmas or "Towers of Silence," where the dead are exposed to the elements rather than buried, to avoid contaminating the soil. This practice, though misunderstood by outsiders, is rooted in the deep Zoroastrian respect for the purity of the earth and its role as a life-giving force.

Fire, another crucial element in Zoroastrian practice, is not only a symbol of spiritual illumination but also a reminder of the energy that powers the natural world. The care given to sacred fires in Zoroastrian temples mirrors the care that must be given to natural sources of energy, such as the sun's warmth and the vital forces that sustain life. The ethical imperative to protect fire from pollution extends metaphorically to the broader duty of maintaining the purity and sustainability of the earth's resources.

The veneration of animals also forms a part of Zoroastrian environmental ethics. Creatures like dogs and cows are given a special status, believed to possess a direct connection to the divine order. The killing of beneficial animals is considered a grave sin in Zoroastrianism, as it disrupts the balance of creation. Instead, Zoroastrians are encouraged to care for animals, providing them with food and protection, reflecting a broader ethos of compassion and respect for all living beings. This approach is evident in ancient Zoroastrian texts that advocate for the ethical treatment of cattle, recognizing their role in sustaining human life through agriculture and nourishment.

Beyond these specific practices, the Zoroastrian worldview encourages a lifestyle that minimizes harm to the environment. The simplicity of Zoroastrian rituals, which often involve offerings of flowers, fruit, and incense, contrasts with practices that might exploit or degrade natural resources. This restraint is seen as a form of asha in action—a conscious effort to live in harmony with the world rather than exerting dominion over it.

Zoroastrian teachings also emphasize the importance of maintaining a clean and pure environment, both externally and internally. The ritual acts of cleansing and purification extend to the physical spaces Zoroastrians inhabit, whether homes, temples, or public places. This focus on cleanliness is not only a matter of hygiene but a spiritual discipline that mirrors the broader cosmic struggle against impurity and disorder. By keeping their surroundings clean, Zoroastrians believe they contribute to the fight against the forces of Druj, symbolically pushing back against chaos and decay.

In the modern world, where the ecological crisis poses a profound challenge to the survival of our planet, these ancient principles offer a timely perspective. Zoroastrianism's respect for the natural world, its emphasis on the stewardship of resources, and its recognition of the sacredness of all creation resonate deeply with contemporary environmentalism. As societies grapple with climate change, pollution, and the depletion of resources, the Zoroastrian call to live in harmony with nature serves as a reminder of the spiritual dimension of ecological responsibility.

For Zoroastrians today, adapting these ancient teachings to contemporary realities involves balancing tradition with innovation. While the practices of their ancestors may not all be applicable in modern contexts, the underlying principles of respect for nature and sustainable living continue to guide their approach to environmental issues. In communities around the world, Zoroastrians engage in tree-planting drives, water conservation efforts, and environmental advocacy, seeking to live out the ancient mandate to protect and cherish Ahura Mazda's creation.

This sense of duty to the earth, handed down through millennia, underscores the enduring relevance of Zoroastrian environmental ethics. It offers a vision where spirituality and sustainability are not separate, but intertwined, where the care for the world is seen as a reflection of the care for the divine order itself. This perspective encourages not only Zoroastrians but all of humanity to reimagine their relationship with nature, recognizing that in protecting the earth, they are also preserving a sacred trust.

As the exploration of Zoroastrian environmental ethics continues into the next chapter, we will delve deeper into the specific ways in which these teachings have been practiced throughout history and their potential to inspire modern approaches to ecological stewardship. The journey through ancient wisdom reveals pathways that may guide us in addressing the urgent environmental challenges of our time, drawing strength from the enduring principles of Asha and the timeless respect for the natural world.

Throughout the centuries, the Zoroastrian approach to environmental preservation has evolved, reflecting both ancient wisdom and the changing challenges faced by their communities. The principles of reverence for nature and responsible stewardship have remained constant, but the application of these ideas has adapted to the contexts of different eras, especially as Zoroastrians migrated and faced new landscapes and environmental conditions.

The Zoroastrian diaspora, notably the Parsis in India, carried with them a respect for nature that was deeply embedded in their faith. In the Indian subcontinent, the landscape differed significantly from the dry, rugged terrain of ancient Persia, and Zoroastrians had to find new ways to express their environmental values. The ancient principle of maintaining the purity of elements such as water and earth remained crucial, and the Parsis adopted practices that would preserve the sanctity of these elements in their new home.

One notable aspect is the adaptation of the dakhmas, or "Towers of Silence." In India, these structures were carefully placed in natural settings, allowing the elements—sunlight, air, and birds—to return the deceased to the cycle of nature without contaminating the earth. Although the practice of sky burials faced challenges in modern times, including urbanization and concerns over the dwindling population of scavenging birds, the underlying philosophy remains: the deceased should be returned to nature without disrupting the natural balance. This approach exemplifies the Zoroastrian desire to align death rituals with environmental ethics, minimizing the impact on the earth.

In addition to burial practices, the cultivation of sacred spaces such as Atash Behram temples and their surrounding gardens highlights the Zoroastrian emphasis on greenery and nature preservation. These gardens, often filled with lush plants and serene water features, serve as reminders of the connection between spiritual practice and nature. They provide a space for contemplation and community gathering, where the sacredness of the earth is honored through the act of tending to living things. The care given to these gardens reflects the broader Zoroastrian commitment to maintaining harmony with the environment.

In recent decades, as global awareness of environmental degradation has grown, Zoroastrian communities have found new ways to integrate ancient principles with contemporary ecological movements. This adaptation is evident in initiatives such as tree-planting campaigns organized by Zoroastrian associations, efforts to conserve water in arid regions, and educational programs that emphasize the importance of protecting local ecosystems. These modern activities are seen as extensions of the ancient duty to uphold Asha, applying the wisdom of the past to address the pressing concerns of the present.

The focus on water conservation remains particularly strong, echoing the teachings of the Avesta, which extol water as a life-giving force that must be protected from pollution. In places like Iran, where drought and water scarcity are significant challenges, Zoroastrians have been involved in community projects to manage water resources sustainably. This involves not only traditional practices like maintaining qanats—the ancient underground aqueducts—but also supporting modern methods of water recycling and efficient irrigation. The spiritual reverence for water thus finds a new expression in technological solutions aimed at preserving this precious resource for future generations.

The principles of environmental ethics in Zoroastrianism have also found resonance with global movements for ecological preservation and sustainable development. Concepts such as eco-theology—the idea that religious beliefs can inspire environmental activism—have gained traction, with Zoroastrians offering a unique perspective rooted in their ancient traditions. By emphasizing the interconnectedness of all life and the moral responsibility to protect the planet, Zoroastrians contribute a voice that blends spirituality with ecological mindfulness, advocating for a world where the sacredness of nature is recognized and respected.

Moreover, the Zoroastrian belief in the cyclical renewal of the world, embodied in the concept of Frashokereti, holds a powerful message for contemporary environmentalism. This eschatological vision describes a future where the world is purified and restored to its original state of perfection, free from the corruption of evil and decay. This hope for a renewal of creation aligns with modern aspirations for a sustainable future, where human actions can lead to the healing of ecological damage and the restoration of balance in the natural world.

In regions where Zoroastrians have migrated, such as North America, Australia, and Europe, their environmental ethics have been further influenced by local conservation efforts and the emphasis on reducing carbon footprints. Zoroastrian youth, in particular, have become involved in environmental activism, creating dialogues between their religious heritage and contemporary science-based approaches to climate change. This engagement reflects a willingness to reinterpret ancient teachings in light of new knowledge, ensuring that the core values of respect for nature continue to guide their actions.

The role of festivals, too, has taken on new significance in the context of environmental consciousness. Celebrations like Nowruz, the Persian New Year, have traditionally involved rituals that honor the arrival of spring and the renewal of life. In modern times, Zoroastrians have used these occasions to promote environmental awareness, organizing events that highlight the importance of planting trees, cleaning public spaces, and fostering a deeper appreciation for the natural world. These activities serve as a bridge between the spiritual and ecological dimensions of Zoroastrianism, connecting ancient seasonal rites with contemporary calls for environmental stewardship.

As these practices have evolved, they have not been without challenges. The tension between maintaining traditional customs and adapting to new environmental contexts has sometimes led to difficult decisions within the community. Yet, the ability to adapt while holding true to core principles has been a defining feature of Zoroastrian resilience. It reflects the belief that the essence of Asha remains unchanged, even as the ways in which it is expressed may shift with time and circumstance.

Zoroastrian environmental ethics offer a framework for viewing the world that transcends mere resource management. It is a vision where the natural world is both a gift and a responsibility, a source of spiritual inspiration that requires care and respect. As global communities grapple with the realities of climate change, pollution, and biodiversity loss, the ancient wisdom of Zoroastrianism serves as a reminder that the quest for sustainability is not just a practical endeavor, but a profoundly spiritual one.

In exploring the depth of these teachings, we find that Zoroastrianism encourages a perspective where humans are not dominators of the earth, but participants in its divine story— entrusted with a role that is both humble and sacred. This perspective invites all people, regardless of their background, to see the preservation of the environment as a shared moral duty, and to seek ways to live in harmony with the natural world.

As we turn our attention to the next chapters, the enduring relevance of these environmental principles will continue to unfold. The integration of ancient beliefs with contemporary ecological challenges provides a path forward, suggesting that the wisdom of the past can illuminate the way toward a more sustainable and spiritually attuned future. Through the lens of Zoroastrianism, the call to protect our world resonates not only as a matter of survival but as an act of devotion to the enduring principles that bind all life together.

Chapter 27
Truth and Honesty

Truth, in Zoroastrianism, is not a mere concept but the very essence of cosmic order, embodied in the principle of Asha. Asha is the fundamental truth that underlies all creation, a universal law governing the balance between light and darkness, good and evil, order and chaos. This is not just a passive reality but a dynamic force, shaping the actions of every believer, guiding them toward righteousness and moral integrity. The Zoroastrian understanding of truth, therefore, permeates all aspects of life, forming the core of spiritual practice and societal values.

At the heart of Zoroastrian ethics lies the triad Humata, Hukhta, Hvarshta—Good Thoughts, Good Words, and Good Deeds. This triad represents the embodiment of Asha in human conduct, urging individuals to align their thoughts, speech, and actions with the cosmic order. To think truthfully is to harmonize one's inner world with the divine principles of Ahura Mazda; to speak truthfully is to bring clarity and honesty into the world; and to act truthfully is to manifest Asha in everyday interactions.

The importance of truth in Zoroastrianism extends to the responsibilities of community and leadership. From the ancient courts of Persian emperors to the modern gatherings of Zoroastrian associations, the expectation that leaders uphold Asha is paramount. The words of Zarathustra, as recorded in the Gathas, emphasize the duty of rulers to act as shepherds of their people, ensuring that their governance is rooted in justice and truth. This expectation is not limited to political authority but is also seen in the role of Mobeds, the priests who are entrusted with interpreting the sacred texts and guiding the community. For a Mobed, truthfulness is essential not only in the performance of rituals but in the preservation of the teachings of Zarathustra, ensuring that the wisdom of the Avesta is conveyed without distortion.

In everyday life, the pursuit of truth is a personal commitment for every Zoroastrian. This commitment is most evident in the emphasis on honesty in all dealings, whether in business, family relationships, or social interactions. In traditional Zoroastrian communities, the reputation of an individual is closely tied to their adherence to the principles of Asha. Being known as a person of truth and integrity is considered one of the highest honors, reflecting a life that mirrors the cosmic order.

The Zoroastrian respect for truth is also evident in their legal traditions, where truth-telling is a central tenet. In ancient Persia, legal proceedings were intertwined with religious values, and witnesses were expected to swear oaths in the presence of fire, symbolizing the light of Ahura Mazda. The act of speaking falsehoods was seen not only as a crime against the community but as a betrayal of divine trust, an act that disrupted the balance of Asha and invoked the forces of Druj—the lie and deceit.

Zarathustra's teachings highlight the cosmic struggle between Asha and Druj, not just as a mythological conflict but as a battle that plays out within each individual. Every choice to uphold truth, no matter how small, is seen as a stand against the darkness of deceit. In the Zoroastrian understanding, the path of Asha is a path of inner discipline, where the mind must be vigilant against the temptations of falsehood, self-deception, and moral compromise. This vigilance is considered a form of spiritual warfare, aligning one's soul with the forces of light and pushing back against the encroaching shadows.

Even in the private sphere, the influence of Asha shapes the Zoroastrian approach to personal reflection and self-improvement. Followers are encouraged to regularly examine their own thoughts and actions, asking themselves whether they align with the principles of truth. This introspection is not meant to induce guilt but to foster a spirit of constant growth, a desire to become ever more attuned to the will of Ahura Mazda. Through prayer and meditation, Zoroastrians seek to purify their minds of thoughts that might lead them astray, reaffirming their commitment to a life lived in accordance with divine order.

One of the ways this focus on truth manifests is through the Zoroastrian calendar, particularly in festivals like Mehregan and Nowruz, which celebrate the renewal of creation and the triumph of light over darkness. During these celebrations, acts of reconciliation and truth-telling are encouraged. Communities come together to resolve disputes, mend broken relationships, and reaffirm bonds of honesty and trust. This practice reflects a belief that collective harmony is inseparable from individual integrity; that the well-being of the community is directly linked to the moral character of its members.

In the Zoroastrian diaspora, where communities have found themselves in diverse cultural contexts, the value of truth has provided a moral compass. Living as minorities, often in regions where their traditions are unfamiliar, Zoroastrians have relied on the universal appeal of truthfulness as a way to bridge cultural divides and build relationships with their neighbors. This commitment to truth, honesty, and fair dealings has helped Zoroastrians earn a reputation as trustworthy and ethical, whether in trade, education, or public service.

As the world has evolved, so too have the challenges to maintaining truthfulness. In contemporary society, Zoroastrians face the complexities of modern communication, where misinformation and half-truths can easily spread. Yet, the teachings of Asha remain a guiding light, offering a timeless standard against which all claims must be measured. For many Zoroastrians, this means being critical consumers of information, applying a discerning eye to the media they consume, and speaking out against falsehoods in both public and private spheres.

The centrality of truth in Zoroastrianism also extends to the concept of Daena, which can be understood as both a "religious vision" and "inner conscience." Daena represents the light of insight that guides an individual's understanding of Asha. It is through Daena that a person perceives the truth of the world and their own place within it. In Zoroastrian thought, Daena is not static; it is nurtured through study, prayer, and ethical living. A strong Daena allows one to perceive the underlying unity of Asha in the universe, even amid the chaos and complexities of everyday life.

Thus, the commitment to truth in Zoroastrianism is not simply about avoiding lies or deceit. It is a holistic way of living that seeks alignment with the deepest truths of existence. By living in accordance with Asha, a Zoroastrian strives to bring harmony to both their inner world and the world around them, embodying the teachings of Zarathustra in each interaction. In this way, truth becomes a bridge between the earthly and the divine, a means by which humans can participate in the eternal dance between order and chaos.

As we move deeper into the exploration of Zoroastrianism, the next chapter will examine how these principles of truthfulness are put into practice in various contexts, shedding light on the challenges and rewards of living by Asha in a complex and ever-changing world.

The Zoroastrian principles of truth and honesty extend beyond the realm of personal morality and touch upon all aspects of societal and spiritual life, deeply influencing how followers of the faith navigate their interactions with the broader world. For Zoroastrians, living in accordance with Asha, or the cosmic truth, means embodying honesty not only as an individual virtue but as a communal ethos, shaping the way communities build trust and engage with the challenges of modernity.

In business and trade, Zoroastrians have long held a reputation for integrity, often seen as reliable partners who prioritize fairness and transparency. This legacy, tracing back to ancient Persia, reflects a deep cultural value that views deceit in economic dealings as a manifestation of Druj, the cosmic lie. To deceive in commerce is to disrupt the balance of Asha, introducing disorder into the fabric of human interactions. Historically, this has led Zoroastrian merchants to establish codes of conduct that emphasize fair trade, honest communication, and respect for contracts, creating a foundation of trust that spans generations.

The application of these principles in business is not simply a pragmatic choice but a spiritual practice. Each honest transaction is seen as an opportunity to align with Ahura Mazda's vision of a just and harmonious world. In this way, everyday actions become a form of worship, a means of bringing the divine order of Asha into the material world. The commitment to honesty is reflected in the stories and proverbs passed down within Zoroastrian communities, emphasizing that wealth earned through truthful means carries a blessing, while gains acquired through deceit carry a hidden cost.

Within the family unit, honesty is the cornerstone of relationships. Zoroastrian teachings encourage open communication between parents and children, spouses, and extended family members. This openness is seen as a way to nurture mutual understanding and to foster a home environment that mirrors the clarity and transparency of Asha. Disagreements are to be approached with a spirit of truthfulness, where each party seeks to understand and convey their perspective honestly, without manipulation or hidden agendas. The home, in this sense, becomes a reflection of the greater cosmic struggle, where truth and transparency are the tools to maintain harmony against the encroachment of misunderstanding and discord.

However, the path of honesty is not without its complexities. In modern times, Zoroastrians, like others, face ethical dilemmas where truth can conflict with compassion or privacy. The teachings of Zarathustra do not prescribe rigid answers for every situation but instead emphasize the importance of intention and the pursuit of righteousness. When facing difficult choices, Zoroastrians are encouraged to reflect on the principles of Asha, seeking a course of action that upholds the spirit of truth while considering the well-being of others. This nuanced approach acknowledges that truthfulness is not always straightforward and that wisdom must guide its practice.

One example of this is the Zoroastrian approach to family secrets and sensitive truths. In situations where revealing certain truths could cause unnecessary harm or distress, discretion may be employed, as long as the intention aligns with compassion and the broader pursuit of Asha. This balance between truth and kindness illustrates the depth of Zoroastrian ethics, which seeks to harmonize principles rather than enforce them rigidly.

In community settings, the value of honesty is central to maintaining unity and trust. Zoroastrian communal gatherings, such as those during festivals like Nowruz or religious ceremonies, are moments when the bonds of trust within the community are reinforced. During these gatherings, the exchange of stories, teachings, and personal experiences often centers around the importance of upholding truth in the face of external challenges, whether political, social, or cultural. Through these narratives, community members are reminded of their shared commitment to Asha and the strength that comes from collective integrity.

In the Zoroastrian diaspora, the emphasis on honesty has played a crucial role in maintaining the faith's identity amidst a diversity of cultures and religions. As Zoroastrians settled in new regions, from India to the West, they carried with them the reputation of being people of their word—trustworthy, diligent, and fair. This reputation not only helped establish strong relationships with other communities but also served as a way to preserve their distinct cultural and religious identity. Honesty became a bridge that allowed Zoroastrians to integrate while retaining their core values, showing that adherence to Asha is not an obstacle to coexistence but a path toward mutual respect.

In the digital age, Zoroastrians face new challenges in upholding truth in a world where information is abundant, yet often unreliable. The teachings of Zarathustra, with their emphasis on discernment and clarity, offer guidance in navigating the complexities of modern media. Zoroastrians are encouraged to question sources, seek knowledge that aligns with the principles of Asha, and avoid spreading falsehoods. This commitment to truth in the digital realm is seen as an extension of the ancient battle between Asha and Druj, where the lies and deceptions of misinformation threaten to distort reality and create division.

At the same time, Zoroastrian communities have used digital platforms to promote transparency and dialogue within their own ranks, addressing issues of governance, leadership, and community welfare. In this way, the digital sphere becomes a space where the values of truth and honesty can be reimagined and adapted, ensuring that the timeless principles of Asha remain relevant in an ever-changing world.

The legal traditions of Zoroastrianism, which have evolved alongside its ethical teachings, continue to emphasize truth-telling as a fundamental duty. In traditional Zoroastrian legal systems, oaths and vows are considered sacred, carrying spiritual as well as social consequences. To break a vow or to bear false witness is seen not only as a transgression against society but as an act that disrupts the spiritual harmony of the universe. Modern Zoroastrian communities, even those who are integrated into secular legal systems, maintain a deep respect for the power of the spoken word, viewing promises and commitments as extensions of their covenant with Ahura Mazda.

The concept of Frashokereti, the ultimate renewal of the world in Zoroastrian eschatology, is deeply tied to the practice of truth. It is believed that in the final days, the power of Asha will prevail over all forms of Druj, leading to a world where truth is absolute and unchallenged. This vision of a future where deception no longer holds sway inspires Zoroastrians to strive for truth in their own lives, seeing each honest act as a step toward this divine restoration. It is a belief that their commitment to truth in the present contributes to a greater cosmic narrative, where the struggle between light and darkness will culminate in a world of perfect clarity.

Thus, truth and honesty in Zoroastrianism are not merely ethical recommendations but profound commitments that shape the identity and destiny of each follower. They are threads that weave through personal, communal, and cosmic dimensions of life, creating a fabric that connects the mundane with the divine. Through their dedication to these values, Zoroastrians continue to honor the legacy of Zarathustra, keeping alive the flame of Asha in a world that constantly tests the resilience of truth.

This exploration of truth within the Zoroastrian tradition reveals a nuanced and evolving approach to honesty, one that adapts to the needs of each era while remaining anchored in timeless principles. As we delve further, the subsequent chapters will turn towards the future, examining how Zoroastrianism faces the challenges of preserving its traditions and adapting to the changing dynamics of the modern world.

Chapter 28
The Future of Zoroastrianism

Zoroastrianism, one of the world's oldest living religions, faces a complex web of challenges as it moves into the future. Though rooted in ancient traditions and rich with teachings that have guided followers for millennia, the faith now contends with significant threats to its continuity. Central among these challenges are the declining number of adherents, the geographic dispersion of communities, and the need to adapt to the rapid cultural and social changes of the modern era.

At the heart of the challenge is the dwindling number of Zoroastrians worldwide. In its homeland of Iran, where Zoroastrianism once held a position of prominence, the community has shrunk dramatically, a result of centuries of persecution, migration, and conversion pressures following the Islamic conquest. Today, Iran's Zoroastrian population is a small fraction of what it once was, confined to a few cities and villages where the echoes of ancient rituals still resonate but in quieter tones. This contraction has led to fears of extinction, with community elders worried about the loss of language, cultural practices, and religious rites that have been passed down through generations.

Outside of Iran, India has become a critical center for Zoroastrian life through the Parsi community. The Parsis, who fled Persia to avoid religious persecution over a thousand years ago, have thrived in India, becoming one of the most prominent Zoroastrian diaspora communities. Yet even among the Parsis, there are concerns about demographic decline. With a small population and low birth rates, the community has faced internal debates over issues like intermarriage and the inclusion of new members, struggles that reflect the tension between preserving tradition and embracing change. The question of who qualifies as a Zoroastrian has become a sensitive topic, dividing opinions and shaping the future of the faith.

The dispersion of Zoroastrian communities, from North America to Australia, adds another layer of complexity. While the diaspora has provided new opportunities for cultural exchange and the spread of Zoroastrian ideals beyond their traditional borders, it has also led to fragmentation. Communities that once thrived through close-knit social structures now find themselves spread across continents, each adapting to local contexts while striving to maintain a shared identity. This dispersion has necessitated new approaches to maintaining community cohesion, with increasing reliance on digital communication and online religious services to bridge the geographical divide. Virtual platforms have allowed Zoroastrians from different parts of the world to connect, but they also highlight the challenge of sustaining a sense of unity in the face of diverse cultural influences.

In this changing landscape, some of the most pressing concerns center around the adaptation of ancient practices to contemporary life. The rituals, prayers, and customs that have been faithfully preserved over centuries often require reinterpretation to remain relevant. For example, younger generations of Zoroastrians, particularly those raised in Western countries, seek ways to integrate their faith into their daily lives in ways that resonate with modern values and lifestyles. This has led to discussions about the role of gender equality in Zoroastrianism, the interpretation of traditional purity laws, and the incorporation of environmental consciousness into religious practice. While some see these changes as necessary for the survival of the faith, others view them as potential compromises to the integrity of Zoroastrian teachings.

At the same time, the survival of Zoroastrianism depends not only on adaptation but also on a profound sense of cultural pride and a desire to reconnect with its roots. In Iran, there has been a resurgence of interest among some younger Iranians in their pre-Islamic heritage, which includes Zoroastrianism. This has led to a renewed appreciation for the religion's role in shaping Persian history and identity, as well as increased interest in ancient Zoroastrian sites and practices. For many, this represents a form of cultural resistance and a reclaiming of an identity that has been overshadowed by centuries of external pressures.

Beyond Iran and India, global Zoroastrian organizations have emerged, working to unify the scattered communities and ensure that Zoroastrian teachings are not lost to time. These organizations, such as the World Zoroastrian Congress, hold regular events and conferences, bringing together Zoroastrians from different parts of the world to share their experiences and discuss the challenges they face. Through these gatherings, Zoroastrians have sought to find common ground on issues like education, cultural preservation, and the role of the religion in a world that often seems at odds with ancient beliefs.

In this context, the use of technology has become a double-edged sword. Digital platforms have allowed for the preservation of sacred texts, online prayer gatherings, and the sharing of teachings, making the faith more accessible to those who may live far from traditional centers of worship. Yet, the digital world also presents challenges, as the virtual realm can dilute the sense of physical community that has been so central to Zoroastrian identity. The transition from fire temples, with their tangible sacred flames, to online worship raises questions about how to maintain the sanctity of rituals in a virtual space.

As Zoroastrianism looks to the future, it must also contend with the question of how to attract and retain younger generations. Many young Zoroastrians feel a deep connection to their heritage but struggle to find a place for their beliefs in a world that is increasingly secular and fast-paced. Initiatives aimed at youth engagement have sought to address this gap, offering camps, educational programs, and cultural activities that emphasize the relevance of Zoroastrian ethics, such as environmental stewardship and social justice, to contemporary global issues. These efforts are designed not only to educate but to inspire a sense of purpose and connection to the faith.

Moreover, Zoroastrianism's emphasis on free will and individual responsibility remains a potent message for modern times. The concept of choosing Asha—truth and righteousness—over Druj—falsehood and chaos—resonates with those searching for ethical clarity amidst the complexities of modern life. This timeless struggle offers a spiritual framework that can be particularly appealing to those who feel disconnected from other religious traditions or disillusioned with materialism. It presents Zoroastrianism not as a relic of the past but as a philosophy with profound contemporary relevance.

Yet, despite these efforts, there is an underlying sense of urgency within the community. The prospect of demographic decline and cultural assimilation looms large, leading to existential questions about what Zoroastrianism might look like in another century. Will the core of the faith be preserved through adaptation, or will it transform into something unrecognizable to its ancestors? The answers to these questions remain uncertain, shaped by the choices of individuals, communities, and leaders who grapple with the balance between tradition and change.

The future of Zoroastrianism is thus a tapestry woven from threads of hope, resilience, and the weight of history. As the world changes around it, Zoroastrianism finds itself at a crossroads, where the enduring wisdom of Zarathustra must meet the demands of a new era. The unfolding story is not one of decline but of transformation, as the ancient flame of Ahura Mazda's teachings continues to find ways to burn brightly, even in unfamiliar landscapes.

The journey toward the future of Zoroastrianism is marked by both uncertainty and a quiet determination to preserve its essence. While demographic challenges and the pressures of modernization pose significant hurdles, there are also initiatives and movements within the global Zoroastrian community that seek to rejuvenate and revitalize the faith. These efforts blend respect for tradition with a willingness to engage with contemporary society, offering hope for a future where Zoroastrianism remains relevant while staying true to its core principles.

One of the central aspects of this revitalization is the effort to reconnect Zoroastrians with their heritage through education. Across the world, educational programs have been established to teach younger generations about the teachings of Zarathustra, the principles of Asha, and the rich history of ancient Persia. These programs often go beyond simple religious instruction, integrating lessons on Zoroastrian history, language, and culture to foster a deeper sense of identity. In the digital age, such education extends to online platforms, where webinars, virtual discussions, and digital archives allow Zoroastrians to access knowledge irrespective of their geographic location.

Global gatherings, such as the World Zoroastrian Youth Congress, play a vital role in this process. These events provide a platform for young Zoroastrians to meet, exchange ideas, and reflect on what it means to be Zoroastrian in today's world. They offer a space where participants can celebrate their heritage while also discussing the challenges of maintaining faith in a rapidly changing environment. These congresses, often filled with workshops, lectures, and cultural exchanges, aim to foster a sense of unity among Zoroastrians from diverse backgrounds, emphasizing that, despite their small numbers, they are part of a global family.

Efforts to promote inclusivity and adapt to contemporary social values have also gained traction, especially in diaspora communities. For many years, debates over the admission of individuals of mixed heritage into the fold of Zoroastrianism have stirred controversy. In places like India, where traditional rules around Zoroastrian identity have been more rigid, these discussions have taken on new urgency. Progressive groups argue for a more inclusive interpretation, suggesting that the focus should be on preserving the teachings and values of the faith rather than strictly maintaining bloodlines. This perspective is driven by a recognition that adaptation may be key to ensuring the survival of the religion in the long term.

In contrast, there are also voices within the community that emphasize the importance of preserving ancient customs and practices without dilution. For these traditionalists, the rituals, the purity laws, and the practices surrounding fire temples represent a direct link to their ancestors and to Zarathustra's original teachings. They worry that too much adaptation risks losing the essence of Zoroastrianism, transforming it into something unrecognizable. The dialogue between these progressive and conservative perspectives is one of the defining features of Zoroastrianism's evolution, as the community seeks a balance that honors the past while navigating the demands of the present.

Technology has become an unexpected ally in the preservation and promotion of Zoroastrianism. The use of social media, websites, and online communities has allowed Zoroastrians to stay connected, share resources, and foster a sense of community even across great distances. Online platforms like Instagram, YouTube, and dedicated Zoroastrian apps feature teachings from priests, discussions on religious practices, and virtual tours of historical Zoroastrian sites. For many younger Zoroastrians, these digital spaces are where they first encounter the deeper aspects of their faith, making them invaluable in bridging the generational gap.

This digital transformation extends to religious practices as well. With the advent of online prayer groups and virtual rituals, many Zoroastrians have found new ways to engage in communal worship, even if they live far from a traditional fire temple. These virtual gatherings offer a new kind of accessibility, making it possible for Zoroastrians who might otherwise feel isolated to participate in the spiritual life of their community. Yet, this shift is not without its challenges, as it raises questions about how to maintain the sacredness and spiritual energy of rituals when they are conducted through a screen rather than in the hallowed spaces of a temple.

In recent years, there has also been a renewed emphasis on Zoroastrian principles that align closely with modern concerns, such as environmentalism and social responsibility. The emphasis on Asha—representing truth, righteousness, and cosmic order—resonates strongly with global movements focused on sustainability and ecological preservation. For example, some Zoroastrian groups have initiated projects that aim to protect natural resources, emphasizing that caring for the Earth is a reflection of their duty as custodians of Ahura Mazda's creation. By framing ancient teachings in terms that address contemporary issues, these initiatives offer a way for Zoroastrianism to engage with broader societal concerns.

The role of globalization cannot be understated in shaping the future of Zoroastrianism. As communities continue to spread and adapt, they find themselves interacting with other cultures, religions, and philosophies. This interaction has the potential to enrich Zoroastrianism, introducing new perspectives and ways of interpreting ancient texts. However, it also poses risks of cultural assimilation and the dilution of unique religious identities. Many Zoroastrians find themselves walking a delicate line between embracing global citizenship and maintaining a distinct spiritual and cultural identity.

In this global context, the preservation of traditional knowledge becomes even more crucial. The older generation holds a treasure trove of oral traditions, stories, and interpretations of sacred texts that are not always found in written form. Efforts are being made to document these oral histories, ensuring that the wisdom and experiences of elders are not lost to time. This preservation of oral knowledge complements the written texts like the Avesta, offering a more holistic understanding of Zoroastrian teachings that is grounded in lived experience.

Another area of focus has been the promotion of Zoroastrianism as a source of philosophical and ethical guidance in the modern world. Scholars and thinkers within the community have sought to highlight the universal aspects of Zoroastrian philosophy, such as the emphasis on free will, the importance of moral choice, and the eternal struggle between good and evil. These themes, while deeply rooted in the Zoroastrian worldview, also offer valuable insights into the human condition, making them relevant to a broader audience beyond the confines of the religion itself.

Looking ahead, the future of Zoroastrianism is likely to be shaped by a mosaic of efforts: some aimed at maintaining traditional practices, others seeking to reframe ancient wisdom in modern contexts, and yet others focused on building connections across the dispersed global community. The outcome of these efforts remains uncertain, but the commitment to keeping the flame of Zoroastrianism alive burns bright. It is a journey defined by both continuity and transformation, where ancient prayers meet digital screens, and the whispers of Zarathustra's voice find echoes in the bustling world of the twenty-first century.

This chapter of Zoroastrianism's story is still being written, and it is being shaped by countless individual choices— by families deciding to teach their children ancient prayers, by young Zoroastrians questioning and redefining what it means to belong, and by community leaders striving to maintain a sense of unity across continents. Amidst the challenges, there is also a sense of renewal, as Zoroastrianism finds ways to adapt without losing the spiritual essence that has guided its followers for thousands of years.

In this evolving narrative, the future of Zoroastrianism remains a testament to the enduring power of faith, tradition, and the unwavering hope that, despite all odds, the teachings of Zarathustra will continue to guide seekers toward the light of Asha for generations to come.

Chapter 29
Daily Rules and Practices

The rhythm of daily life for a Zoroastrian is steeped in rituals that maintain a connection to Ahura Mazda and reinforce a sense of spiritual discipline. These practices form the backbone of a Zoroastrian's journey through the world, offering structure and a sense of purpose rooted in ancient wisdom. From the moment one awakens to the time of rest, the day unfolds as a series of opportunities to express gratitude, uphold purity, and align oneself with the cosmic order of Asha.

Central to the daily practices is the recitation of prayers, or manthras, which are not merely spoken words but sacred vibrations believed to invoke spiritual power. The Avesta provides a wealth of these prayers, with the Ashem Vohu and Yatha Ahu Vairyo being among the most frequently recited. These prayers are said at various moments throughout the day— upon waking, before meals, during the lighting of the sacred fire, and before sleep—each time seeking to renew the bond with Ahura Mazda and the principles of truth and righteousness. Reciting these manthras is a way to align one's thoughts with the divine and remind oneself of the eternal struggle against falsehood and disorder.

Purity, both physical and spiritual, plays a significant role in Zoroastrian daily life. Ablutions, known as padyab, involve washing the hands, face, and other parts of the body, often accompanied by the recitation of a prayer. This act symbolizes the cleansing of not only physical impurities but also the removal of negative thoughts or influences. Such acts of purification are performed before prayer and other religious duties, reinforcing the concept that purity of body and mind are prerequisites for approaching the divine.

Fire, as the symbol of divine light, holds a prominent place in daily rituals. At home, many Zoroastrians maintain a small flame or atash dadgah as a focal point for their prayers, honoring the sacred element that represents the presence of Ahura Mazda. The tending of this flame—whether it involves lighting a lamp or kindling incense—serves as a reminder of the divine fire that burns within and around all creation. For those who cannot access a fire temple daily, this practice becomes a personal altar, a space where devotion and reflection converge.

In the structure of a typical day, three primary prayer times are observed, each aligned with the natural progression of the sun: dawn (Havan), midday (Rapithwin), and evening (Uzirin). These times are not arbitrary but deeply connected to the cycles of nature, reflecting the Zoroastrian belief in the sacredness of creation. Morning prayers celebrate the rising sun, which symbolizes the triumph of light over darkness. Midday prayers acknowledge the peak of the sun's power, a time for reaffirming strength and clarity. Evening prayers, as the sun descends, represent a time for introspection, gratitude, and seeking protection against the forces of darkness. These rhythms connect the individual to the broader universe, turning each day into a microcosm of the cosmic struggle between order and chaos.

The practice of Kusti prayers is another foundational aspect of daily life. The Kusti, a sacred cord woven from wool, is wrapped around the waist over the Sudreh, an inner garment that represents the path of righteousness. The ritual of untying and retying the Kusti is performed several times a day—upon waking, before eating, and before sleeping—each time accompanied by specific prayers. The act of retying the Kusti symbolizes a recommitment to the Zoroastrian faith, to the triad of good thoughts, good words, and good deeds. For many, this ritual becomes a moment of pause, a chance to refocus amidst the demands of daily life and to renew their spiritual armor against the temptations of Druj.

Zoroastrian dietary customs also reflect the broader religious philosophy, emphasizing moderation, respect for life, and gratitude. Meals begin with a simple prayer, offering thanks for the food and recognizing it as a gift of Ahura Mazda. This ritual underscores the interconnectedness between the material and spiritual worlds, reminding the faithful that every act, even eating, has a spiritual dimension. In some traditions, Zoroastrians avoid consuming certain foods that are believed to disrupt spiritual balance, though dietary practices can vary widely across communities.

In addition to the structured rituals, Zoroastrianism encourages the practice of Frashokereti in daily life—the idea of working towards the renewal of the world through individual actions. This concept suggests that every thought and deed contributes to the broader struggle to bring about a world free of suffering and falsehood. Acts of kindness, generosity towards those in need, and efforts to protect the natural world are all seen as extensions of this divine duty. Thus, Zoroastrianism integrates spirituality with social responsibility, making daily life an ongoing expression of devotion and service.

Zoroastrians are also mindful of the care of the deceased, which reflects the emphasis on purity. The tradition of not burying the dead in the earth, to avoid polluting the sacred elements of earth and fire, leads to the unique practice of exposure in the Dakhma or Tower of Silence. While this practice is not directly part of daily routines, it illustrates the broader worldview in which each element of nature must be treated with reverence. Daily life, in this way, is constantly attuned to the cosmic laws and the balance between the physical and spiritual realms.

Beyond the prayers and rituals, the everyday behavior of a Zoroastrian is guided by the moral teachings of the religion. Truthfulness, respect for others, diligence in work, and maintaining a peaceful household are seen as manifestations of living in accordance with Asha. In this way, even the most mundane activities—like interactions with neighbors, the conduct of business, or the care of family—are imbued with spiritual significance. The ideal Zoroastrian life is one where every action, however small, contributes to the harmony of the world and reflects the values imparted by Zarathustra.

The emphasis on community also plays a crucial role in daily practices. Zoroastrians are encouraged to gather for communal prayers, festivals, and charity events, reinforcing a sense of unity and shared purpose. Even in the diaspora, where distances may separate individuals from fire temples or larger Zoroastrian communities, many maintain ties through online groups, local associations, and virtual prayer meetings. These gatherings, whether in person or virtual, provide a space for collective reflection, support, and the strengthening of communal bonds. The sense of belonging to a tradition that spans millennia offers a powerful source of continuity, particularly in the face of modern challenges.

At its heart, the daily practices of Zoroastrianism reflect a profound mindfulness—a constant awareness of one's role in the cosmic order and the responsibility that comes with it. In these routines, the faithful find a rhythm that connects them to their ancestors and to the teachings of Zarathustra, even as they navigate the complexities of contemporary life. The rituals, whether ancient or adapted, serve as reminders that the struggle between Asha and Druj is not merely a grand cosmic battle but a series of choices made every day. Through these practices, Zoroastrians strive to live in harmony with the eternal flame, walking a path illuminated by the light of Ahura Mazda.

While the core practices of Zoroastrian daily life center on universal rituals, prayers, and purification, the diversity within the faith has given rise to variations that adapt these traditions to the cultural, social, and geographical realities of each community. Across the world, Zoroastrians in the diaspora have tailored their routines, balancing the adherence to ancient traditions with the challenges of living in modern, often non-Zoroastrian, environments. This chapter delves into the nuances of these adaptations and the ways in which ancient practices continue to resonate, even as they transform to meet contemporary needs.

One of the most profound variations in daily practices emerges in how different Zoroastrian communities maintain the rituals of purification. The practice of padyab—ritual washing—remains a central tenet, but in places where water might be scarce, such as in urban centers or arid regions, adaptations have been made. Some communities have introduced simplified versions, using minimal water or focusing more on the symbolic recitation of prayers rather than the physical washing itself. This flexibility reflects the pragmatic approach embedded in Zoroastrianism, where the essence of the ritual—the purification of thought and intention—can be preserved, even if the form must evolve.

The ritual of maintaining the Kusti and Sudreh, too, has taken on new interpretations among diaspora communities. While the fundamental act of tying the Kusti and reciting the accompanying prayers remains consistent, the frequency and timing of these practices can vary. For Zoroastrians balancing demanding work schedules or living in regions with differing daily rhythms, the ritual is sometimes adjusted to suit their lifestyle. Yet, even in these adapted forms, the core intent—a daily reminder of the covenant with Ahura Mazda and the values of truth and righteousness—remains intact. For many, this adaptability is a testament to the resilience of the Zoroastrian spirit.

The presence of fire in Zoroastrian practice, particularly in the home, has also undergone significant changes in response to modern living conditions. In traditional settings, families would maintain a dedicated space for a lamp or small fire, symbolizing the presence of divine light. However, in contemporary urban dwellings or regions where open flames may pose safety concerns, many Zoroastrians have shifted to using electric lights or symbolic lamps. The flame, real or symbolic, continues to be the focal point of prayers, a reminder of the eternal fire that signifies Ahura Mazda's presence in every corner of the world.

While these adaptations allow Zoroastrians to continue their practices in diverse environments, there remains a deep sense of reverence for the original customs. This respect for tradition is particularly visible during life events that involve specific rituals, such as weddings, births, and funerals. Zoroastrian wedding ceremonies, for instance, involve a combination of ancient rites, such as the exchange of rings before a fire and the recitation of manthras, alongside more modern elements that reflect the culture of the region where the ceremony takes place. Even as these ceremonies evolve, they retain their essence—a celebration of the divine union and the affirmation of values that will guide the couple's life together.

Similarly, the customs surrounding death and mourning in Zoroastrianism have had to adapt. Traditionally, the Dakhma or Tower of Silence was used for sky burials, but in many parts of the world, such practices are not legally permitted. As a result, some Zoroastrian communities have shifted to burial or cremation, but always with a strong emphasis on purity and respect for the elements. For example, burial rites might include placing the body in a cement-lined grave to prevent contact with the earth, reflecting the ongoing respect for the sacredness of the natural world. These adjustments show how Zoroastrians navigate the delicate balance between adhering to ancient beliefs and accommodating contemporary legal and environmental constraints.

Daily prayer times, too, face adaptation challenges in a world where the pace of life often differs significantly from that of ancient agrarian societies. For many Zoroastrians, the traditional times for prayers at dawn, noon, and sunset can be difficult to observe rigidly due to work or school commitments. In response, some have found creative solutions, such as reciting shorter versions of the manthras during breaks or using digital prayer apps that provide reminders throughout the day. These modern tools serve as bridges, connecting the past with the present, allowing individuals to carry the rhythm of Zoroastrian devotion into the fabric of their daily routines.

Another example of adaptation is the celebration of Zoroastrian festivals in different parts of the world. In regions where Zoroastrians are a minority, festivals like Nowruz or Yalda are often celebrated with smaller gatherings in private homes or community centers rather than grand public festivities. Yet, even in these intimate settings, the core elements remain: the lighting of candles, the offering of prayers, the sharing of food, and the telling of stories that connect the community to their roots. This continuity ensures that the essence of these festivals—gratitude, renewal, and the celebration of life—remains vibrant, even as the scale of celebration adjusts to the realities of diaspora life.

The challenge of maintaining purity and ethical conduct in a diverse world has also led to thoughtful reflections within Zoroastrian communities. Living in multicultural societies often means engaging with customs and practices that differ from traditional Zoroastrian values. For example, maintaining dietary purity, especially the avoidance of certain foods or the ritual sanctification of meals, can be difficult in a globalized world where foods from many cultures are readily available. In response, some Zoroastrians focus more on the spirit of the practice—expressing gratitude for all meals and striving for moderation—rather than strictly adhering to ancient dietary laws. This focus on intention over form allows the faithful to adapt without losing the moral essence of their practices.

In the context of technology, many Zoroastrians have embraced online platforms as a means to stay connected to their faith. Virtual fire temples, online prayer meetings, and digital archives of sacred texts have emerged as vital resources for those who live far from physical Zoroastrian centers. For younger generations, these platforms offer a way to engage with their heritage in a manner that feels accessible and relevant. At the same time, they pose questions about how the faith might evolve—how can the warmth and intimacy of a community gathering around a fire be translated into a virtual space? How does the experience of reciting prayers alone in front of a screen differ from doing so in a shared, physical space?

Despite these adaptations, the essence of Zoroastrian practice—its emphasis on maintaining a connection with the divine, fostering community bonds, and upholding a life aligned with Asha—remains unwavering. The Zoroastrian belief in free will encourages each individual to choose how best to integrate their traditions into the modern world, while always striving to preserve the underlying values taught by Zarathustra. This approach allows the faith to be dynamic, adapting to new contexts without sacrificing the wisdom and guidance of ancient teachings.

The continued relevance of these practices highlights the resilience and flexibility of Zoroastrianism. Whether in a bustling city or a remote village, each Zoroastrian's daily routine is a testament to the enduring power of a faith that values both tradition and the capacity for renewal. As they navigate the complexities of modern life, Zoroastrians around the world continue to find ways to keep the flame of their faith alive, letting it illuminate their paths just as it did for their ancestors. Through these practices—both ancient and newly adapted—they remain deeply connected to a spiritual heritage that spans millennia, yet is ever-present in the choices they make each day.

Chapter 30
Symbolism

Zoroastrianism is rich with a symbolic language that transcends words, weaving a tapestry that connects the visible world with the spiritual realms. Among these symbols, each carries layers of meaning, a conduit through which the faithful can better understand the mysteries of the cosmos and their own place within it. From the iconic image of the Faravahar to the enduring presence of the sacred fire, Zoroastrian symbols offer a visual and spiritual map that guides followers on their journey through life.

The Faravahar is perhaps the most recognizable symbol of Zoroastrianism, a winged figure that embodies the essence of human spirit and divine guidance. Its intricate design, featuring a human figure emerging from a circle with wings and a tail feather, holds multiple layers of meaning. The central human figure represents the soul, reaching outwards toward Ahura Mazda, suggesting the aspirational nature of the spirit's journey. The circle that encircles the figure is a reminder of eternity, the cyclical nature of life, death, and rebirth. The two wings, each composed of three layers, are thought to represent Humata, Hukhta, and Hvarshta—good thoughts, good words, and good deeds—guiding the faithful toward righteousness.

The Faravahar is not just an abstract representation but a practical reminder of the moral and spiritual duties of every Zoroastrian. It encourages introspection, asking the faithful to align their actions with the principles of Asha. Whether carved into the stone of ancient temples or worn as a pendant, it serves as a constant symbol of the pursuit of spiritual elevation, anchoring

Zoroastrians in their daily moral struggles. In modern times, it has also become a cultural emblem, a connection to Persian heritage for many, including those outside the Zoroastrian faith, symbolizing values of resilience, dignity, and the quest for wisdom.

Equally central to Zoroastrian symbolism is the sacred fire, which holds a place of profound reverence within the faith. Fire is not merely an element; it represents the divine light of Ahura Mazda, embodying purity, truth, and the energy that sustains life. In temples, the fire is kept burning continually, representing the eternal presence of Ahura Mazda. To Zoroastrians, fire is a living entity, a manifestation of divine energy that can purify the mind and spirit. Its warmth and glow are seen as the physical embodiment of spiritual illumination, guiding believers towards clarity and understanding in a world filled with shadows.

Beyond the temple, fire also plays a role in the everyday lives of Zoroastrians. The lighting of a small lamp during prayers at home serves as a connection to this eternal flame, a personal reflection of the greater cosmic order. The flame is not just an object of veneration; it is a participant in the believer's dialogue with the divine. Its flickering light, responding to the breath of the wind, symbolizes the ever-present interaction between the material and spiritual realms. The fire's ability to transform the physical—turning wood into ash, for example—mirrors the spiritual journey from ignorance to enlightenment, a transformation that each soul must undergo.

Water, too, holds deep symbolic significance within Zoroastrianism. It represents the purity and life-giving force of the divine, complementing the cleansing power of fire. Sacred springs and rivers are regarded as vessels of Asha, embodying the creative power of Ahura Mazda. Water is central to many Zoroastrian rituals, from the simple act of washing hands before prayer to more elaborate purification ceremonies. It serves as a medium through which the faithful can connect with the divine, washing away not just physical impurities but also the subtle influences of Druj—the forces of deception and chaos.

In Zoroastrian cosmology, each element—fire, water, earth, and air—is part of a sacred balance, reflecting the interplay between the material and spiritual worlds. This reverence extends to mountains, trees, and other natural features, each seen as a manifestation of the divine presence in the world. The mountains of Iran, for instance, have long been considered places of spiritual retreat, where the isolation from society allows one to connect more deeply with Ahura Mazda's creation. For centuries, Zoroastrian pilgrims have sought these natural sanctuaries for contemplation and prayer, believing that the physical heights of the mountains bring them closer to spiritual enlightenment.

Another symbol that resonates deeply with Zoroastrian believers is the Asha Vahishta, the embodiment of truth and righteousness. Unlike fire or the Faravahar, Asha is not a physical symbol but a guiding principle that permeates the practice and philosophy of Zoroastrianism. It is often visualized in the balance between light and darkness, or the straight and unwavering path, reminding the faithful of the cosmic struggle between order and chaos. In prayers and rituals, Asha is invoked as a force that aligns the individual's actions with the divine plan, a way to live in harmony with the universe. It teaches that by pursuing truth in every thought, word, and deed, one contributes to the broader cosmic order and the triumph of light over darkness.

The importance of Asha is also reflected in the symbolism of Zoroastrian ethics, where truth becomes a powerful weapon against the deceit of Druj. The concept of Mithra—contracts or agreements—plays a crucial role here, symbolizing the sacredness of truthfulness and the moral consequences of breaking one's word. Mithra is more than a legal principle; it is a spiritual bond that holds the fabric of society together. When a person keeps their promises, they reinforce the fabric of Asha; when they break them, they invite the disorder of Druj into the world. Thus, Mithra serves as a reminder that integrity is not just a personal virtue but a cosmic duty, binding the individual to the community and the divine.

Symbols in Zoroastrianism are also tools of meditation and contemplation, offering layers of meaning to be explored over a lifetime. Take, for example, the sacred thread of the Kusti, wrapped around the waist over the Sudreh, a simple white garment. The act of tying the Kusti is a symbolic reaffirmation of the believer's commitment to the path of Asha, binding oneself to the divine covenant. It is an outward symbol of an inward journey, a way of reminding oneself of the constant battle between good and evil that takes place within. The threads of the Kusti, interwoven with prayers, represent the interconnectedness of thought, word, and action—each strand contributing to the larger fabric of one's life.

In this chapter, we begin to see how the symbols of Zoroastrianism—be they physical like the Faravahar and the sacred fire, or conceptual like Asha—create a language through which the Zoroastrian worldview is expressed. They are not merely relics of an ancient faith but living symbols, continuously interpreted and reinterpreted by each generation of believers. They form a bridge between the ancient teachings of Zarathustra and the experiences of Zoroastrians living in a modern, rapidly changing world. In them, the essence of Zoroastrian philosophy comes alive, offering a profound means to understand the universe and one's place within it.

These symbols carry a timeless message, echoing across the ages: that the struggle between light and darkness, order and chaos, is not just a cosmic battle but a deeply personal one, fought within the heart of every believer. Through the lens of these sacred symbols, Zoroastrians find both a connection to their ancient roots and a compass to navigate the complexities of the present world. They serve as a reminder that, even in the face of profound change, the essence of the Zoroastrian faith—its reverence for the divine, its pursuit of truth, and its commitment to the path of Asha—remains as enduring as the flame that has burned in Zoroastrian temples for millennia.

As the symbols of Zoroastrianism unfold their layers, they serve as more than mere representations; they are instruments that carry the teachings of the faith into the daily lives of its followers. These symbols become part of the rituals, the architecture, and even the art that permeates Zoroastrian communities. They shape the way believers perceive their place in the universe, influencing their actions, ethics, and the pursuit of the divine.

One such symbol that extends its presence beyond temples and prayers is the Ahura Mazda's Fire. Not limited to sacred spaces, this fire often inspires artistic representations, appearing in Zoroastrian art as a radiant flame encircled by intricate designs. In ancient carvings and reliefs, one finds the sacred fire depicted alongside kings and priests, underscoring its role as a divine witness to earthly events. These artistic renderings of fire suggest its dual nature—both a protector and a purifier—guiding rulers and devotees alike. Within the glow of this sacred fire lies the unspoken promise of divine light guiding humanity through periods of darkness.

In the fire temples, the Atash Behram and other sacred fires are kept with meticulous care, each flame representing a different level of ritual purity. The presence of these varying grades of fire—Atash Dadgah, Atash Adaran, and Atash Behram—serves as a reminder that even within the purity of fire, there are hierarchies and pathways, much like the spiritual journeys of individuals. The gradations of sacred fire symbolize the stages of spiritual elevation, suggesting that the journey toward Ahura Mazda is layered and progressive. This hierarchy of fire is not static; it is a living tradition, evolving with the community's needs, yet ever rooted in the ancient wisdom of Zarathustra's teachings.

The Faravahar too has found its place beyond religious contexts, becoming a symbol of Persian identity and resilience, especially among the Zoroastrian diaspora. This dual role—both as a spiritual guide and a cultural emblem—demonstrates the adaptability of Zoroastrian symbols. For those in the diaspora, it becomes a bridge, connecting them to their spiritual and cultural roots even when far from their ancestral lands. When engraved on walls or worn as jewelry, the Faravahar transcends the boundaries between the sacred and the everyday, offering a silent reminder of the enduring legacy of Zoroastrian ideals.

In addition to fire and the Faravahar, there is the Khvarenah, a concept that, while more abstract, plays a crucial role in Zoroastrian thought. Khvarenah represents divine glory or fortune, an ethereal radiance bestowed by Ahura Mazda on righteous individuals. This aura of glory, often depicted as a luminous halo or radiating energy around kings and heroes in ancient Persian art, signifies divine favor and the inner light of truth. To Zoroastrians, Khvarenah is not simply a mystical concept; it is a state to strive for, achieved through devotion, moral strength, and alignment with Asha. It embodies the belief that spiritual brightness is reflected in the material world, and those who live in harmony with the cosmic order shine with an inner light that others can perceive.

The presence of Khvarenah in ancient texts and its visual representation in art indicate a deep intertwining of spiritual aspiration and worldly authority. Kings and leaders were seen as bearers of Khvarenah, responsible for upholding divine law in their realms. This understanding reinforced the idea that earthly power should align with spiritual principles, reflecting the Zoroastrian ethos where governance is a sacred duty. In the modern context, while monarchies have faded, the concept of Khvarenah continues to inspire Zoroastrians to pursue leadership in ways that serve the greater good, guided by the same ideals of light and righteousness.

Turning to rituals, the Kusti and Sudreh form another vital symbolic pair, embodying the commitment of each Zoroastrian to their faith. The Sudreh, a white cotton garment worn close to the body, symbolizes purity and spiritual armor against the forces of Druj. The Kusti, a long woolen cord, is wrapped around the waist three times, symbolizing the three principles of good thoughts, good words, and good deeds. The act of untying and retying the

Kusti during daily prayers becomes a moment of renewal, a conscious re-alignment with the path of Asha.

This daily ritual transforms the mundane into the sacred, turning the act of dressing into a spiritual practice. It serves as a reminder that the battle between Asha and Druj is not just a cosmic struggle but an internal one, playing out in the choices and actions of every individual. Each time a Zoroastrian recites the prayer while tying the Kusti, they reaffirm their commitment to fight against the influences of falsehood and chaos, grounding themselves in the ancient tradition that has guided their ancestors for millennia.

Zoroastrian symbolism is also evident in architecture, particularly in the design of fire temples. These structures are often built with a focus on simplicity and harmony with nature, embodying the Zoroastrian reverence for the physical world as a manifestation of divine creation. Within the temple, the sacred fire is housed in a domed sanctuary, where the curved ceiling represents the vault of heaven and the cosmic order. This architectural design is not merely functional; it creates a space where the worshipper feels the embrace of the universe, standing between earth and sky as they offer their prayers.

In ancient Persian architecture, motifs of cypress trees and lions are often carved into stone, symbols of life, strength, and divine protection. The cypress, evergreen and enduring, symbolizes the eternal spirit that withstands the cycles of time. The lion, fierce and majestic, represents the guardianship of divine order, much like the role of Ahura Mazda as protector of truth. These symbols, seen in palaces and ancient ruins, connect Zoroastrian teachings to the physical spaces where communities once gathered, offering a tangible link to the spiritual ideals that shaped their world.

While the material manifestations of these symbols provide a glimpse into the Zoroastrian worldview, their power lies in the way they shape the inner life of believers. They are not static images but dynamic expressions, constantly reinterpreted as the world changes. The symbols serve as a language through which the mysteries of the universe are communicated, reminding each generation of the eternal principles that lie at the heart of their faith.

The adaptability of these symbols has allowed Zoroastrianism to survive through centuries of change and challenge, from the ancient Persian empires to the present-day diaspora. They hold a mirror to the soul, reflecting the Zoroastrian belief that the world is a reflection of the divine order, and that every action taken in the physical realm echoes in the spiritual. As Zoroastrians light a candle, don the Sudreh and Kusti, or contemplate the eternal flame within a fire temple, they participate in a tradition that transcends time, finding in these ancient symbols a source of strength and a path to understanding the mysteries of existence.

Through this intricate web of symbols, Zoroastrianism speaks to the universal human quest for meaning, weaving a connection between the temporal and the eternal. Each symbol serves as a thread, drawing the faithful deeper into the fabric of their tradition, guiding them through the complexities of life with a promise of divine presence and order. In these symbols, the enduring light of Ahura Mazda shines, casting its rays across centuries, illuminating the path toward a world where Asha prevails over the darkness of Druj.

Chapter 31
Connection with Science and Philosophy

The teachings of Zoroastrianism, while deeply rooted in ancient spirituality, hold a unique resonance with modern scientific thought and philosophical inquiry. There is an inherent order in the Zoroastrian worldview—a cosmic blueprint designed by Ahura Mazda—that finds parallels in scientific understandings of the universe. This chapter explores these intersections, revealing how Zoroastrian concepts align with, and sometimes anticipate, contemporary ideas about the natural world and humanity's place within it.

Central to Zoroastrian cosmology is the belief in an ordered universe, governed by the principles of Asha, or truth and order. This vision of an intricately structured cosmos shares affinities with scientific explorations into the laws that govern physical reality. Just as Asha represents a cosmic harmony in Zoroastrianism, science seeks to uncover the underlying patterns that bring coherence to the universe—from the dance of subatomic particles to the gravitational forces that shape galaxies. For Zoroastrians, the universe is not a random collection of matter but a creation imbued with purpose, where every element, from the smallest drop of water to the most distant star, follows a divine order set forth by Ahura Mazda.

This sense of cosmic order is particularly mirrored in the field of cosmology. The Zoroastrian narrative of creation speaks of the universe emerging through a series of structured stages, each representing aspects of divine intent. Science, through disciplines like astrophysics and cosmology, offers its own narrative of creation: the Big Bang theory and the formation of stars, planets, and galaxies. While these perspectives differ in their methodologies—one emerging from mystical insight, the other from empirical observation—they share a profound curiosity about the origins of existence. Zoroastrianism's focus on an orderly cosmos finds an echo in the scientific pursuit to map the universe's structure, suggesting a deep, albeit metaphorical, kinship between the ancient and the modern.

The concept of Asha as a guiding force extends to the Zoroastrian understanding of nature and its cycles. It holds that the world operates according to a divine rhythm, evident in the changing of seasons, the cycles of life, and the interplay between the elements. Modern ecology, with its focus on ecosystems and the interdependence of life forms, resonates with this perspective. Just as Zoroastrian teachings emphasize the need to maintain balance and harmony with the natural world, ecological science recognizes the delicate equilibrium required to sustain life on Earth. In both, there is a recognition that disrupting the balance—whether through the forces of Druj or through environmental degradation—can lead to chaos and suffering.

Furthermore, the Zoroastrian emphasis on individual responsibility in maintaining this balance parallels the ethical considerations that underpin environmental science today. The call to care for Asha by protecting water, air, and soil can be seen as an early articulation of the principles that guide modern environmental stewardship. Zoroastrian rituals that honor the natural elements, such as the reverence for fire, water, and earth, serve as a reminder of the interconnectedness of all life—an understanding that aligns closely with the ecological principle that human well-being is tied to the health of the planet.

Philosophically, Zoroastrianism's emphasis on free will and moral choice intersects with the existential questions posed by Western and Eastern philosophy. The struggle between Asha and Druj, central to the Zoroastrian worldview, presents a vision of life as a series of moral choices, where humans are endowed with the power to shape their destiny. This mirrors existentialist thought, which emphasizes individual agency and the search for meaning within the constraints of the human condition. Zoroastrian teachings suggest that through the exercise of free will, one can align with the cosmic order, contributing to the ultimate triumph of good over evil. It is a vision of life that embraces both personal responsibility and the profound impact of each choice on the broader cosmic drama.

In dialogue with the deterministic philosophies that sometimes dominate scientific thought, Zoroastrianism offers a perspective that affirms the human capacity to change the course of events. While the laws of physics might govern the behavior of matter, Zoroastrianism suggests that the moral universe is shaped by conscious actions. This belief in the power of human choice stands as a counterpoint to ideas of a universe governed solely by impersonal forces, presenting instead a world where each decision ripples through the fabric of reality, influencing the balance between Asha and Druj.

The dualistic nature of Zoroastrianism, with its clear distinction between good and evil, light and darkness, also offers an intriguing parallel to discussions in metaphysics about the nature of reality and the existence of dualities. Concepts such as the mind-body problem, the interplay between material reality and consciousness, and the search for ultimate truth find a kindred spirit in Zoroastrianism's exploration of spiritual and material realms. The notion that spiritual forces like Asha can manifest in physical realities invites a broader philosophical question: Can morality shape the material world, just as physical laws shape the cosmos?

This metaphysical inquiry extends into the realm of ethics, where Zoroastrianism's teachings offer a foundation for understanding the nature of good and the role of humanity in its pursuit. The philosophical debates that have long pondered the nature of virtue, justice, and the purpose of human life find echoes in the Zoroastrian call to cultivate Humata, Hukhta, Hvarshta—good thoughts, good words, good deeds. Zoroastrian ethics, with its focus on the active practice of virtue, aligns with the moral philosophy that seeks to define a path toward the good life, suggesting that true wisdom lies in the alignment of thought, speech, and action.

Zoroastrianism's influence can even be traced in the realm of ethics that underpins modern human rights. Its teachings about the inherent dignity of individuals, the emphasis on truth, and the need to strive for justice resonate with contemporary ideals of equality and human dignity. Scholars and philosophers have noted the parallels between Zoroastrian concepts of moral order and the principles that later influenced Enlightenment thought. This ancient perspective, rooted in the mystical teachings of Zarathustra, offers a reminder that the search for justice and truth is a timeless endeavor, one that transcends the boundaries of culture and history.

Thus, the dialogue between Zoroastrianism and modern science and philosophy is not one of opposition but of a shared quest for understanding the mysteries of existence. Whether through the lens of spiritual revelation or through the rigors of scientific inquiry, both seek to answer the same fundamental questions: What is the nature of reality? What is the role of humanity within the cosmos? And how can one live in harmony with the truth that underlies all creation?

In exploring these connections, Zoroastrianism demonstrates its capacity to engage with the world of ideas beyond its ancient origins. It offers a perspective where the material and spiritual worlds are interwoven, each influencing the other. This vision encourages a synthesis of ancient wisdom and modern knowledge, suggesting that the search for truth is a journey that spans millennia, with each era adding its voice to the chorus of understanding.

As the chapters unfold, the Zoroastrian view of the universe continues to reveal its depths, inviting reflection on how ancient spiritual insights remain relevant in contemporary discussions about the nature of reality and the human role within it. The journey through these intersections between Zoroastrian thought, science, and philosophy invites a deeper appreciation of the enduring quest for knowledge and the mysteries that continue to captivate the human spirit.

Building upon the initial exploration of the connections between Zoroastrianism and modern scientific and philosophical thought, this chapter delves deeper into the dialogues that have emerged between ancient Zoroastrian teachings and the broader currents of philosophical inquiry. Here, we uncover how the intricate principles of Zoroastrianism have found resonance in various schools of thought across both Eastern and Western traditions, offering new dimensions of understanding to timeless questions about existence, morality, and the nature of the cosmos.

One of the most fascinating aspects of Zoroastrian thought is its nuanced approach to dualism, which has become a topic of extensive discussion in philosophy. While Zoroastrianism is often noted for its clear distinctions between good and evil—embodied in the cosmic opposition between Asha (order, truth) and Druj (chaos, deceit)—this dualism is not a simplistic division. It acknowledges the complex interplay between these forces, recognizing that the material world is the stage upon which the moral struggle unfolds. This perspective has drawn parallels with the dualistic philosophies found in the works of figures like Plato, who also grappled with the tension between the ideal (the realm of forms) and the physical world.

Zoroastrianism's influence on Western thought is perhaps most evident in the ancient Greek encounter with Persian ideas. Philosophers such as Heraclitus, who spoke of the world as being in a state of flux governed by a kind of divine reason (Logos), may have been indirectly influenced by Zoroastrian ideas of an ordered cosmos guided by Asha. The exchanges between ancient Persian and Greek thinkers highlight a historical cross-pollination that shaped the philosophical landscapes of both regions, leaving traces in concepts of cosmic order and the nature of the divine.

In the Eastern philosophical traditions, especially within Indian philosophy, the echoes of Zoroastrian thought are equally profound. The interactions between the early followers of Zoroastrianism and Vedic culture led to a sharing of metaphysical ideas that influenced both traditions. Concepts such as the eternal struggle between light and darkness can be seen reflected in the dualistic themes found in Hindu and later Buddhist cosmology. This dialogue contributed to a broader understanding of the spiritual battle between enlightenment and ignorance, creating a rich tapestry of ideas that enriched both religious landscapes.

Beyond the ancient world, Zoroastrian dualism also invites comparisons with the Manichean and Gnostic traditions, which flourished in the early centuries of the Common Era. These movements, like Zoroastrianism, emphasized the struggle between light and darkness, and the material world's role in that cosmic conflict. Though distinct in their theological frameworks, the thematic similarities suggest that Zoroastrian ideas about the nature of good, evil, and cosmic struggle resonated deeply with the spiritual currents of the time, shaping the mystical outlooks that later influenced Christian and Islamic mysticism.

Turning to the modern era, Zoroastrian concepts continue to find a place in philosophical discussions about ethics and morality. The Zoroastrian emphasis on the role of individual choice in shaping one's destiny mirrors the existentialist focus on personal responsibility, as articulated by thinkers like Jean-Paul Sartre and Albert Camus. For Zoroastrians, the act of choosing Asha over Druj is not just a religious duty but an affirmation of one's agency within the cosmos—a theme that resonates with existentialist ideas about creating meaning through action in an indifferent universe. This shared emphasis on the weight of individual choice underscores a timeless concern with the nature of freedom and the burden of ethical responsibility.

Moreover, Zoroastrian ideas about the cyclical nature of the universe and the concept of Frashokereti—the renewal of the world—find a parallel in contemporary debates within philosophy of time and cosmology. The Zoroastrian vision of a cosmos that undergoes periods of decay followed by ultimate renewal aligns with certain interpretations of time as non-linear, a view that has gained traction in both Eastern philosophies and in modern physics through theories of a cyclical universe. It invites reflection on how ancient visions of cosmic renewal might intersect with scientific theories of entropy, the Big Crunch, or the potential rebirth of the universe.

In engaging with these philosophical currents, Zoroastrianism also offers a framework for understanding the relationship between ethics and the physical world. The Zoroastrian commitment to Asha as an active force that shapes both spiritual and material reality suggests a dynamic interplay between thought and being. This perspective resonates with certain aspects of idealist philosophy, which holds that consciousness and ideas play a fundamental role in shaping reality. Yet, Zoroastrianism remains distinct in its insistence that ethical action is essential for bringing about change, positioning it closer to pragmatist philosophies that value the practical application of ideas in shaping the world.

Zoroastrianism's vision of a harmonious universe also engages with contemporary scientific discourse on sustainability and the ethical treatment of the environment. The ancient teachings about the sanctity of natural elements and the duty to maintain the balance of the Earth find a parallel in modern environmental ethics, where the recognition of interconnectivity between life forms has led to a deeper awareness of humanity's responsibility toward the planet. This alignment suggests that the ancient Zoroastrian reverence for nature offers timeless insights into contemporary discussions on ecological responsibility and the need for sustainable living practices.

In dialogues with scientific perspectives on the nature of consciousness, Zoroastrianism's teachings about the soul and its journey post-death offer an early articulation of questions that continue to intrigue neuroscientists and philosophers alike. The journey of the soul across the Chinvat Bridge—a passage that symbolizes the transition from the material to the spiritual realm—raises questions about the nature of consciousness, the possibility of an afterlife, and the relationship between mind and matter. While science remains focused on empirical evidence, Zoroastrian spiritual insights provide a poetic counterpoint, suggesting that the mysteries of consciousness may extend beyond the physical confines of the brain.

In the modern era, Zoroastrianism's influence has extended to thinkers and spiritual seekers who are drawn to its emphasis on cosmic order, ethical living, and the quest for truth. Its principles have inspired a resurgence of interest among those who see in Zoroastrianism a spiritual path that bridges the gap between ancient wisdom and modern challenges. The emphasis on truth (Asha), the battle against deceit (Druj), and the pursuit of a life aligned with higher principles speaks to those seeking a moral framework that remains relevant amidst contemporary complexities.

Ultimately, Zoroastrianism's ongoing dialogue with science and philosophy demonstrates its capacity to evolve and engage with the changing landscape of human knowledge. It offers a perspective that is both ancient and forward-looking, suggesting that the questions posed by Zarathustra continue to resonate in the hearts and minds of those who seek to understand the nature of existence. The teachings of Zoroastrianism provide a reminder that in the search for truth, one must look both outward, toward the vast mysteries of the cosmos, and inward, toward the moral choices that shape the human soul.

In this continued exploration of Zoroastrianism's philosophical dimensions, the reader is invited to reflect on how ancient teachings can illuminate modern discussions, offering a bridge between the mysticism of the past and the rationality of the present. It is in this synthesis that Zoroastrianism reveals its enduring relevance, a testament to the timeless human quest for wisdom, meaning, and a deeper understanding of the universe.

Chapter 32
Famous Zoroastrians

The journey through Zoroastrianism's long and rich history brings us to those figures who, across centuries, have embodied the teachings of Zarathustra and played a vital role in the preservation and propagation of the faith. These individuals, from ancient sages to contemporary leaders, are not just guardians of a spiritual tradition but are also symbols of resilience and adaptation in the face of immense cultural shifts. Their stories reveal the enduring spirit of Zoroastrianism, providing a bridge between ancient wisdom and modern expressions of faith.

Among the earliest and most significant figures is the legendary Darius I, the king of the Achaemenid Empire, whose rule in the 6th century BCE marked a time when Zoroastrianism was intertwined with the governance of one of the world's great empires. Darius's inscriptions, particularly those at Behistun, speak to his devotion to Ahura Mazda, emphasizing the role of divine support in his right to rule. His patronage of Zoroastrian rituals and the protection of fire temples reinforced the connection between statecraft and spiritual duty. Although Darius's reign came centuries after Zarathustra's lifetime, his support helped institutionalize the faith, allowing it to flourish alongside the imperial ambitions of Persia.

Another pivotal figure in the early history of Zoroastrianism is the priestly scholar Tansar, who lived during the Sassanian period (224-651 CE). Tansar is often credited with systematizing Zoroastrian teachings and solidifying the canon of the Avesta, the sacred texts that form the core of Zoroastrian scriptures. His influence in organizing the religious structure of the Sassanian state cannot be overstated, as he worked to establish a centralized religious authority, which helped the faith resist external influences and internal fragmentation. Tansar's efforts ensured that the teachings of Zarathustra remained a cohesive and structured tradition during a time of great political and social transformation in Persia.

With the advent of the Islamic conquest of Persia in the 7th century, Zoroastrianism faced a dramatic shift. The story of the faithful Mobedan (priests) like Adurfarnbag Farrokhzad is crucial during this time. Adurfarnbag, a prominent Zoroastrian priest, worked tirelessly to preserve the spiritual texts and traditions of Zoroastrianism during an era of increasing suppression. His writings and commentaries on the Avesta provided a lifeline for the continuity of Zoroastrian knowledge in the face of adversity. His commitment to maintaining the purity of the rituals and the transmission of knowledge in secret gatherings exemplified the resilience of the Zoroastrian spirit in a time of great change.

Moving forward to the era of migration and diaspora, the story of the Parsi community in India offers a testament to the adaptability of Zoroastrian traditions. One cannot speak of this period without mentioning the figure of Dadabhai Naoroji, a pioneering Parsi leader known for his role in Indian politics as the first Asian to serve in the British Parliament in the late 19th century. Naoroji's advocacy for Indian independence and his belief in social reform were deeply influenced by his Zoroastrian values, particularly the emphasis on truth (Asha) and social justice. He used his platform to speak not only for the rights of Indians but also to ensure that the Parsi community's heritage and values were respected within the broader fabric of Indian society.

In the modern era, another significant figure is Dastur Dr. Firoze M. Kotwal, a high-ranking Mobed who has become a prominent voice for the Zoroastrian faith in contemporary times. Dr. Kotwal's scholarly work and dedication to the preservation of traditional rituals have made him a respected authority within the Zoroastrian community. His efforts in documenting and teaching the ancient rites, as well as his openness to engaging with modern questions about faith and identity, make him a key figure in the ongoing dialogue about Zoroastrianism's place in the modern world. Dr. Kotwal's leadership has helped maintain the delicate balance between honoring the past and addressing the needs of a globalized Zoroastrian community.

Beyond the religious leaders, Zoroastrianism has also seen the emergence of figures in literature and the arts who have drawn inspiration from its rich symbolism and philosophy. Among these, Keki N. Daruwalla, an acclaimed Indian poet, stands out. His poetry often reflects the themes of fire, light, and the struggle between order and chaos—motifs deeply embedded in the Zoroastrian worldview. Through his work, Daruwalla has brought the spirit of Zoroastrian philosophy into the literary mainstream, offering a poetic reflection of the Zoroastrian ethos to a wider audience.

In the field of science, the legacy of Zubin Mehta, a renowned conductor, provides an example of how Zoroastrian values can permeate diverse aspects of life. Although his work is primarily in the realm of classical music, Mehta's approach to leadership in orchestras around the world reflects the discipline and passion that echo the Zoroastrian principles of striving for excellence and harmony. His contributions to the world of music have earned him international acclaim, and he has often spoken of the importance of his Parsi heritage in shaping his values and worldview.

Each of these individuals, across different eras and domains, reflects a unique facet of Zoroastrianism's impact on the world. They embody the teachings of Zarathustra through their dedication to truth, their resilience in the face of adversity, and their commitment to serving their communities. Through their lives, the ancient values of Zoroastrianism find new expressions, showing that even as the world changes, the core principles of this ancient faith continue to inspire.

As the chapter unfolds, readers are invited to consider how the contributions of these figures have shaped the course of

Zoroastrianism's history, keeping alive a tradition that might have otherwise faded into obscurity. Their stories serve as a reminder that the essence of a spiritual path is not only in its doctrines but also in the lives of those who live it. From royal courts to the diaspora and from sacred temples to the stages of global symphonies, the spirit of Zoroastrianism endures, adapting and finding new forms in each generation that rises to carry its torch.

As Zoroastrianism navigates the waves of history, its survival and influence are closely tied to the efforts of extraordinary individuals who have helped to sustain its teachings across generations. These figures, emerging from various corners of the world, represent the faith's adaptability and its ability to remain relevant even in times of profound transformation. Their contributions in philosophy, human rights, literature, and beyond, continue to inspire Zoroastrians and non-Zoroastrians alike, demonstrating the power of their heritage and the enduring message of Zarathustra.

One of the most prominent contemporary figures is Rohinton Mistry, a renowned novelist whose works have shed light on the Parsi Zoroastrian experience in modern India. His acclaimed novels, such as A Fine Balance and Family Matters, delve into the challenges faced by the Parsi community, touching upon themes of identity, tradition, and the tensions between maintaining ancient customs while adapting to a rapidly changing world. Mistry's storytelling offers a window into the everyday lives of Zoroastrians, capturing the complexities of a community striving to preserve its heritage amidst the pressures of modernity. Through his literature, Mistry preserves the spirit of Zoroastrian values, such as the pursuit of truth (Asha) and the struggle for justice, presenting them to a global audience in a deeply human context.

In the realm of social activism, Cyrus Habib, a former Lieutenant Governor of Washington State, has emerged as a symbol of perseverance and progress. As a blind politician of Zoroastrian heritage, Habib has faced challenges that he has turned into opportunities for advocacy and change. His commitment to equity, disability rights, and public service is deeply rooted in the Zoroastrian ideals of serving others and striving for the common good. Habib's career reflects a modern interpretation of Zoroastrianism's teachings, demonstrating how the principles of moral duty and the fight for justice can be applied to contemporary issues in governance and society. His work serves as an inspiration for young Zoroastrians who seek to make a difference in their communities while staying true to the ethical foundations of their faith.

In addition to these cultural and political figures, Zoroastrianism has also made its mark in the world of academia, with scholars like Jamsheed Choksy offering a critical bridge between ancient texts and contemporary understanding. Choksy's extensive research on the history and religious practices of Zoroastrianism has been instrumental in bringing the depth of the faith's philosophical and theological ideas to a broader scholarly audience. His work explores the intersections of Zoroastrianism with other world religions and cultures, revealing how Zoroastrian concepts of dualism, morality, and cosmology have influenced global religious thought. Choksy's scholarship has helped to elevate the study of Zoroastrianism, ensuring that its complexities and historical significance are recognized within the field of religious studies.

Among the many notable Zoroastrians who have contributed to science and technology, Farrokh Bulsara, known to the world as Freddie Mercury, stands as a unique figure. Although primarily known as the legendary lead singer of Queen, Mercury's Parsi background and Zoroastrian upbringing in Zanzibar and India played a subtle role in shaping his perspective on life. While he rarely spoke publicly about his faith, the themes of duality and the internal struggle between good and evil present in some of his lyrics echo the core Zoroastrian beliefs. Mercury's global impact through music illustrates how the values and experiences of a Zoroastrian upbringing can permeate and influence even the most unexpected realms of creativity and self-expression.

The contributions of Zoroastrians extend beyond individuals and into the philanthropic initiatives that have shaped communities worldwide. One such example is the Tata family in India, whose industrial empire has been intertwined with a commitment to social welfare and progress. Jamsetji Tata, the founder of Tata Group, was driven by a vision of industrialization that went hand-in-hand with social responsibility. He invested in education, healthcare, and community development, principles that reflect the Zoroastrian ideals of stewardship and the betterment of society. Today, the Tata Trusts continue this legacy, funding initiatives that aim to uplift communities and foster innovation, embodying the Zoroastrian ethic of using wealth for the greater good.

Another important contemporary figure is Dr. Meher Master-Moos, a Zoroastrian leader who has worked tirelessly to promote interfaith dialogue and understanding. As the president of the Zoroastrian College in India, Dr. Master-Moos has been a bridge-builder between Zoroastrianism and other world religions, fostering a spirit of cooperation and mutual respect. Her efforts to preserve Zoroastrian teachings through education, while also advocating for harmony among different faiths, embody the core Zoroastrian value of striving for unity in diversity. Through her work, Dr. Master-Moos ensures that the wisdom of Zoroastrian teachings remains accessible and relevant in a pluralistic world, while also nurturing a sense of pride and identity among Zoroastrian youth.

The global diaspora has also seen Zoroastrians like Fali Nariman, a distinguished jurist in India, making significant contributions to the field of law. Known for his expertise in constitutional law, Nariman has been a defender of civil liberties and human rights, often drawing upon the Zoroastrian emphasis on justice and the moral duty to stand against falsehood. His legal work has shaped the development of constitutional jurisprudence in India, and his dedication to upholding the principles of fairness and equity has earned him a reputation as one of the leading legal minds of his generation. Nariman's career reflects how

Zoroastrian principles can find expression through a lifelong commitment to the rule of law and the protection of human dignity.

As this final chapter closes, it is clear that the contributions of these famous Zoroastrians are not isolated acts but part of a larger tapestry of resilience, innovation, and faith. Their lives demonstrate that Zoroastrianism, while rooted in ancient traditions, continues to inspire action and creativity in new and unexpected ways. These individuals have carried the torch of Zarathustra's teachings across the centuries, adapting them to the challenges and opportunities of each era. In doing so, they have kept the essence of the faith alive, proving that the core values of Asha, truth, and service to humanity remain timeless.

The stories of these Zoroastrians serve as a beacon for future generations, reminding them that the principles of their faith can be a source of strength and guidance, no matter the challenges they face. Through their dedication, creativity, and moral courage, they have ensured that the legacy of Zoroastrianism will continue to shine brightly in the world, offering a path of wisdom and hope for all who seek it.

Epilogue

The path we have traveled has brought us to the edge of a horizon where the sacred and the profane meet, where light and darkness face each other in a final embrace before dawn. Ahura Mazda and Angra Mainyu continue their struggle, but now, you understand that this battle also resides within you. The choices made, the silences kept, each act of kindness or shadow, all resonate within the fabric of the cosmos.

What Zarathustra envisioned was not just a world divided between good and evil, but the possibility of redemption, of renewal. The promise of Frashokereti, the renewal of the world, is a symbol of a future where shadows dissipate, and the truth of Asha triumphs over the veils of Druj. But this promise is not a divine gift handed without effort; it is a construction, a work that demands the commitment of every being that breathes under the sky.

While the sacred fire burns silently in the temples, as a testament to the eternal presence of Ahura Mazda, you, who have reached the end of these pages, now carry a spark of that flame within your spirit. It is a legacy that transcends the ages, a connection between yesterday and tomorrow, between the visible and the invisible. The ancient wisdom that rests here becomes yours, ready to guide your steps, but also to challenge you to be more than just an observer.

You are called to be a guardian of creation, to keep the flame of truth alive in the face of the storms that Angra Mainyu casts upon the world. And though the journey may be arduous, though the darkness may try to swallow the light, the destiny of creation rests in the hands of those who dare to keep their gaze fixed on the promise of a new dawn.

Now, as you close this book, know that your role in the great narrative of the cosmos has only just begun. May the echo of Zarathustra's words resonate in your heart, reminding you that, in every moment, there is the opportunity to choose light, to live in harmony with Asha. May you find the courage to face the shadows, and may the flame of wisdom guide your steps, until the day when the world, at last, shines with the purity of the restored creation.